YOU DECIDE!

YOU DECIDE!
Controversial Cases in American Politics
Second Edition

Edward Drachman and Robert Langran

ROWMAN & LITTLEFIELD PUBLISHERS, INC.
Lanham • Boulder • New York • Toronto • Plymouth, UK

ROWMAN & LITTLEFIELD PUBLISHERS, INC.

Published in the United States of America
by Rowman & Littlefield Publishers, Inc.
A wholly owned subsidary of The Rowman & Littlefield Publishing Group, Inc.
4501 Forbes Boulevard, Suite 200, Lanham, Maryland 20706
www.rowmanlittlefield.com

Estover Road
Plymouth PL6 7PY
United Kingdom

British Library Cataloguing in Publication Information Available

Library of Congress Cataloging-in-Publication Data:
Drachman, Edward R., 1940–
  You decide : controversial cases in American politics / Edward Drachman and Robert Langran. — 2nd ed.
    p. cm.
  First ed. entered under Alan Shank.
  Includes bibliographical references and index.
  ISBN-13: 978-0-7425-3805-4 (pbk. : alk. paper)
  ISBN-10: 0-7425-3805-2 (pbk. : alk. paper)
  1. Political planning—United States—Case studies. I. Langran, Robert. II. Shank, Alan, 1936– Controversial cases in American politics. III. Title.
  JK468.P64S48 2008
  320.60973—dc22   2007004533

Printed in the United States of America

∞™ The paper used in this publication meets the minimum requirements of American National Standard
for Information Sciences—Permanence of Paper for Printed Library Materials, ANSI/NISO Z39.48-1992.

Contents

Introduction

To instructors of American politics courses:

THE SECOND EDITION OF *You Decide! Controversial Cases in American Politics* is a collection of fourteen original case studies. The book provides a unique and innovative way to learn more about American government by examining contending points of view on controversial issues. Our cases encourage readers to make choices from various options that might help resolve the case controversies.

As veteran teachers of both introductory and advanced American politics courses at SUNY Geneseo and Villanova University, we have developed, field-tested, and refined the case method of teaching over a period of several years. *You Decide!* contains three types of cases. First, six *retrospective* cases deal with controversies in which political, judicial, and/or policy decisions have been made. These decisions have been debated for many years and continue to be a source of controversy. These cases consider policy options that might have yielded more favorable resolution of the problem(s). The six retrospective cases include interpretation of the Constitution (Case 1), the response of the media to Danish cartoons of the Prophet Muhammad (Case 6), campaign finance reform (Case 8), the Electoral College (Case 10), use of the filibuster in Congress (Case 11), and presidential power during wartime (Case 12).

Second, five *contemporary* cases consider American political and policy controversies that are still in search of a solution. The policy options identified in these cases will most likely be debated for many years before the controversies can be resolved. The five contemporary cases deal with illegal immigration (Case 2), affirmative action (Case 4), bilingual education (Case 5), school vouchers (Case 7), and the Iraq War (Case 14).

Finally, three *hybrid* cases include both the past resolution of a policy problem (retrospective) and contemporary issues with unresolved controversies. These cases include organized school prayer (Case 3), voting and redistricting (Case 9), and the Supreme Court (Case 13).

Our fourteen cases provide opportunities for students of American politics to decide how controversial political and policy issues should be resolved. Each case is introduced with a provocative question to set the stage for analysis and decision making. Following a brief case snapshot, the major controversies are summarized. These are provided to identify the key issues, conflicts, arguments, and different viewpoints contained in the case.

Next, the historical background of the case provides a chronological narrative to explain how the issue developed over time. Key events and major participants and their competing views are identified. The goal is to depict the clash of ideas and interests, the struggle between contending groups, and the different points of view that emerged in a long-standing or seemingly insoluble dilemma. The historical background section captures the reader's attention by providing a foundation for considering options to resolve the case controversy.

The policy options section provides an outline of alternative solutions to the case controversies. These solutions intentionally cover a wide range of possibilities. The goal is to stimulate the student's active participation as a problem solver. Policy options provide opportunities to decide the best way to resolve the case controversies. We do not include all possible solutions in the policy options. We encourage students to develop other solutions that might resolve case controversies more effectively.

Each case ends with a conclusion that summarizes the case controversies and options. The goal is to suggest probable future directions of the case controversy, as most case issues will remain debatable for many years.

The fourteen cases also include useful supplements to encourage active decision making. First, a series of discussion questions highlight and review the major case issues. Second, the class activity section suggests how policy options might be applied in discussions, debates, and other formats. Finally, there are suggestions for further reading, including useful websites.

We have four additional suggestions for students to consider in becoming effective problem solvers and decision makers of the case controversies:

- *Rational Actor Approach*: The student assesses the evidence provided, analyzes the case controversies, and makes a reasoned judgment concerning which option best resolves the controversies. The selected option is justified by a carefully reasoned argument that defends the preferred choice over the other options. The rational actor approach can be used in class reports and short papers in which students are asked to defend their preferred choice in resolving case controversies.
- *Advocacy Approach*: The student defends one of the options that best represents a particular point of view in resolving the case controversies. The point of view could be ideological, partisan, or representative of a group or organization involved in the case. The advocacy approach can be used in role-playing exercises in small discussion groups.
- *Political Decision Approach*: The student tries to fashion a solution from one or a combination of options that can satisfy a variety of contending viewpoints. In this approach, the decision maker seeks a solution that results from negotiation, bargaining, and compromise. Discussion groups can assist in facilitating the political approach.
- *Leadership Approach*: The student assumes the role of one of the key players in the case and selects an option that can be used as the basis for persuading others. In this approach, the leader needs to decide how best to convince others through rhetorical, moral, political, and other appeals. The goal is to persuade others involved in the case that it is in their own self-interest to accept the leader's preferred choice. Student presentations to small groups in which one person assumes the role of a leader is a way of facilitating this approach.

We have found that case studies work very well in the classroom by stimulating student debate, discussion, and research on term paper topics. The case approach is a valuable technique for student learning. It differs from traditional lecture and class discussion. By using cases, the instructor becomes a resource person in assisting students. The instructor is also a facilitator by encouraging students to become actively engaged in seeking solutions to political and policy controversies. As a result, the cases encourage both instructors and students to interact more closely and to become partners in the learning process.

Each case in this book is presented without commitment to a particular goal, viewpoint, or ideology. We present a variety of approaches to each controversy. We want students to reach their own conclusions in resolving case controversies. We hope that students will use critical thinking in selecting among their decision options.

Our case studies can be used to supplement any standard text on American politics. The book is designed primarily for use in the introductory American politics course, including the Advanced Placement program of the College Board that is offered in many secondary schools. Some of the cases can also be used for more advanced courses in American public policy. We suggest that instructors use the cases after introducing course topics and readings. Instructors should present the case issues to the class before students get involved in discussion and evaluation.

Our case book is a product of a joint effort by the coauthors, each of whom wrote seven cases. Edward Drachman, professor of political science at SUNY, Geneseo, wrote cases 2 through 7 and 14; and Robert Langran, professor of political science at Villanova University, wrote cases 1 and 8 through 13. We would like to thank students at both Geneseo and Villanova for their valuable assistance with several of the cases. Geneseo students who helped were Lis Garner (research and preparation of the Danish cartoons case); Chris Browne (research and writing of the Iraq case); and David Murphy and Mike Bagel (feedback on the final draft of Professor Drachman's cases). The Villanova students were in Professor Langran's graduate course on Congress and wrote the first drafts of the following case studies: Daniel Morris (original intent and eminent domain); Meredith Bullamore (campaign reform); Laura Coppeto (redistricting); Joshua Rucci (Electoral College); Rachel Hadley (filibuster); and Ashley C. Blaschak (presidential power in wartime). In addition, former Villanova graduate student Jeremy Johnson helped oversee these seven case studies, and current Villanova graduate student Brian Buechel helped put them into a consistent format. Professors Drachman and Langran would also like to thank Villanova's department secretary, Karen Wolfe, for helping to prepare the manuscript for submission to the publisher; and Rowman & Littlefield's political science editor Niels Aaboe for his encouragement and assistance in completion of this book project and Elaine McGarraugh, production editor, for her helpful suggestions to improve the readibility of the text.

To the students:

You, the students, will now examine fourteen cases and controversies in American politics. You have the opportunity to become directly involved in discussing, debating, evaluating, and solving controversial issues. We ask you to judge whether the case controversies can be resolved or why some of them will remain difficult problems for the foreseeable future. We ask you to consider the policy options critically, carefully, and completely. We also strongly encourage you to develop your own option(s) that can contribute to public debate on these controversial issues. In the final analysis, *You Decide!*

1

The Constitution

Case 1
Is Original Intent the Proper Model for Constitutional Interpretation?

Case Snapshot

Twin vacancies on the U.S. Supreme Court that arose in 2005 have once again sparked national interest in the Constitution and its various models of interpretation. Add to this the Republican platform of advocating and appointing "strict constructionist" judges, and the debate over constitutional interpretation is given temporal relevance. The contemporary debate is, however, usually shrouded with political rhetoric, and theories are often presented in binary conservative and liberal terms. Does this results-oriented rhetoric sidestep more important issues of judicial and political philosophy? If so, will the use of a jurisprudence of original intent allow us as a society to remain loyal to the ideals of the established republic? Did the Founders desire their intentions to guide interpretation in forthcoming decades? And if so, how does one discern the collective intent of the fifty-five delegates when history tells us of their bitter divisions and debates? Whereas many notable conservatives are now (and have been) advocating original intent as a theory of interpretation, still others cry for a different approach, one that is potentially more useful in accommodating changing societal ideals and political surroundings. What do you think about the nature of the Constitution? Should judges defer to the original intentions of the Founders, or will a theory of the "living Constitution" better serve our needs of adapting to a constantly altering social climate?

In today's politically polarized society, the stakes in the debate are immense. Over the past forty years or so, Supreme Court decisions have legalized abortions, made available a plethora of rights to criminal defendants, liberalized obscenity and pornography laws, placed restrictions on the death penalty, and hindered (and even blocked) state support for religion. Most of these decisions have been decried as liberal attempts to legislate from the bench. Will a return to original intent change the direction of the judicial branch? You decide!

Major Case Controversies

1. *The Founding Fathers recognized the need for a written Constitution, as opposed to the un-written common law pervasive in England.* A great deal of reflection and debate went into the forging of this document, and many concessions were made to entice the necessary states to ratify.
2. *In 1803, in the case Marbury v. Madison, the Supreme Court assumed the power of judicial review.* With this power, the Court can determine the constitutionality of the laws of the land. What is necessary to properly carry out this power is a question for interpretation.
3. *The model of original intent seeks to interpret the Constitution in light of those who drafted and ratified it.* This is subject to controversy because there likely exists no collective intent upon which to base interpretation. Rather, the Constitution was forged on compromises and accommodations.
4. *In recent decades, various liberal judges have embraced the idea of a living Constitution.* But opponents contend that the text of the Constitution is not malleable, aside from changes that may be made according to the amendment process set forth in Article V.
5. *The current Supreme Court is divided over reliance on originalism.* Justice Antonin Scalia, for example, is an originalist/textualist in that he looks at the text of the Constitution and statutes in arriving at decisions, whereas Justice Stephen Breyer takes a more pragmatic approach to constitutional issues, so that instead of embracing any kind of judicial doctrine, he prefers to decide cases in a way that will produce continuity in law.
6. *There is growing debate both within and without the Supreme Court over use of international law in the Court's decisions.* Justices Ruth Bader Ginsburg and Anthony Kennedy at times resort to this whereas Justice Scalia opposes it. Do we know where the other judges stand, especially the Chief Justice?

Background of the Case

The model of original intent resurged after a period of liberalism, which surfaced with the triumph of the New Deal and persevered via the Warren Court in the 1960s and onward.

For example, the Court began to uphold most of the important New Deal measures beginning with the 1937 case of *National Labor Relations Board v. Jones & Laughlin Steel Corporation* (sustaining the National Labor Relations Act). Then in the 1960s the Court rendered many liberal decisions such as in the 1966 *Miranda v. Arizona* case in which it told the police what they must tell a suspect upon apprehension. In reaction to these types of decisions, Attorney General Edwin Meese in 1985 published an article advocating a return to a "jurisprudence of original intention." It was his view that the Founders intended for federal judges to "resist any political effort to depart from the literal provisions of the Constitution. The text of the document and the original intention of those who framed it would be the judicial standard in giving effect to the Constitution." Furthermore, Meese wrote that legal scholars and judges should attempt to discern and resurrect the original meaning as the sole guide for judgment. What is interesting is Meese's interchanging use of intent, text, and meaning (a relationship that will be developed in more detail later in this chapter). This minor point of contention notwithstanding, his article effectively set the scene for the contemporary debate over constitutional review. Since then, Meese's "originalism" has become the dogma for conservative critics of the judicial branch. It needs to be noted that original intent is often synonymous with originalism, and the two terms are often carelessly interchanged. In fact, originalism developed as a broader doctrine, and has since been clarified and broken down into a family of theories, including original intent.

The call for a jurisprudence of original intent correlated with the realignment of American politics in the 1980s, led by the conservative administration of President Ronald Reagan. The use of original intent was intended to curb judicial discretion in favor of returning to the core principles of the American Founding, namely, a limited government operating under a written constitution. In the 1990s the original intent jurisprudence gained support in the academic community. Supported by strong intellectual currents in philosophical and political theory, American judges and legal scholars are once again embracing a theory of original intent. It is necessary, then, to determine whether original intent is the proper model of interpretation. To do so, we will need to look at the following items. First, we will examine whose intentions count for the model and whether or not the Founders may have wanted their intentions to guide future generations. Then, these historical reflections will bow to a systematic comparative effort, and we will look at both other theories in the originalist family and other, nonoriginalist methods.

The Model of Original Intent

Whose Intentions?

In broad terms, original intent is a doctrine of constitutional interpretation holding that judges should interpret the written Constitution in a manner consistent with the intentions of those who framed and ratified it. Advocates are known for an insistence that constitutional meaning is perpetually fixed. Who fixed it is a minor point of contention among contemporary originalists. So, whose intentions count? Some will say the drafters of the specific constitutional language. Others focus on the Framers, or those fifty-five men present at the Philadelphia Convention in 1787. Another group might strive to discern the intent of the ratifiers (those members of the state legislatures who voted to ratify the Constitution and its following amendments), and still others concentrate on the *vox populi*, whose interests were represented by the ratifiers. These potential discrepancies need only be noted, and do not affect the basic maxim of the model of original intent, which is this: Once the meaning of the Constitution (and other constructed statutes) is settled by whatever body, that meaning is not open-ended and would not and should not evolve. For the purposes of our analysis, we will refer to the intent of the "Founders," meaning those persons involved with the drafting and ratifying of the text, although most writers use "Founders" and "Framers" interchangeably. Using the model of original intent involves a detailed study of a variety of sources. Included are, foremost and most obviously, the Constitution, but also the writings of the authors and the records of the Constitutional Convention, used in an attempt to discern the original intent of the Founders. Some useful texts are *The Federalist Papers*, Farrand's *Records of the Constitutional Convention*, William Blackstone's *Commentaries on the Laws of England*, and James Madison's *Notes of Debates in the Federal Convention of 1787*. This raises another interesting issue, and that is the importance of history on the model of original intent.

The Intentions of the Founders?

Some will argue that the job of discerning original intent may be better suited for historians than sitting judges, and there may be some truth to this, considering the hardships involved. James Madison knew full well the frustrations involved, having undertaken a study of the histories of distinguished confederacies throughout antiquity. Perhaps that is why he embraced the Machiavellian concept of *ridurre ai principii*, the belief that a periodic return to the founding principles was necessary for the survival of the republic. If these principles were not intermittently returned to, history might bury them in silence. Accordingly, Madison himself undertook the task of taking detailed notes and observations during the Convention.

So, did the Founders mean for their intent to guide the interpretations of future generations? Some will say yes, citing their willingness to break with the English tradition of unwritten common law as evidence. Putting a constitution in writing might seem counterintuitive if the intent and meaning of that constitution is allowed to wander aimlessly through time. If this is the case, why was there no stenographer present to keep an official record for reasons of publication? Why were not Madison's notes published until after his death? Were the Founders concerned with appearances, worried that exposing the proceedings might hurt chances of ratification? The answers are not clear, and will vary from scholar to scholar, but whether or not the Founders meant for their intentions to be used for interpretation may become irrelevant when considering another problem—the lack of history. The model of original intent will have history as its guiding force. Thus, an absence of records (some say Madison's and Farrand's are insufficient and ill-kept) may in fact render this model impossible. Those opposed to original intent will argue that even if ample records were available, the Supreme Court lacks the resources to conduct the necessary historical analysis and research. Perhaps because of these potential shortcomings, originalists began to abandon parts of this general model.

Intent vs. Text and Meaning

The model of original intent must be further developed if we are to accurately assess its merit. Originalists, in the broadest sense, agree that the current meaning of the Constitution and laws should be determined only in accordance with their meaning at the time in which they were promulgated. In other words, the meaning of the Constitution was fixed at the moment of its adoption by the states. Disputes can arise, however, within this general camp. While agreeing that the "intent" of the Constitution is binding, originalists frequently disagree over how to conceptualize this intent, be it through text, intended meaning, or commonly understood meaning. For the sake of clarity, we will delineate the various factions of originalism.

Supporters of original intent, which is our concern here, adhere to the old idea that the Supreme Court should interpret the Constitution according to the understanding of it by the Founders. It is clear today that many of the intentions of the Founders remain, as elements of the earliest American government prevail today: government by consent of the governed, a bill of rights applying to all branches of government, majority rule under a carefully constructed system of restraints, federalism, a single executive, a bicameral legislature, an independent judiciary, a system of checks and balances, and a representative government with elections at predetermined times. Additionally, the underpinnings of liberty and equality that the Founders strove for have been advanced and enhanced throughout history with various amendments. The issue gets complicated, however, upon more detailed analysis of the model of original intent.

This particular jurisprudence has several potential advantages. Advocates of original intent claim that this model will lessen the risk that is intrinsic in a more interpretative approach. In this way, judges are less likely to inject their own personal values into their decisions about the meaning of the Constitution. Critics of judicial activism claim that all too often, judges will displace the law with their personal predilections. This is a potential weakness inherent in the judiciary. Original intent can help by creating a criterion distinct from those preferences of the judge. Adherence to the Founders' intent will allow a judge to remain objective. This is, however, also where the model can begin to break down. Critics of the model of original intent (often originalists of a different breed) claim that because the intent of the Founders is unclear in many cases, such as slavery, judges will have no choice but to enforce their own interpretations—the very flaw that the model ostensibly seeks to avoid. Consider this example. *Dred Scott v. Sandford* was decided in 1857 and was the first invalidation of a federal law since the Court's establishment of judicial review in 1803. Since the Founders were indeterminate in their treatment of slavery, the various branches of government were consequently given significant freedom of choice. Chief Justice Roger Taney of Maryland headed the Supreme Court that heard the case. A dominant question of national politics at the time was slavery, and Taney's majority opinion used powerful language, holding that slaves were at the time of the Founding "considered as a subordinate and inferior class of beings, who had been subjugated by the dominant race, and whether emancipated or not, yet remained subject to their authority, and had no rights and privileges but such as those who held the power and the Government might choose to grant them." Taney, and those supporting him, tried to justify the *Dred Scott* decision by appealing to the intentions of the Founders. Since there was no explicit provision that could be read to confer a right to own slaves, Taney employed his own thoughts concerning what he thought to be the intentions of the Founders. (Interestingly, in his dissent Justice Benjamin Curtis notes the danger in using the intentions of the Founders to veil a judge's own views.) In a definitive statement on a jurisprudence of original intent, Taney wrote:

> No one, we presume, supposes that any change in public opinion or feeling, in relation to this unfortunate race ... should induce the Court to give the words of the Constitution a more liberal construction in their favor than they were intended to bear when the instrument was framed and adopted .... [W]hile it remains unaltered, it must be construed now as it was understood at the time of its adoption .... [I]t speaks with the same meaning and intent with which it spoke when it came from the hand of the framers.

And here is Justice Curtis:

> [W]hen a strict interpretation of the Constitution, according to the fixed rules which govern the interpretation of laws, is abandoned, and the theoretical opinions of individuals are allowed to control its meaning, we have no longer a Constitution; we are under the government of individual men, who for the time being have power to declare what the Constitution is, according to their own views of what it ought to mean.

So the model of original intent strives to be politically neutral, but this becomes difficult for historically fuzzy cases. Perhaps this is why many originalists have instead embraced the theory of *original meaning*. Original meaning applies to the literal wording of the Constitution and all its provisions, and the model is allied with what scholars have deemed textualism.

Textualism intends to achieve the sort of personal detachment from judicial policy for which the original intent model strives, but may fall short. In deference to the written Constitution, it is easier to remain objective in the decision-making process. Thus, the danger of the judge enforcing his or her own personal values under the guise of the Founders' intentions is lessened. By relying on the text, judges are less likely (and less able) to rationalize political outcomes with ad hoc reasoning, something for which judicial activists are often criticized. Contrary to claims on the political left and right, original meaning/textualism is not a results-oriented jurisprudence.

In fact, the method, properly applied, is indeed politically neutral. The model will only lead to ideological results if ideological positions are legislated, and even then, the results will still be bound to the degree of that position. Thus, it significantly reduces the risk of judicial policy making by those judges who stray from the literal meaning of constitutional language. Also, textualists are less likely to face the problem of conceptualizing a collective and authoritative intent. The approach may also encourage more stable constitutional scholarship by placing emphasis on the text rather than shaky historical analysis. Textualism might then reduce the need to engage in complicated historical research and analysis, which may be both time-consuming and expensive. Additionally, consider that the text of the Constitution is likely more authoritative than the intent of the Founders because only the text was presented to the ratifying bodies. American constitutional text is indeed determinate when compared to the unwritten British constitution to which the document was no doubt compared.

But how useful is text without context? Should judges go any distance to account for the will of the Founders? Is there a spirit *and* letter of the law? These questions present difficulty for this model, which is why some judges instead embrace original understanding (or intent).

Original understanding differs from both original intent and original meaning/textualism. Original understanding is used to examine the interpretations and beliefs formed by those original ratifiers. So, for example, interpretation of the Twenty-seventh Amendment (ratified on May 7, 1992, 203 years after it was proposed) would focus exclusively on the impressions of those twentieth-century ratifiers, and not the colonial framers. This model might be useful as the legitimacy and supremacy of the Constitution as a source of law is derived from the populist schema in which it was ratified.

Objections to Original Intent

Like most other models of interpretation, original intent (and originalism in general) has its critics. Some would argue that a jurisprudence of original intent fails because it assumes the existence of one, collective intent. It is known, however, because of various supporting documents, like notes on the Philadelphia convention, that the Founders did not have the same convictions. Thus, an opposing school of thought has emerged over the years, one advocating a living Constitution. An early advocate of this school of thought was Justice Oliver Wendell Holmes, whose ideas have gained support and strength over time. Former Supreme Court Justice William Brennan was a big proponent of the living Constitution theory and opposed former Attorney General Meese when the latter made his call for original intent. The theory has been termed and/or associated with judicial activism, and is rooted in a potential fundamental flaw in adherence to the original documents of the Founders. For originalists, variations from the intent of the Founders can only be justified if they are required by controlling precedent (and even the importance of precedence will differ amongst originalist judges). Some people have grown to believe that this is simply indefensible, citing a logical limit to the amount that the dead Founders may govern from the grave. In 1910, the Supreme Court agreed, writing in the case *Weems v. United States*:

> Time works changes, brings into existence new conditions and purposes. Therefore a principle to be vital must be capable of wider application than the mischief which gave it birth. This is particularly true of constitutions. They are not ephemeral enactments . . . . In the application of a constitution, therefore, our contemplation cannot be only of what has been but of what may be.

Advocates of a living Constitution claim that the Constitution was written by a small number of white males (no women, Native Americans, African Americans, etc.) who may or may not have had any concern for those people outside their particular demographic. Therefore, the original intent theory cannot include these nonparticipants. Howard Zinn makes this point in his book *A People's History of the United States*.

Charles Beard, in his book *An Economic Interpretation of the Constitution*, claims that the overwhelming majority of the Framers were economic beneficiaries from the adoption of the Constitution, which again works against the original intent theory. Supporters also note that if the Constitution is to continue to unify the nation, it cannot be "frozen" in the eighteenth century. Standards of interpretation will almost inevitably evolve, and amendments will be made if the Constitution is to speak with the same authority and relevance as it did in the past. In this way, the changing needs of societies will continue to be accommodated.

It needs to be noted that the notion of a living Constitution is not a theory of interpretation, as is the model of original intent. Rather, it is a characterization that is often associated with nonoriginalist doctrines. Accordingly, the living Constitution is often interchanged with judicial pragmatism. For example, a judge embracing a living Constitution will interpret constitutional language such as "equal rights" based on contemporary standards of equality, not those standards of the American Founding. In this way, many legal scholars have come to view the relationship of original intent and the living Constitution as dichotomous. But does it have to be? After all, did not the Founders *intend* for amendments to be made, providing a detailed process for the American populace to do so? Is insisting on a certain amount of flexibility and accepting that many constitutional provisions are intentionally broad totally inconsistent with the ideals of the Founders? Or is a living Constitution a dead constitution? In other words, if the Constitution can mean anything, does it mean anything?

Policy Options

Various models of interpretation are perhaps more obvious in scholarly work done by political scientists than in opinions handed down by federal judges. Supreme Court justices, however, will generally have discernible judicial philosophies. By examining these philosophies, one can see two things: (1) how the models of original intent and the notion of a living Constitution affect the outcome of cases that consequently affect the nation on social, political, and economic issues; and (2) the interplay of these models within the overall dynamic of the Court. The following philosophies characterize (in the broadest sense) the approaches of the members of today's Supreme Court:

1. *A delicate adherence to the text of the Constitution and federal statutes.* This is the approach taken by the Court's leading originalist/textualist, Justice Antonin Scalia. His colleague, Justice Clarence Thomas, also embraces this method. Although the two justices often agree when deciding cases, they will occasionally diverge, usually based on preference for *stare decisis* in a given case. *Stare decisis* means to let the decision stand, and it is used to build decisions upon previous decisions involving the same point of law, therefore forming precedents and making the law more certain. This approach also discounts the use and importance of legislative history when interpreting statutes.
2. *Judicial minimalism with a strong deference to settled law.* Although labeled a conservative by most advocates and opponents during his confirmation hearings, Chief Justice John

Roberts Jr. is proving himself to be heavily deferential, especially in cases that are considered settled. This approach emphasizes the importance of *stare decisis* in maintaining stability and legitimacy for the law. It seems as if Justice Samuel Alito Jr. is also of this mold, with strokes of evenhandedness pervasive in his opinions. Alito, although often philosophically associated with Scalia, values the importance of legislative history, which at times places the two at odds.

3. *A conservative/libertarian mix with* no *defined judicial philosophy.* Such is the case with Justice Anthony Kennedy who, with the retirement of Justice Sandra Day O'Connor, has become a doctrinal fulcrum on the Court. He is known for a broad reading of certain clauses, such as the Due Process Clause of the Fourteenth Amendment, but seems to use ad hoc reasoning in other opinions. He is also criticized for his citing of international law—law from the various European countries, as well as from the European Union, and others—a concept that originalists find outrageous.

4. *A pragmatic approach to constitutional issues.* Justices taking this approach are less concerned with embracing any kind of judicial doctrine than they are with deciding cases in such a way that will produce continuity in law. Justices David Souter and Stephen Breyer are known to be moderate pragmatists on the Court. Another, more liberal Justice, Ruth Bader Ginsburg, tends to evade doctrinal categorization and cites international law in justification of her opinions.

5. *Liberal, but not pragmatic, originalist, etc.* Justice John Paul Stevens is difficult to label. Although he is associated with the liberal bloc of the Court, he will often take distinctive, individual approaches to cases, straying from an early judicial career marked by conservative decisions.

Conclusion

The further removed We the People become from the American founding, the more concern will naturally arise that our source of supreme law, the Constitution, remains accommodating to evolving societal norms. Some judges believe that the best way to ensure this is to embrace the notion of a living Constitution. This approach, while not characterized by a particular judicial methodology, attempts to interpret the Constitution and its various provisions in a modern context. Others will embrace the model of original intent, or one of its sister theories, and abide by the principles held true by those who drafted and ratified the words of the Constitution.

Historically, the idea of a written constitution was better suited to a nation still wary of the specter of a monarchy. By putting the Constitution in writing (and having it pass through the populist stages of ratification), the Founders ensured that Americans would forever have a benchmark upon which to measure the law and its interplay with government and human rights. Should the Constitution, then, be safeguarded against encroaches by activist judges, or should judges properly interpret these notions of justice and liberty by contemporary standards?

The fall and winter 2005–2006 battles over Supreme Court nominees Chief Justice Roberts and Associate Justice Alito have once again emphasized the importance of constitutional interpretation and its potential effect on society en masse. Modern concerns have focused on judicial activism, which can take on various forms. On the political right, judicial critics claim that liberal judges use the idea of a living Constitution only to justify results-oriented, policy-driven decisions. This reckless abandon will weaken the structure of constitutional law by writing and rewriting laws that do not properly correlate with the vision of the Founders. Conversely, liberal critics claim that "bad" forms of originalism, especially original intent, will essentially do the same thing, by inserting a conservative policy agenda in the place of the potentially unknowable intent of the Founders.

Are we stuck then between Scylla and Charybdis? Or do the strengths of either model merit their use? Or perhaps there is a pragmatic medium that can remain true to the ideals of the Founders? The debate is ongoing.

Discussion Questions

1. Should the American people in the twenty-first century be bound by the original intent of the Framers (those who actually attended the 1787 Constitutional Convention)?
2. Why might the Founders (the Framers plus others from that era who were involved with the drafting and ratifying of the Constitution) have wanted their intent to guide future interpretation of the Constitution? Why might they have not wanted this?
3. What are some of the theoretical strengths of the model of original intent? Is original meaning/textualism a better way to achieve the goal of the originalists?
4. What problems do issues such as slavery in the *Dred Scott* case pose for the model of original intent?
5. Does the fact that the American Constitution is written and was born after careful reflection and ratification support the argument for original intent?
6. Which faction of originalism might yield the most desirable results—original intent, meaning, or understanding. Why?
7. What are the strengths and limitations of the notion of a living Constitution?
8. What other approaches might judges use to properly interpret the Constitution?

Class Activities

1. Debate the relative merits of the theory of original intent and the view of a living Constitution and discuss what approach the Founders would have favored.
2. Divide the class into three groups. Groups 1 and 2 will defend either original intent or the living Constitution. Group 3 will ask questions to both groups on the legitimacy of each approach and possible weaknesses/reforms.

Suggestions for Further Reading

Barton, David. *Original Intent: The Courts, the Constitution, and Religion.* Aledo, TX: Wall Builder Press, 1996.

Bassham, Gregory. *Original Intent and the Constitution: A Philosophical Study.* Lanham, MD: Rowman & Littlefield, 1992.

Belz, Herman. *A Living Constitution or Fundamental Law? American Constitutionalism in Historical Perspective.* Lanham, MD: Rowman & Littlefield, 1998.

Bork, Robert H. *The Tempting of America: The Political Seduction of the Law.* New York: Free Press, 1990.

Carter, Lief H., and Thomas F. Burke. *Reason in Law.* New York: Pearson, 2005.

Fisher, Louis. *Constitutional Dialogues: Interpretation as Political Process.* Princeton: Princeton University Press, 1988.

Goldstein, Leslie Friedman. *In Defense of the Text: Democracy and Constitutional Theory.* Savage, MD: Rowman & Littlefield, 1991.

Levy, Leonard W. *Original Intent and the Framers' Constitution.* New York: Macmillan, 1988.

Lynch, Joseph, M. *Negotiating the Constitution: The Earliest Debates over Original Intent.* Ithaca, NY: Cornell University Press, 1999.

Maltz, Earl M. *Rethinking Constitutional Law: Originalism, Interventionism, and the Politics of Judicial Review.* Lawrence: University Press of Kansas, 1994.

Rakove, Jack N. *Original Meanings: Politics and Ideas in the Making of the Constitution.* New York: Knopf, 1996.

Smith, Rogers. *Civic Ideals: Conflicting Patterns of Citizenship in U.S. History.* New Haven: Yale University Press, 1997.

Whittington, Keith E. *Constitutional Interpretation: Textual Meaning, Original Intent, and Judicial Review.* Lawrence: University Press of Kansas, 1999.

Helpful Websites

www.earlyamerica.com/review/fall98/original.html. This website argues for original intent.

http://people.brandeis.edu/~teuber/origintent.html. This website claims that the drafters of the Constitution took steps to block efforts to recover their original intent.

2

Federalism

Case 2

Should Undocumented Students Qualify for In-State Tuition Benefits from Public Colleges and Universities?

Case Snapshot

AT THE DAWN OF THE TWENTY-FIRST CENTURY, immigrants started coming to the United States in near record numbers, reminiscent of the great waves that engulfed its shores at the beginning of the previous century. Yet most immigrants now come from Mexico and countries of Central America, the Caribbean, and South Asia rather than Europe, and unlike ever before many more are here illegally. Prior to World War I almost all immigrants were allowed into this country; the two main exceptions were those barred for reasons of health or, in the case of Chinese, "racial unassimilability." When Congress imposed immigration quotas after World War I, it also created the phenomenon of illegal immigration. Most illegal immigrants enter the U.S. by sneaking across the border with Mexico. Others come with stolen or fraudulent documents; still others (approximately 45 percent of the total number of illegals) simply overstay their visas. According to a report by the Pew Hispanic Center, as of March 2006 almost 12 million illegal immigrants were living in the United States. Moreover, this number was expected to increase by an estimated 850,000 a year if current trends hold. According to the U.S. Constitution, the federal government has plenary (complete or full) power over immigration. Over the years, the Supreme Court has repeatedly reaffirmed this by consistently deferring to the federal government on any conflict between state and federal laws regarding immigration. However, fast-growing illegal immigration has complicated matters, resulting in the development of a two-tier responsibility for immigration. Congress clearly retains plenary power to regulate admission and expulsion of immigrants, but by not adequately policing this country's borders it has left the states with the responsibility of providing benefits for increasing numbers of illegal immigrants residing within their borders. In addition to emergency medical care, one of the most important, costly, and contentious benefits states provide to illegal immigrants is education. In *Plyler v. Doe* (1982), the Supreme Court ruled that states must provide all persons, including undocumented children, equal access to K–12 public education. However, this decision left unanswered the main question of this case: Should states provide all persons with equal access to public postsecondary education by making undocumented students eligible for much lower in-state tuition? You decide!

Major Case Controversies

1. *Congress clearly has plenary (complete) power over immigration based on these major constitutional clauses: supremacy (of the federal government) in any conflict between federal laws and state laws, commerce, uniform rule of naturalization, citizenship, and "necessary and proper."* But under the police power of the Tenth Amendment states can pass laws and regulations that involve the health, safety, welfare, and education of their residents, including illegal immigrants.
2. *Some argue there should be a difference in treatment between illegal immigrants who have sneaked across the border or passed through border controls with false documents and those who have entered this country legally but for whatever reason(s) overstayed their visas.*
3. *Over the years, a number of special categories of immigrants have evolved that further complicate the federalism issue:* refugees (people who flee their countries because of a well-founded fear of persecution based on race, religion, nationality, membership in a particular social group, or political belief); people with temporary protected status (aliens admitted to the United States under emergency, usually humanitarian conditions, like El Salvadorans escaping war and Hondurans fleeing after Hurricane Mitch); and people who are in the process of applying for asylum or another legal residency status.
4. *It is questionable whether constitutionally Congress can delegate to the states certain powers over immigration* (e.g., the proposed DREAM Act, which would authorize states to give in-state tuition benefits to undocumented students). A different interpretation of the Constitution holds that the tuition issue falls under the states' police power.
5. *There is a contradiction between the fact that Congress has plenary power over immigration, yet does not provide financial assistance to the states to provide benefits for undocumented immigrants.*
6. *In Plyler v. Doe, the Supreme Court ruled that states must provide free public education (K–12) to all persons living inside their borders, but it was silent on postsecondary education.* Would states be violating the Equal Protection Clause of the Fourteenth Amendment if they did not allow all persons within their borders to qualify for in-state tuition? Would they also be violating Title VI of the Civil Rights Act of 1964, which prohibits discrimination based on immigration status?
7. *The in-state tuition issue is further clouded by Title IV of the Higher Education Act of 1965, which forbids undocumented students from receiving federal aid for postsecondary education, and two 1996 federal laws* (the Personal Responsibility and Work Opportunity Reconciliation Act [PRWORA] and the Illegal Immigration Reform and Immigration Responsibility Act [IIRIRA]), both of which aim to deny undocumented students state or local benefits for college education.
8. *Most states interpret federal law to mean undocumented students are ineligible for government financial aid to state colleges.* Thus, even when undocumented students qualify for in-state tuition they are ineligible for financial aid, which very often makes college attendance prohibitively expensive.

9. *Currently, whether undocumented students are eligible for in-state college tuition depends on which state they live in.* As of spring 2007, ten states offer in-state tuition to undocumented students. A number of others are considering doing this. However, other states have denied in-state tuition benefits. Should each state decide for itself on this issue, or should there be a uniform national policy?

10. *There is controversy over whether Americans should help illegal immigrants already in this country.* One position, such as that taken by some leaders in the Catholic Church, is that helping illegal immigrants is the just, moral, fair, and humane policy; accordingly, these leaders believe that it is their duty to disobey any law that may be passed which criminalizes illegal immigrants. An opposing position, which also claims the moral high ground, is that Americans should not help people who break the laws of this country, and that illegal immigrants should not have any advantages, such as in-state tuition, that are not made available to all legal residents—in accordance with their interpretation of PRWORA and IIRIRA.

11. *It is uncertain at which level of government the in-state college tuition controversy should be addressed.* Congress may let each state decide for itself on immigration questions, possibly by referendum; it could also defer to the Supreme Court, which may or may not address the issue head-on.

Background of the Case

According to the U.S. Constitution, Congress has plenary power to regulate immigration. When the Homeland Security Act of 2002 created the Department of Homeland Security, the Immigration and Naturalization Service (INS) was soon abolished. Since March 1, 2003, immigration has been administered by the Bureau of Immigration and Customs (ICE), located within the directorate of Border and Transportation Security (BTS).

One of the biggest problems the government has to deal with is illegal immigration. There are more illegal immigrants than ever before, now numbering around 12 million. Each year approximately 500,000 enter the United States from Mexico alone by sneaking across the border or crossing with fraudulent or stolen documents; some even have been smuggled into the U.S. from countries such as the People's Republic of China. Others are here illegally because they overstayed their legal visas (e.g., tourist visas, H–1B visas that attract high-tech workers, and F–1 student visas that bring international students to our colleges). Still others are considered illegal while they await processing for asylum or immigrant status.

The majority of illegal immigrants live in six states (California, Texas, Florida, New York, Illinois, and New Jersey). However, this demographic pattern is changing as the bulk of the most recent rapid growth has been in the Southwest, the Rocky Mountains, the Midwest, and the Southeast—especially North Carolina and Georgia. Many illegal immigrants would live in this country legally, but immigrant visas granted each year are very limited by statute (5,000 permanent visas worldwide for unskilled workers) and the process of applying and waiting for legal status is long and drawn-out. For example, Mexicans who are naturalized U.S. citizens have to wait at least twelve years to bring an adult child to live in the U.S.; and those who are legal residents must wait up to seven years to bring in a spouse or young children. This frustrating situation results in a big backlog of applicants, only some of whom eventually will be approved.

Most illegal immigrants come to the U.S. to get better-paying jobs. Like most Americans, they pursue the American dream of a better life than they left behind. Education is the key to fulfillment of this dream. Neither federal nor state law forbids undocumented students from attending college, but in effect many are turned away for financial reasons.

Access to postsecondary education remains severely constrained by federal laws that prevent undocumented students from receiving financial assistance to attend college. Title IV of the Higher Education Act of 1965 forbids undocumented students from receiving federal aid for postsecondary education. In addition, the Personal Responsibility and Work Opportunity Reconciliation Act (PRWORA) and the Illegal Immigration Reform and Immigration Responsibility Act (IIRIRA), both enacted in 1996 on a wave of anti-immigrant sentiment sweeping the country, aim to exclude undocumented students from receiving state or local benefits for postsecondary education.

PRWORA and IIRIRA have sparked a national debate. They have forced states to grapple over how or even whether to comply, both because of differing interpretations of these laws and their questionable constitutionality. Moreover, with ineffective federal policing of U.S. borders, by default as well as devolution of power, states have had to assume increased responsibility for dealing with undocumented immigrants within their borders. The financial burden of providing a wide range of benefits has been especially troublesome. Some states with the largest numbers of undocumented immigrants, including California, Texas, Arizona, New Jersey, and Florida, have even sued the federal government to reimburse their costs of services. However, the courts have consistently rebuffed these efforts. The leading case is *Chiles v. United States* (1994), where the U.S. District Court in Miami, Florida, found that a Florida lawsuit presented "a non-justiciable political question, inappropriate for judicial resolution because it requires the Court to adjudicate in areas of foreign policy, national defense, immigration, and the allocation of federal resources." The court concluded that "reimbursement should be considered as a political rather than judicial matter." One thing the court suggested states might do when seeking financial relief for services for undocumented immigrants is to lobby the federal government.

The Controversy over Proposition 187 in California

One of the most costly and politically contentious benefits that states have been wrangling over is education. This is especially true where there are the largest numbers of both legal and illegal immigrants, like California. Upset by what they considered an unfair heavy financial burden, in 1994 voters in this state tried to deny health care, welfare benefits, and educational services (including postsecondary education) to undocumented immigrants through passage of Proposition 187. Supporters argued that welfare, medical, and educational benefits were magnets that drew undocumented immigrants to California; that the federal government had fallen down on its responsibility of policing the country's borders; and that California should show the way in stopping the subsidization of undocumented immigrants—to the tune then of roughly $5 billion a year. This proposition passed easily, with a majority of voters believing that it would not only save money but also ease the problem of overcrowded public school classrooms on all levels.

Almost immediately, a host of civil rights groups challenged Proposition 187 in court. They maintained it would not accomplish its main goal of curbing illegal immigration. More specifically, they claimed that it would do nothing to beef up enforcement of border crossings; nor would it penalize employers who hire undocumented immigrants. The proposition would also create a "police state mentality," for it would force public officials to deny services to anyone they suspected of being an undocumented immigrant. Opponents of the proposition estimated that approximately 400,000 students would be kicked out of school. Because most would not be deported, they would probably just hang out, have insufficient education to get a good job, and get into trouble. Students who might have become contributing workers and solid citizens instead might turn up on the rubbish heap—through no fault of their own. States might also lose federal education funds if school districts disclosed information from education records in violation of the Family Educational Rights and Privacy Act (FERPA).

Finally, opponents of Proposition 187 argued that the proposition was unconstitutional because it violated the Supremacy, Equal Protection, and Due Process Clauses of the U.S. Constitution. Moreover, it contradicted Supreme Court decisions in two landmark cases: *DeCanas v. Bica* (1976) and *Plyler v. Doe* (1982). *DeCanas* dealt mainly with issues of supremacy and preemption. It held that federal power to regulate immigration did not preempt a California statute that prohibited an employer from knowingly employing an illegal alien because the state law was consonant with federal law. Thus, states could regulate aliens under their traditional police power so long as their regulations furthered legitimate state interests and were "consistent with pertinent federal laws." This case is widely cited in the controversy over awarding of state benefits to undocumented immigrants, including in-state tuition. However, the more directly relevant case is *Plyler v. Doe* (1982) which held that undocumented children were entitled to K–12 public school education under the Due Process and Equal Protection Clauses of the Fourteenth Amendment. Although this case did not address postsecondary education, many people believe that by extension its decision and arguments have an important bearing on the in-state college tuition controversy.

The Impact of *Plyler v. Doe* on K–12 Public Education

The *Plyler* case involved a law enacted by the Texas state legislature in May 1975 authorizing local school districts to bar undocumented children (mainly from Mexico) from enrolling in public schools if they chose to do so. The alternative, chosen by the Tyler Independent School District, was to charge these children tuition.

In 1977, defense attorneys filed a class-action suit on behalf of "certain school-age children of Mexican origin residing in Smith County, Texas, who could not establish that they had been legally admitted into the United States" against the State of Texas, the Texas Education Agency, and several Texas school districts. A federal district court ruled in both 1977 and 1980 that state law violated the Equal Protection Clause of the Fourteenth Amendment. A court injunction then barred both the state and the Tyler school board from denying free public education to undocumented children. After a federal appeals court in 1981 upheld the district court rulings, the Tyler school board and school superintendent James Plyler appealed to the U.S. Supreme Court. The key constitutional questions were whether the Equal Protection Clause applied to undocumented children, and if so, whether they were entitled to a free public school education.

The Supreme Court, in a 5–4 decision, upheld the basic arguments of the defense lawyers, which were supported by briefs from a wide array of civil rights and political activist groups. The majority opinion, written by Justice William J. Brennan Jr. (with Justices Harry Blackmun, John Paul Stevens, Thurgood Marshall, and Lewis F. Powell Jr. concurring), held that denying undocumented children access to free public education "imposes a lifetime hardship on a discrete class of children not accountable for their disabling status [and that] the stigma of illiteracy will mark them for the rest of their lives."

More specifically, the defense argued the following:

- children of illegal immigrants were indeed "persons" living under the jurisdiction of the State of Texas and thus under the Fourteenth Amendment were entitled to equal access to public education;
- every person had the right to equal educational opportunity, reflecting the landmark decision in *Brown v. Board of Education* (1954);
- although the right to education did not meet the test of a "fundamental right" (citing the U.S. Supreme Court decision in *San Antonio Independent School District v. Rodriguez* [1973]), it was more than an ordinary right;
- education was "not merely some government 'benefit' indistinguishable from other forms of social welfare legislation," but an important interest that plays a "fundamental role in maintaining the fabric of our society";
- "[c]harging tuition to undocumented children constitutes a ludicrously ineffectual attempt to stem the tide of illegal immigration";
- although "illegal aliens" were not an inherently "suspect" class entitled to strict scrutiny protection under the Equal Protection Clause, their situation merited an "intermediate level of scrutiny";
- denying undocumented students free public education was not justified by any "substantial state interest";
- undocumented immigrants come to the U.S. mainly for jobs, not public benefits;
- not educating undocumented children would mean even higher future costs (e.g., in terms of jobs, welfare, health care, and crime);
- undocumented children were "basically indistinguishable" from legal resident alien children as regards educational cost to the state;
- undocumented children should not be punished for decisions made by their parents;
- denying free public education to all children would deleteriously split some immigrant families as some children would be born in Mexico and some in the U.S.; and
- in the future many of these undocumented children would seek legal residence and/or U.S. citizenship and thus everyone, the undocumented children as well as the State of Texas, would benefit.

Brennan concluded that "there is no assurance that a child subject to deportation will ever be deported. An illegal entrant might be granted federal permission to continue to reside in this country, or even to become a citizen . . . . It would of course be most difficult for the State of Texas to justify denial of education to a child enjoying an inchoate federal permission to remain." In other words, Brennan was arguing that the federal government, by its lax enforcement of immigration laws, was in effect accepting the consequence that undocumented immigrants should be entitled to government benefits. But should they be entitled to both federal and state benefits? If so, which, if any, may be proscribed, and for what reason(s)?

The *Plyler* decision was hailed by its supporters but reviled by its opponents. Supporters considered it a major victory for civil rights, equity, and pragmatism. Opponents, however, argued that the reasoning in the majority opinion was flawed because it misconstrued the original intent of the Equal Protection Clause, which they claimed was supposed to prevent discrimination against free slaves. Chief Justice Warren Burger, who wrote the dissent (with Justices Sandra Day O'Connor, William H. Rehnquist, and Byron White concurring), made these additional points:

- "By definition, illegal aliens have no right whatever to be here, and the state may reasonably, and constitutionally, elect not to provide them with government services at the expense of those who are lawfully in the state."
- The financial burden of illegal immigration on Texas was a rational consideration for its policy response.
- "The Texas law might also be justified as a means of deterring unlawful immigration."
- The issue at hand should be decided by Congress rather than the Supreme Court.

On a personal level, Burger was sympathetic to the plight of undocumented children. He agreed that "it is senseless . . . to deprive any children . . . of an elementary education" and that "it would be folly—and wrong—to tolerate creation of a segment of society made up of illiterate persons . . . . However, the Constitution does not constitute us as 'Platonic Guardians' nor does it vest in this Court the authority to strike down laws because they do not meet our standards of desirable social policy, 'wisdom,' or 'common sense.'"

Though remaining controversial, the *Plyler* decision cleared the air on providing free K–12 education to undocumented children. However, it left open the question whether its ruling could be more broadly applied to postsecondary education. In recent years, the debate over whether undocumented students have a right to a college education has come to the fore and is conjuring up many of the same arguments found in the *Plyler* case.

States Decide for Themselves Whether Undocumented Immigrants Are Eligible for In-State Tuition

An estimated 65,000 undocumented students graduate every year from the country's secondary schools, about 37,000 of whom are Latino. Thus, the number of students in question is substantial. Moreover, only about 5–10 percent of this number goes on to postsecondary education, compared to about 75 percent of their classmates. Presumably, inability to pay for education beyond high school and worry over not being able to work legally in a profession account for this significant disparity. Thus far at least, the simmering controversy over equal access to a college education has been more over fairness, finances, legality, and politics than on importance of a college degree in today's world. Arguably, the key issue in equal access is whether undocumented students are eligible for in-state tuition to public colleges and universities. Both supporters and opponents in this debate make impassioned and meritorious arguments.

The major supporting arguments for in-state tuition reflect or extend some of the same ones made in the majority opinion of the *Plyler* decision.

- Undocumented students should not be punished for the unlawful actions of their parents.
- Many undocumented immigrant children drop out of high school or do not take a college preparatory program because they don't believe they can afford college. Nationally, the dropout rate is highest among Latino youth. The difference between in-state and out-of-state tuition is substantial and would make a significant difference in their decisions about postsecondary education. Thus, many undocumented students who otherwise would enroll in college cannot afford to do so. This is damaging psychologically and emotionally to these students, as well as a terrible waste of talent and potential.
- For the most part, undocumented students are in this country to stay. Therefore, it is in the public interest to allow them to reach their full potential through a college education. For

many students in today's world, higher education is necessary for success in their career, so denying undocumented students access to college would mean lifelong punishment. The alternative, as noted in the *Plyler* decision, is to create a discrete, permanent underclass continuing to live with an "enduring disability." In addition, from an economic point of view, college graduates generally pay more in taxes and cost government less in criminal justice and welfare expenses than high school dropouts.

- Most undocumented immigrants come to this country for jobs, not education benefits.
- Enrollment of undocumented students adds important diversity to the student body.
- Undocumented students would not necessarily take the seats of legal immigrants or legal residents or receive preference for admission based on their immigration status. Instead, they would be part of the general in-state applicant pool.
- IIRIRA violates the U.S. Constitution, since the federal government cannot determine how states award in-state benefits such as in-state college tuition. Moreover, states like Texas and California believe that their laws allowing in-state tuition for undocumented students avoid conflict with federal law by omitting references to tuition benefits on the basis of state residency. Instead, these laws focus on where students graduate from high school and whether they sign a pledge to apply for permanent residency as soon as they are eligible.
- Public colleges and universities cannot discriminate against undocumented students in enrollment, as this would violate the Equal Protection Clause of the Fourteenth Amendment. It would also violate Title VI of the Civil Rights Act of 1964, which prohibits discrimination based on immigration status. Barring undocumented students from enrollment (de facto because of cost) could be considered "alienage discrimination," which would generally require strict scrutiny from the Supreme Court. The Court thus far has generally not applied strict scrutiny to federal laws based on alienage.
- Denying in-state tuition to undocumented students violates moral principles. As one observer argued: "Their sacred dignity as children of God . . . gives them basic rights that cannot be declared 'illegal' by any government, such as the right to life, and the essentials necessary to the living of a dignified life, such as shelter, health care and education."

Opponents of in-state tuition for undocumented students make these main arguments, some of which echo the minority opinion in *Plyler*:

- States should not subsidize lawbreakers. Some critics like U.S. Representative Tom Tancredo (R-CO) even call for deportation of undocumented students. Tancredo, a candidate for president in the 2008 elections, founded the Congressional Immigration Reform Caucus that aims to restrict both legal and illegal immigration. He is also a leading opponent of granting undocumented students eligibility for in-state college tuition.
- State laws that grant in-state tuition to undocumented students violate the Supremacy Clause of the U.S. Constitution, which gives Congress plenary power over immigration, and the Equal Protection Clause because they treat this group more favorably than out-of-state U.S citizens.
- States should not have to pay benefits to undocumented students when the federal government has failed in its responsibility to keep illegal immigrants out of the country.
- Undocumented students cannot establish state residency, a usual requirement of eligibility for in-state tuition. Opponents of in-state tuition cite, for example, the decision in *Regents of the University of California v. Superior Court of Los Angeles County* (1990), known as the

"Bradford decision," which held that undocumented students could not establish state residency to become eligible for in-state tuition.

- Giving in-state tuition to undocumented students would demean those immigrants who play by the rules and would shamefully devalue the privilege of U.S. citizenship.
- Making undocumented students eligible for in-state tuition would encourage further illegal immigration.
- Most states, in the public interest, mandate at least a ninth-grade education for all their residents. Moreover, while K–12 public education is free, postsecondary education is not; nor is it seen as necessary.
- Because of the global war on terror, undocumented students pose an unacceptable security risk to the country.
- Large waves of immigrants coming largely from Mexico, both legal and illegal, are adversely transforming the traditional culture and national identity of this country. Two recent books spotlight this argument. In *Who Are We? The Challenges of American Identity*, Professor Samuel P. Huntington argues that this surge of heavy Hispanic immigration poses a threat to America's shared values, culture, and community, which serve as the basis of liberal democracy. And in *Mexifornia: A State of Becoming*, Professor Victor Davis Hanson warns that California (the state with the largest illegal immigrant population) will continue morphing into "Mexifornia"—unless this country focuses more on assimilation and more rigorously restricts the flow of immigration.
- The intent of Congress, indicated primarily through enactment of PRWORA and IIRIRA, is to deny undocumented students financial assistance to attend college. IIRIRA provides that a public postsecondary educational institution may not grant in-state tuition benefits to undocumented students unless such an institution also grants the same benefit to out-of-state U.S. citizens or legal residents. Thus, when state laws like those in Texas and California allow in-state tuition based on criteria other than state residency, they contravene the intent if not the actual wording of these 1996 federal laws.

Differing Interpretations of the Intent of Congress

There is widespread disagreement over what Congress meant when enacting PRWORA and IIRIRA. The key dispute is over Section 505 of IIRIRA, which stipulates that "an alien who is not lawfully present in the United States shall not be eligible for in-state tuition on the basis of residence within a State (or political subdivision) or for any postsecondary benefit *unless* [our italics] a citizen or national of the United States is eligible for such benefit . . . without regard to whether the citizen or national is such a resident." Differing interpretations of this stipulation have led states to adopt a wide variety of policies on eligibility of undocumented students for in-state tuition.

Most states, believing that their policy abides by federal law, do not allow in-state tuition for undocumented students. Their position is that Congress clearly intended to make illegal immigrants ineligible for a wide array of state and local benefits, including postsecondary education. One example is a referendum adopted in the key border state of Arizona. In November 2004 Arizona voters overwhelmingly passed Proposition 200, which forbade the granting of state benefits, including in-state tuition, to undocumented immigrants. This referendum decision is reminiscent of Proposition 187, passed by California voters in 1994 but ruled unconstitutional several years later for having violated *Plyer* and the Supremacy Clause of the Constitution. Whether the Arizona law will pass constitutional muster is unclear.

Other states, however, have interpreted Section 505 of IIRIRA differently. They look, for instance, to the arguments made by Professor Michael A. Olivas from the University of Houston Law Center who contends that Congress does not have the authority to regulate state benefits for postsecondary education. According to Olivas, even if Congress does have this authority, it left a loophole in Section 505. Olivas concludes that the word "unless" allows states to enact student legislation that can circumvent official state residency laws.

In accordance with the "loophole" interpretation of IIRIRA, a growing number of states have passed laws making undocumented students eligible for in-state tuition under certain specified conditions. In June 2001, Texas became the first state to do so. Since then, nine other states (California, Utah, New York, Illinois, Oklahoma, Washington, Kansas, New Mexico, and Nebraska) have passed similar legislation. Only three of these states (Texas, Oklahoma, and New Mexico) offer state financial aid to undocumented students. State laws allowing undocumented students eligibility for in-state tuition avoid official residency requirements. Instead, with some variation, they make undocumented students eligible if they have lived in the state for a certain number of years, graduated from a high school in their state, and signed an affidavit pledging to apply for permanent residency as soon as they were eligible.

Two states that allow in-state tuition for undocumented students have been taken to court for violation of federal law and the Constitution. On July 19, 2004, a number of students with Kansas residency sued the state for denying them in-state tuition benefits (*Day v. Sebelius*). Their basic charge was that the Kansas law violated PRWORA and IIRIRA, as well as the Equal Protection Clause of the Fourteenth Amendment. On July 5, 2005, U.S. District Court Judge Richard Rogers ruled in favor of Governor Kathleen Sebelius. It remains to be seen whether this decision will be upheld upon appeal. And in California, a lawsuit filed in December 2005 by former San Diego congressman Brian Bilbray has challenged a 2001 state law (AB540) which, under certain conditions such as graduation from a California high school, makes undocumented students eligible for in-state tuition to the state's public colleges and universities. Bilbray contends that California law violates PWRORA and IIRIRA and is unfair to out-of-state American citizens and legal residents who do not qualify for in-state tuition. How this case turns out will have an important influence on the in-state tuition issue around the country.

The Proposed DREAM Act

What is the likelihood that the dreams of undocumented students for postsecondary education can be realized? After passage of PRWORA and IIRIRA, a number of federal legislators, believing these laws were not in the best interest of the country, sought to amend or repeal them. In 2001, Senators Orrin Hatch (R-UT) and Richard Durbin (D-IL) introduced the Development and Education for Alien Minors Act (DREAM Act). At the same time, Representatives Christopher Cannon (R-UT), Lucille Roybal-Allard (D-CA), and Howard Berman (D-CA) introduced the Student Adjustment Act.

The main thrust of the proposed legislation is to repeal Section 505 of IIRIRA. This would clearly allow states to make their own determination on eligibility for in-state tuition. The DREAM Act would grant conditional permanent resident status for six years to undocumented students if they came to the U.S. before age sixteen; have good moral character; have no criminal record; have lived in the U.S. continuously for at least five years at the time of the law's enactment; have graduated from high school; and have been accepted at a two- or four-year college. The Student Adjustment Act has similar provisions.

Debate over passage of federal legislation allowing in-state tuition has been joined. Supporters include a number of civil rights, labor, and political organizations such as People for the

American Way, the National Council of La Raza, the American Immigration Lawyers Association (AILA), the Mexican American Legal Defense and Education Fund (MALDEF), the AFL-CIO, and the "I Have a Dream" Foundation. Leading opponents are the Center for Immigration Studies (CIS) and the Federation for Immigration Reform (FAIR), and conservative columnists like Phyllis Schlafly. For example, FAIR has called the DREAM Act "a massive illegal amnesty program, disguised as an educational initiative." Schlafly argues that U.S. taxpayers should not reward illegal immigrants by subsidizing their college tuition, "especially when U.S. parents are struggling to pay college expenses for their own children."

Congressional backers of the DREAM and Student Adjustment Acts have repeatedly introduced these bills for discussion, but so far they have not received enough votes to pass. They have become part of a broader attempt by Congress at immigration reform. When or whether these bills will eventually be enacted remains to be seen.

Policy Options

Options Dealing with the Overall Problem of Illegal Immigration

1. *Legalize all undocumented immigrants.* This would mean enactment of legislation that would offer amnesty to illegal immigrants now living in the United States. Such legislation would reflect the main thrust of the 1986 Simpson-Mazzoli law enacted under the Reagan administration, which provided legalized status to approximately 3 million illegal immigrants and barred employers from knowingly hiring them. Some argue that amnesty in any current legislation should be offered only to those illegal immigrants who do not have a criminal record, are verifiably employed, pledge to learn English, pay back taxes, and even pay a fine. They could also be placed on the path toward earned citizenship, but probably at the end of the line after those who are applying legally for citizenship. A related question is whether illegal immigrants who may become U.S. citizens should have the right to become dual citizens by retaining their Mexican citizenship.

2. *Establish a guest worker program, such as one modeled after the Bracero program (1942–1964).* There are many versions of this type of program, such as that proposed by President George W. Bush. What they all have in common is recognition of the country's need for guest workers and allowance for them to stay here for a certain amount of time; they could also return to Mexico and come back to this country without a hassle.

3. *Deport all undocumented immigrants.* Representative Tancredo is a leading proponent of this position. The assumption is that because illegal immigrants by definition have broken the law, they have no right to remain in this country. Opponents argue that deportation is both unrealistic and inhumane, as many illegal immigrants have put down roots in this country; moreover, some have divided families with some children born in Mexico and some in the U.S. (often referred to pejoratively as "anchor babies").

4. *Open up the U.S. border with Mexico.* The idea is that it is unrealistic to try to seal this country's border with Mexico. Moreover, workers should be allowed to cross borders to help a state's economy, just like free trade, which encourages capital and goods to cross borders with minimal restrictions. For comparison purposes, most people may move freely within the various countries of the European Union. In addition, from a moral point of view, there is the argument that borders discriminate unfairly against the poorest and most politically powerless people. The only people who should be barred from

entering the U.S. are suspected criminals, terrorists, and those with contagious diseases. There are three main criticisms of the open border option: Each country has the sovereign right to control its borders; U.S. workers, especially minorities at the bottom of the economic ladder, would be hurt by illegal immigrants, who would take jobs and depress wages; and the U.S. would face an untenable security problem.

5. *Enforce existing immigration laws much more thoroughly and perhaps on all government levels.* This position maintains that the U.S., as a sovereign country, has the right to monitor who enters the country but so far has not demonstrated either the will or power to do so. Moreover, in the current global war on terror, it is foolish to believe that illegal immigrants do not pose a serious security risk to the American public. Some groups of private citizens, such as the Minuteman Project, have already taken it upon themselves to help border patrols secure the border and pressure government officials to enforce immigration laws. Supporters of this position also contend that state and local authorities, by default, should be allowed to enforce immigration laws. As part of a unified policy this would mean, for example, cracking down on employers who intentionally hire illegal workers and on landlords who knowingly rent to illegal immigrants. States like Colorado and Georgia have already taken action against illegal immigrants. So have towns like Hazelton, Pennsylvania. In March 2007, Hazelton's laws were put to the legal test in a trial that, for the first time, dealt with whether a town has the right to act on its own to curb illegal immigration. The American Civil Liberties Union argued that Hazelton's laws were unconstitutional because they encroached on the exclusive federal domain over regulation of immigration. Yet Judicial Watch, a Washington-based conservative interest group, maintained that the town's ordinances were constitutional because they were "in harmony with federal law." The decision of the federal court on Hazelton's laws, expected later in the spring, will have enormous influence throughout the country as many localities face a similar dilemma over illegal immigration.

6. *Build a seven-hundred-mile-long fence between Mexico and the U.S. along the most porous areas of the border.* On October 26, 2006, President Bush signed the Secure Fence Act of 2006, which authorized the building of a barrier along parts of the U.S.-Mexico border. Supporters of this position argue that this would be the most effective way to control the illegal immigration problem. A physical barrier would not shut off all illegal immigration, but would reduce it significantly and make it much more manageable. They point to the "success" of Operation Gatekeeper in the early 1990s with the construction of a fence and stepped up enforcement around the point of entry in San Diego. This resulted in a dramatic decrease in the number of attempted crossings. Opponents counter that this operation merely pushed illegal immigrants toward the Texas and Arizona borders, and that it made the crossing more risky, which led to increased deaths of migrants. Moreover, opponents argue that building a fence damages the image of the U.S. as a democracy and conjures up unflattering comparisons to the Berlin Wall under communism. Some, like Senator Arlen Specter (R-PA), recommend building a "virtual wall" that would utilize overhead telemetry, unmanned drones, and beefed-up patrols to make the border more secure. How successful this would be is uncertain.

7. *Send National Guard troops to help shore up the U.S.-Mexican border.* President Bush proposed this measure in a nationally televised speech to the nation on May 15, 2006. According to the president, the approximately 6,000 troops that would be deployed along the border by 2008 would support border patrol officers but not participate in law enforcement. States would have to pay for the cost of Guard deployment, though the federal gov-

ernment would front the money (approximately $2 billion) and require reimbursement; and states may opt out if they wish. Governors in the four border states most affected by illegal immigration were divided over the president's proposal. Janet Napolitano (D-AZ) and Rick Perry (R-TX) indicated that this extra enforcement would reduce the flow of illegal immigrants. However, Arnold Schwarzenegger (R-CA) and Bill Richardson (D-NM) expressed concern that the Guard would not have a significant impact on border security; it should not be involved in border security; it is not trained for this mission; its deployment along the border would stretch the U.S. military too thin when it is already pressed hard to do its job in Iraq and Afghanistan; and the Guard deployed along the border in the affected states might not be available for other emergencies such as natural disasters. The governors also were disappointed by what they believed was the lack of sufficient consultation by the White House. The first National Guard troops, sent from Utah to the Arizona-Mexico border, began their assignment in the first week of June 2006.

8. *Help and/or pressure Mexico and other countries that send the largest number of illegal immigrants to the United States to improve their economies and living conditions.* This might mean, for example, urging these countries to improve workers' wages, rights, and on-the-job health and safety. One target area could be the maquiladoras (small-business enterprises) along the Mexican side of the border with the United States. Under this option, presumably working in the U.S. would be less attractive to foreign workers.

9. *Resist any law that criminalizes illegal immigrants and those who try to help them.* A number of leaders in the Catholic Church support this position on the basis of biblical morality. For example, Roger Mahony, cardinal archbishop of Los Angeles, contends that providing help to the poor and needy is a higher calling than support for any unjust and inhumane government law.

Options Dealing with Undocumented Students Seeking In-State Tuition

1. *Disallow eligibility to all undocumented students for in-state tuition.* As lawbreakers, they do not deserve any public benefits. Indeed, even consider deporting them to their country of origin.

2. *Make only certain categories of undocumented students eligible for in-state tuition.* For example, allow in-state tuition only to undocumented students whose parents did not sneak into the U.S. or come here with fraudulent documents, or whose cases for asylum and/or legal residency are pending.

3. *Pass a federal law (e.g., the DREAM Act) that would allow each state to decide for itself whether undocumented students are eligible for in-state tuition.* This would mean, among other things, repealing the restrictive clauses of benefit allowance in IIRIRA.

4. *Let the Supreme Court resolve the in-state tuition issue.* This can be done by deferring to Congress, which has plenary power over immigration, which in turn may let the states decide for themselves. Or, the Court can make its own decision, perhaps based on civil rights concerns.

Conclusion

What can we conclude from the growing national debate over whether undocumented students should be eligible for in-state tuition? Arguably, these are the most important considerations:

First, causes of undocumented status vary. Most undocumented immigrants do sneak across this country's borders from Mexico or enter with fraudulent documents, but many others come here legally and overstay their visas. Only the technicality of their legal status, which is often in the process of litigation, keeps many undocumented students from a college education. Second, there is widespread agreement that this country's immigration system is broken. The in-state college tuition controversy reflects this nationwide problem. Third, current state policy toward eligibility of undocumented students for in-state tuition is a mess of confusion and inconsistency, reflecting disagreement over the intent and constitutionality of federal law. Fourth, many undocumented students suffer from serious psychological and emotional distress because of their predicament. Generally, not only can they not afford postsecondary education, but they are reluctant to disclose their undocumented status for fear of deportation or other serious consequences. All this has kept the number of undocumented students who actually enroll in public colleges and universities very low.

Undocumented students who are now forced to live in the shadows of society and in legal limbo comprise a large and growing untapped resource in this country. In most states, they cannot afford to enroll in public colleges and universities because they are ineligible for in-state tuition. However, even when then do qualify they face additional formidable barriers in pursuit of the American dream. Under federal law they remain ineligible for financial assistance and cannot work legally. Moreover, under the Real ID Act enacted by Congress in May 2005 (set to go into effect in 2008) they will be unable to obtain a driver's license. Therefore, the issue of eligibility for in-state college tuition must be considered part of the much larger problem of comprehensive immigration reform.

Ultimately, the outcome of the whole array of issues involving illegal immigration will be decided in the court of public opinion. Those who try to improve the lot of undocumented immigrants will face tough sledding as the American public in general, while somewhat supportive of legal immigration, wants to crack down on illegal immigration. Recent public opinion polls (see, e.g., *Time Magazine*, April 2, 2006) confirm this conclusion. Consequently, any improvements for the undocumented probably will come only over time.

In a climate where so many Americans believe that undocumented immigrants compete unfairly for jobs, depress wages, receive public benefits they don't deserve, adversely affect the country's identity, and endanger national security, the undocumented face daunting opposition. Yet the undocumented also have their fervent supporters who realize potential college graduates are a valuable national resource that should be tapped rather than rejected. Results of the November 2006 elections reflect both sides of this controversy. In Arizona, residents passed a initiative referendum denying in-state tuition benefits to undocumented students. In March 2007 the state's Board of Regents gave universities permission to implement this referendum. Arizona students will now have to prove U.S. citizenship by presenting an Arizona driver's license issued after 1996, a passport or birth certificate—unless they have already completed the federal Free Application for Federal Student Aid (FAFSA) form that screens for U.S. citizenship.

Yet in Massachusetts, voters elected as governor Democrat Devon Patrick, who pledged to push legislation approving in-state tuition for undocumented immigrants to the state's public colleges and universities. This position is the direct opposite of that held by his predecessor, Republican Mitt Romney, who is a candidate for president in the 2008 elections. Last, in Texas where about 10 percent of the country's illegal immigrants live, there is a bill proposed to deny services and benefits to children of undocumented immigrants—*including those who are U.S. citizens.* This bill presents the first major legal challenge to citizenship granted automatically to those born in the U.S. irrespective of parental citizenship. Therefore, it goes beyond California's Proposition 187, ruled unconstitutional in 1994, that would have denied various benefits to illegal immigrants but not citizenship to their children born in the U.S. How the controversy over benefits will eventually play out nationally remains to be seen.

Discussion Questions

1. Is it fair that states have to pay for the education of large numbers of undocumented students largely because the federal government has failed to adequately police the country's borders?
2. Should an undocumented student receive any benefit not available to every citizen or legal resident of the United States?
3. Irrespective of the legality issue, does providing undocumented students access to a college education make sense from an economic point of view?
4. Is it acceptable that states disproportionately face the problem of educating undocumented students based on favorite destinations of their illegal immigrant parents (often border states like California, Texas, and Arizona)?
5. Is it fair to deprive undocumented students, most of whom did not make the decision themselves to come to the United States, of an opportunity for postsecondary education?
6. Do you believe that undocumented students should be considered a "suspect class" deserving strict scrutiny by the courts on discrimination issues such as access to in-state college tuition?
7. Do you believe illegal immigrants should be subjected to a civil or criminal penalty? If a criminal penalty, a felony or misdemeanor? Whatever the category of penalty, should all or just some illegal immigrants be deported—depending on how long they have been in the U.S., whether they are employed, and whether they have a criminal record?
8. Would you favor building a barrier along part of the U.S.-Mexico border to keep undocumented immigrants from entering the U.S.? Would you still favor a barrier even if it led to an increase in the number of undocumented immigrants already in the U.S. because going to and from Mexico would be so much harder?

Class Activities

1. Class debates the arguments of the Court in *Plyler v. Doe*. Include in the debate whether the Court's decision should be extended from K–12 education to a college education.
2. Class debates whether Congress should pass the DREAM Act. Include in the debate the need for broader, more comprehensive immigration reform. Related issues might include the advisability of an amnesty program and the building of a barrier between Mexico and the United States.

Suggestions for Further Reading

Badger, Ellen. "Myths and Realities for Undocumented Students Attending U.S. Colleges and Universities." *Journal of College Admission*, Winter 2002, 10–15.
Bernstein, Nina. "Student's Prize Is a Trip into Immigration Limbo." *New York Times*, April 26, 2006, A1.

Coolidge, Sharon. "Local Authorities Take Border Control into Own Hands." *USA Today*, May 18, 2006, 8A.

Cornhill, June. "Politics and Economics: Should Illegal Immigrants Get Tuition Help?" *Wall Street Journal*, February 22, 2006, A4.

Daniels, Roger. *Guarding the Golden Door: American Immigration Policy and Immigration Issues since 1882*. New York: Hill & Wang, 2004.

Dudley, William, ed. *Illegal Immigration: Opposing Viewpoints*. San Diego: Greenhaven Press, 2002.

Finn, Chester. "Don't Punish Children for Parents' Illegal Entry." *Los Angeles Times*, February 17, 2004, B11.

Hanson, Victor Davis. *Mexifornia: A State of Becoming*. San Francisco: Encounter Books, 2004.

Huntington, Samuel P. *Who Are We? The Challenge of American Identity*. New York: Simon & Schuster, 2004.

Jordan, Miriam. "States and Towns Attempt to Draw the Line on Illegal Immigration." *Wall Street Journal*, July 14, 2006, A1.

Ngai, Mae M. "How Grandma Got Legal." *Los Angeles Times*, May 16, 2006, B13.

Oliver, Jeff. "States Struggle to Cut Costs of Immigration." *Christian Science Monitor*, June 16, 2006, 01.

Preston, Julia. "State Proposals on Illegal Immigration Largely Falter." *New York Times*, May 9, 2006, A17.

Reed, T. R. "Hill Impasse Spurs States to Tackle Illegal Immigration." *Washington Post*, May 3, 2006, A01.

Rhmer, Rebecca Ness. "Taking Back the Power: Federal vs. State Regulation on Postsecondary Education Benefits for Illegal Immigrants." *Washington Law Journal* 44 (May 2005): 603–25.

Romero, Victor C. "Postsecondary School Education Benefits for Undocumented Immigrants: Promises and Pitfalls." *North Carolina Journal of International Law and Commercial Regulation* 27, no. 3 (Spring 2002): 393–418.

Salsbury, Jessica. "Evading 'Residence': Undocumented Students, Higher Education, and the States." *American University Law Review* 53, no. 2 (December 2003): 459–90.

Yates, Laura. "*Plyler v. Doe* and the Rights of Undocumented Immigrants to Higher Education: Should Undocumented Students Be Eligible for In-State College Tuition Rates?" *Washington University Law Quarterly*, Summer 2004, 584–609.

Zolberg, Aristide R. *A Nation of Design: Immigration Policy in the Fashioning of America*. Cambridge, MA: Harvard University Press, 2006.

Helpful Websites

www.aila.org. This site of American immigration lawyers focuses on legal issues generally supportive of and helpful to illegal immigrants.

www.centerforimmigrationstudies.org. This site contains valuable studies and reports that generally oppose illegal immigration.

www.fair.org. This is a website of a major political interest group that opposes illegal immigration.

www.maldef.org. This site of the Mexican American Legal Defense Fund contains studies and reports helpful to illegal immigrants.

www.numbersusa.org. This site contains reports warning of the demographic ramifications and consequences of illegal immigration.

3

Civil Liberties

Case Snapshot

PRAYER IN THE PUBLIC SCHOOLS has long been one of the most controversial, emotional, and contentious issues in American society. There is no complete separation of church and state in the United States. For example, the currency and the oaths sworn in federal courts include reference to God and prayer. These official references stand in stark contrast to what the U.S. Supreme Court has allowed in the public schools. The only formal reference to religion in the U.S. Constitution that relates to school prayer is the First Amendment: "Congress shall make no law respecting an establishment of religion or prohibiting the free exercise thereof." There is no dispute that children have the right to pray in school. Federal guidelines issued in 1995 and updated in 2003 allow student prayers as long as they do not interfere with normal school day activities or requirements. The controversy is over school-sponsored or school-organized prayer. The Supreme Court has recognized the fact that public schools are unique institutions. They must take all children who want to go; school attendance is compulsory; and because schoolchildren are more impressionable and vulnerable than older college students and adults, they need more protection. Beginning with a series of Supreme Court cases after World War II, most notably the landmark decisions of *Engel v. Vitale* (1962) and *Abington Township School District v. Schempp* (1963), the Court has ruled consistently that officially organized prayer in public schools is forbidden because it violates the Establishment Clause of the First Amendment. These prayer decisions have received both strong public support and condemnation. Supporters maintain that the decisions properly safeguard an important civil liberty of keeping government from interfering with religious beliefs and practices. Opponents contend that the Court was misguided in its decisions and seek to change or evade them. Should organized prayer be allowed in public schools? You decide!

Major Case Controversies

1. *There is dispute as to the meaning and original intent of the Founding Fathers on the Establishment and Free Exercise Clauses of the First Amendment.* In general, supporters of organized prayer in the public schools give a narrow interpretation, arguing that the federal government must not prefer one religion over another or establish a national religion. According to this interpretation, public schools should be able to accommodate and even sponsor religious activities, including prayer.

    Opponents of organized prayer give a broader interpretation based on what James Madison called "perfect separation" between government and religion, and on Thomas Jefferson's aim to build "a wall of separation between church and state." Focusing on the Free Expression Clause, government should remain neutral toward religion and not interfere with religious freedom in any way. Still others claim that the original intent was to protect religious minorities from the potentially harmful effects of an established religion. This last interpretation would allow and perhaps even encourage government to affirm the importance of religion in public life.

2. *Some believe that the Supreme Court has been hostile toward religion.* Others believe that the Court has tried to maintain the government's strict neutrality toward religion and that its decisions are consistent with the idea that religion is strictly a private matter.

3. *There is disagreement over whether the framers of the U.S. Constitution believed that the First Amendment should apply only to the federal government.* The Supreme Court first applied First Amendment protection to the states in *Gitlow v. New York* (1925). In this case, the Court decided that free speech was protected by the Due Process Clause of the Fourteenth Amendment. It was not until 1940 that the Supreme Court first applied the First Amendment guarantee of religious freedom to the states through the Fourteenth Amendment. In *Cantwell v. Connecticut,* the Court incorporated the Free Exercise Clause into the Fourteenth Amendment when it decided that three Jehovah's Witnesses could distribute religious pamphlets on the street, solicit contributions for their church, and criticize Catholicism. Then in 1947, the Court incorporated the Establishment Clause into the Fourteenth Amendment when it decided in *Everson v. Board of Education of Ewing Township* that the state of New Jersey's policy of funding children to travel to school on city buses did not violate the Establishment Clause because it benefited the children rather than the state.

4. *Over the years, the Supreme Court has widened its application of what "establishment" covers.* Starting in the early 1960s it has interpreted the First Amendment to mean a ban on organized prayer and Bible reading in public school classrooms. Since then, it has extended this ban to a "moment of silence" and invocations at school activities such as graduation exercises and sporting events—when these activities are seen as government endorsement of religion.

5. *Opponents of government-sponsored school prayer point to an inconsistency of the Supreme Court's ban with some official government practices.* For example, "In God We Trust" is found on our national currency; Moses and the Ten Commandments are featured on the U.S. Supreme Court building; "God Bless America" is sung at official and unofficial events; and Congress opens its sessions with prayers.

6. *Proponents of allowing government-sponsored prayer in public schools trace what they consider the moral decline of our society to the Supreme Court prayer decisions.* Despairing of growing secularization, they blame these decisions for increased sex, violence, drugs, and so on among the school-age population. Opponents argue that this explanation overlooks the complexity of those problems and claim there is no evidence that supports this alleged causal connection.

7. *One widespread opinion is that "majority rules," i.e., organized prayer in the public schools should be allowed if the majority of Americans want it.* The opposing view is that it is uncertain what a majority of Americans want, that difficult civil liberties issues should not be solved by majority rule, and also that minority rights should be secured.

8. *Some believe that the Supreme Court has banned all prayer in the public schools.* However, this is only partially true. According to the 2003 federal guidelines, organized prayer activities are clearly forbidden (e.g., when the teacher reads a prayer to the class), but private prayer has always been permitted. For example, students have the right to pray individually or in groups, they can read their Bibles or other scriptures, pray for good test scores or successful sports actions, say grace before and after meals, or otherwise pray as they wish—as long as they do not violate school rules and policies or disrupt activities. Finally, the constitutionality of some prayer activities is still to be determined, e.g., whether the phrase "under God" should be allowed when schoolchildren recite the Pledge of Allegiance or whether at graduation ceremonies valedictorians on their own initiative may recite a prayer or lead the audience in prayer.

9. *Compulsory, organized prayer in the schools might reduce the chances for sincere, meaningful prayer that would come from the students themselves.*

10. *If organized prayer were permitted in the public schools, attempting to decide which prayers to use would cause divisiveness.* Prayer is a very personal matter. Who would choose the prayer? In a country where there are over 1,500 religious denominations, could one prayer fit all?

11. *With increasing numbers of Muslims in the U.S., the public schools face a new set of issues regarding school prayer.* For example, would it be disruptive when Muslim schoolchildren ask to pray five times a day at specific hours during the school day? And should Muslim students be released from school on Friday to observe the Muslim Sabbath? Moreover, Muslim leaders who believe there should be no separation of government and religion understandably may ask to revisit school prayer cases already decided by the Court.

12. *Religious groups take differing views on the school prayer controversy.* Some like the Christian Coalition strongly support organized prayer in the public schools, whereas others like the National Council of Churches are strongly opposed.

Background of the Case

The Supreme Court's School Prayer Decisions

Although many immigrants came to this country to escape religious persecution, religious tolerance was hardly a hallmark of the colonial period. Members of various sects whose beliefs went against the established Church of England were discriminated against, persecuted, flogged, jailed, exiled, and even executed. For example, Massachusetts banished Roger Williams, a Salem minister, for repudiating the Church of England. Williams and his disciples then founded Providence, Rhode Island. Similar disputes over religious freedom led Anne Hutchinson to found Connecticut and William Penn and Quakers to found Pennsylvania.

In the nineteenth and twentieth centuries, many public schools, especially in the South and the Northeast, allowed organized prayer in a variety of ways. The influence of Protestantism was predominant. There was Bible reading, recitation of various prayers (e.g., the Lord's Prayer), and singing of religious hymns. For example, in the public schools of Boston, Massachusetts (one of the cities that required Bible reading), the teaching of Christmas carols was part of the curriculum. Other school districts, however, prohibited such practices. State supreme courts had a mixed record on this controversy.

Catholic and Jewish leaders resisted what they considered potentially harmful intrusions into their religion when schoolchildren had to sing Protestant hymns and listen to verses from the King James Version of the Bible. Rather than fight the constitutionality of such practices, many Catholic and Jewish parents took their children out of public schools and placed them in newly established parochial schools. However, for the most part, children who were not Protestant just accepted religious practices in school and went along with what, in effect, was state-sponsored religious instruction.

Our Founding Fathers disagreed over the best relationship between government and religion and the value of school prayer. Some like Patrick Henry considered school prayer an important vehicle for promoting virtuous living and good citizenship. In 1790, Sons of Liberty leader Samuel Adams said: "Let . . . philosophers, statesmen and patriots, unite their endeavors to renovate the age by impressing the minds of men with the importance of educating their little boys and girls, inculcating in the minds of youth the fear and love of the Deity . . . and leading them in the study and practice of the exalted virtues of the Christian system." Then in 1798, John Adams stated: "Our Constitution was made only for a moral and religious people. It is wholly inadequate to the government of any other." And in 1799, George Washington noted: "What students should learn in American schools above all is the religion of Jesus Christ."

However, opposing views on the relationship of government and religion of other Founding Fathers prevailed. James Madison, the author of the First Amendment, argued for the "perfect separation" of church and state because he believed that government support for religion diminished religious liberty. And Thomas Jefferson, in his famous letter to the Baptists of Danbury, Connecticut, in 1802, argued that the First Amendment was intended to build "a wall of separation between church and State." Jefferson feared that any government intrusion into religion was dangerous for religious freedom.

When the Supreme Court started to hand down decisions on school prayer after World War II, it consistently ruled against school-sponsored prayer. Starting with the *Cantwell* and *Everson* cases, its rulings became applicable to both the federal and state governments. The Court's decisions have dealt with school prayer in four major areas: official prayer and Bible reading exercises, silent meditation, student use of school facilities for religious purposes, and school functions like graduation and high school football games.

Official Prayer and Bible Reading Exercises

The two main relevant cases are *Engel v. Vitale* (1962) and *Abington Township School District v. Schempp* (1963). In *Engel*, the Court ruled against state-written prayer. In *Abington*, it ruled against the more prevalent practice of Bible reading. Both cases resulted in landmark decisions, arguably as important, far-reaching, and controversial as the school desegregation decision on *Brown v. Board of Education* (1954). Like *Brown*, the school prayer decisions led to angry public protests and attempts at evasion or noncompliance. However, unlike *Brown*, which is now widely accepted, the school prayer decisions are still being contested by school officials, politicians, and the public they serve.

Engel v. Vitale. This case originated when the New York State Board of Regents, a government agency with administrative authority over the public schools, ordered school districts to read this twenty-two-word prayer aloud in class: "Almighty God, we acknowledge our dependence upon Thee, and we beg Thy blessings upon us, our parents, our teachers, and our country." Shortly after this prayer policy was implemented, Steven Engel and several other parents of pupils in the New Hyde Park Union Free School District challenged the constitutionality of the state's school prayer law. They argued that it violated the Establishment Clause of the First Amendment and, by extension, the Fourteenth Amendment, which applied to the states. William Vitale, a member of the Board of Regents, was the defendant. On behalf of the board, he contended that the prayer in question was harmless and nonsectarian and that its recitation was voluntary. Students who did not want to pray could remain silent or leave the room.

The New York Supreme Court ruled that if the schools did not force students to pray, the prayer exercise was constitutional. This court called on the state board of education to establish a process whereby those who did not want to pray could be exempt from the exercise and be protected from "embarrassment and pressures." However, the U.S. Supreme Court said that violation of the Establishment Clause required no proof of coercion. Justice Hugo Black, writing for the majority, based his decision largely on what he thought was the original intent of the Founding Fathers. Justice Potter Stewart issued the only dissent. Using a very narrow interpretation of the Establishment Clause, he argued that the Court had misapplied it in the *Engel* case. Stewart believed that this clause prohibits only the establishment of a state church or state religion. Moreover, he complained that the ruling actually violated the Free Exercise Clause rights of those children who wanted to recite the prayer and that it also ran counter to the country's "spiritual traditions." As evidence of congressional approval of religion, he cited, for example, the motto on the national currency: "In God We Trust."

The *Engel* decision led to a great outcry in the country. There were numerous calls for impeachment of the Court's justices and for constitutional amendments to bypass the Court's decision. Some newspapers ran headlines such as "Court Outlaws God." Other papers, like the *New York Times*, supported it. Recognizing that the New York law led to at least indirect coercion of minorities to conform, the paper argued that "the Constitution was designed precisely to protect minorities." Reaction from the country's religious groups was mixed. In general, Roman Catholic leaders strongly opposed the decision but Protestant and Jewish leaders supported it. President John F. Kennedy, using his bully pulpit, urged the American people to support the decision. For those who opposed the decision, Kennedy pointed to "a very easy remedy." The president called on Americans "to pray ourselves." This "would be a welcome reminder to every American family that we can pray a great deal more at home and attend our churches with a good deal more fidelity, and we can make the true meaning of prayer much more important in the lives of all our children." However, the furor over the decision only increased the next year, when the Court issued a decision against Bible reading in the schools.

Abington Township School District v. Schempp. The Supreme Court decided this case concurrently with *Murray v. Curlett*, which challenged a 1905 Baltimore School Board rule requiring each school day to start with Bible reading, recitation of the Lord's Prayer, or both. The Abington school district in Pennsylvania, in accordance with a 1949 state law, required reading from the King James Version of the Bible at the start of each school day. (The law did not stipulate a specific version of the Bible, but Abington like many other school districts in the state used only the King James Version.) After the Bible reading, which was broadcast over the school's public address system, students rose to hear the Lord's Prayer, which they then repeated in unison. Any teacher who refused to comply with Bible reading could be dismissed. Like the *Engel* case, participation by students was voluntary. They could be excused if their parents wrote a letter to the school. Otherwise, they could leave the classroom, or if they stayed they could choose not to participate in the religious exercises. At the time, four other states required Bible reading before class and this was "optional" in twenty-five other states.

The Schempp family, who were members of the Unitarian Church, challenged the constitutionality of this law. Edward Schempp was upset that teachers and classmates of their children,

Donna and Roger, had labeled them "oddballs" and "atheists" for not participating in the religious exercises. Furthermore, when they were seen outside the classroom, other children thought they were being punished. They also missed announcements read afterward over the public address system.

At first, a federal district court found that the Pennsylvania law, as applied to the states through the Fourteenth Amendment, violated the Establishment Clause of the First Amendment. On appeal, the Supreme Court affirmed this decision and declared the Pennsylvania law unconstitutional.

The Supreme Court held that the Bible reading exercises were "religious exercises, required by the States in violation of the command of the First Amendment that the government maintain strict neutrality, neither aiding nor opposing religion." The Court added that it was "no defense to urge that the religious practices here may be relatively minor encroachments on the First Amendment. The breach of neutrality that is today a trickling stream may all too soon become a raging torrent." Finally, the Court said that even while allowing a written note excusing students, the school still had violated the Establishment Clause.

The Court concluded that the Establishment and Free Exercise Clauses had to be looked at together. It said that for government action to be constitutional, it had to meet the following test: "There must be a secular legislative purpose and primary effect that neither advances nor inhibits religion." A few years later, in *Lemon v. Kurtzman* (1971), the Court added a third test: Government action must not lead to excessive entanglement with religion.

Most school districts complied with the *Engel* and *Abington* decisions, but a few, especially in the South, did not. One survey found that 33.2 percent of the reporting schools had conducted religious services in 1960, but by 1966 only 8 percent did, and in those same years Bible reading in the schools had dropped from 41.8 to 12.9 percent. Some states kept their laws requiring religious exercises, whereas others continued to allow prayer and Bible reading based on tradition. However, compliance with the decisions did not necessarily mean public support. At first, public opinion polls showed only about 24 percent public support. In the following years, public support increased but never reached a majority. Arguably, the main opposition came from the increasingly influential religious Right, which had gathered strength in the 1970s and became a powerful political force in the 1980s when it helped elect Ronald Reagan president. The religious Right saw the Court's decisions against organized school prayer as another indication that liberal activist justices were contributing to the growing secularism and moral decline in the country, especially among the young.

At the same time, there were frequent efforts to skirt the Court's prayer and Bible reading decisions. There were attempts by states to amend their constitutions (e.g., the Becker Amendment in New York), and by Congress to amend the federal Constitution—all without success. Another way was to post the Ten Commandments in the classroom.

Stone v. Graham.   In 1980, the Supreme Court struck down a Kentucky statute which required that a copy of the Ten Commandments, bought with private funds, be posted on the wall of each public school classroom. The statute required the following sentence to be printed below the last commandment: "The secular application of the Ten Commandments is clearly seen in its adoption as the fundamental legal code of Western Civilization and the Common Law of the United States." In a 5–4 decision, the Court concluded that the "preeminent purpose" for this posting requirement was "plainly religious in nature" and thus it was unconstitutional.

Silent Meditation

The main relevant case is *Wallace v. Jaffree* (1985). In 1985 the Supreme Court struck down a 1981 Alabama law that required that each school day begin with a "period of silence . . . for meditation or voluntary prayer." Ishmael Jaffree, a lawyer in Mobile County, charged that Governor George Wallace, other government officials, and public school teachers had violated the constitutional rights of his school-age children when teachers led their classes in prayer at the start of each school day. As a result, Jaffree claimed that they were subjected to "various acts of religious indoctrination" and were ostracized by their classmates for nonparticipation in the prayer sessions. At first, a federal district court in Alabama ruled that the statute was constitutional because it believed the decision in the *Engel* case was wrong. However, a court of appeals reversed the district court, arguing that the statute violated the Establishment Clause. The case was then sent to the Supreme Court.

Arguing before the Court, the state of Alabama pointed out that the law in question was constitutional because it did not prevent prayer, affirm religious belief, or coerce religious exercises. In a friend-of-the-court brief (*amicus curiae*), the Reagan administration supported the state, arguing that the law was "perfectly neutral with respect to religious practices. It neither favors one religion over another nor conveys endorsement of religion." In essence, President Ronald Reagan sought to overturn both *Engel* and *Abington*.

The Supreme Court upheld the court of appeals. It explained that the Alabama legislature enacted its statute on silent meditation "for the sole purpose of expressing the State's endorsement of prayer activities for one minute at the beginning of each school day." The Court took note of a 1978 Alabama law that required a moment of silence at the start of each school day for meditation. This law was clearly constitutional, but the Court pointed out that in 1981 the Alabama legislature had violated the First Amendment by adding "or voluntary prayer." The Court considered this law a backdoor way to support school prayer.

Justice Sandra Day O'Connor, siding with the majority, argued that a state-sponsored moment of silence in the classroom is constitutional if it is not associated with prayer or Bible reading, not used by the state to endorse religious activity, and not involved with influencing students to compromise their beliefs. Justice William Rehnquist dissented, arguing for a narrow interpretation of the Establishment Clause. He contended that it simply "forbade the establishment of a national religion and forbade preference among religious sects or denominations . . . and [it] did not prohibit the federal government from providing nondiscriminatory aid to religion." Rehnquist concluded that the Court should try to accommodate religious practices, which included praying out loud in the classroom, and that the Establishment Clause "does not prohibit Congress or the states from pursuing legitimate secular ends through nondiscriminatory sectarian means."

Student Use of School Facilities for Religious Purposes

An especially touchy constitutional issue is whether students are allowed, on their own initiative, to use school facilities for religious purposes, including prayer. In 1981, in *Widmar v. Vincent*, the Supreme Court ruled that a public university (the University of Missouri at Kansas City) could not bar students from using its facilities for religious worship and discussion. These activities are protected by the Free Speech Clause of the First Amendment. The Court added that student use of campus facilities for religious purposes did not mean university sponsorship of religion, which would be a violation of the Establishment Clause.

In 1990, the Supreme Court applied the *Widmar* decision to the public secondary schools in *Board of Education of Westside Community Schools v. Mergens*. The Court ruled on the constitutionality of a federal statute. The Equal Access Act of 1984 had provided that public secondary schools that receive federal aid and allow noncurriculum-related groups to meet on school grounds during nonteaching times may not deny similar access to religious groups. The Court concluded that the Act was a remedy against "perceived widespread discrimination against religious speech in public schools" and it did not violate the Establishment Clause.

The *Westside* decision was affirmed in 1993. In *Lamb's Chapel v. Center Moriches Union Free School District*, the school contended that allowing religious meetings on school premises would violate the Establishment Clause. But the Court disagreed. It ruled that a school district's refusal to permit a religious group to show a film on family life on school grounds violated the Free Speech Clause of the First Amendment. Because the school routinely permitted social, civic, and recreational groups to use its facilities, prohibiting their use "by any group for religious purposes" would be uniquely discriminatory.

The distinction between school-sponsored prayer and voluntary prayer was again at issue in *Good News Club v. Milford Central School* (2001). In this case, an elementary school had barred a Christian organization for schoolchildren from using a room in after-school activities, including prayer. Ruling against the school district, the Supreme Court decided that the meetings did not violate the Establishment Clause because they were not sponsored by the school, were held after school, and were open to any student with parental permission. Furthermore, excluding such activities could be construed as a violation of free speech. Still to be decided, however, were questions regarding prayer at school graduations and sporting events.

Prayers at School Graduations and Sporting Events

May students pray at graduation? Yes, if they pray silently and the prayer is not required by the school. The key relevant case is *Lee v. Weisman* (1992). In 1991, David Weisman, whose daughter Deborah graduated from the Nathan Bishop Middle School in Providence, Rhode Island, challenged a prayer offered at the graduation exercises by a Jewish rabbi, Leslie Gutterman. The Weisman family is Jewish.

Principal Robert E. Lee had followed the school district's practice of inviting clergy to give invocations and benedictions at the middle and high school graduation ceremonies. Clergy who accepted the offer were given a copy of the school's pamphlet, "Guidelines for Civic Occasions." Rabbi Gutterman gave this invocation, which would be ruled unconstitutional:

God of the Free, Hope of the Brave:
  For the legacy of America where diversity is celebrated and the rights of minorities are protected, we thank You. May these young men and women grow up to enrich it.
  For the liberty of America, we thank you. May these new graduates grow up to guard it.
  For the political process of America in which all its citizens may participate, for its court system where all may seek justice, we thank You. May those we honor this morning always turn to it in trust.
  For the destiny of America, we thank You. May the graduates of Nathan Bishop Middle School so live that they might help to share it.
  May our aspirations for our country and for these young people, who are our hope for the future, be richly fulfilled.

The rabbi added this benediction:

O God, we are grateful to You for having endowed us with the capacity for learning we have celebrated on this joyous commencement.

Happy families give thanks for seeing these children achieve an important milestone. Send your blessings upon the teachers and administrators who helped prepare them.

The graduates now need strength and guidance for the future. Help them to understand that we are not complete with academic knowledge alone. We must each arrive to fulfill what You require from all of us. To do justly, to love mercy, to walk humbly.

We give thanks to You, Lord, for keeping us alive, sustaining us and allowing us to reach this special, happy occasion.

AMEN.

The administration of President George H.W. Bush filed an *amicus curiae* in support of the school district. It argued that government support of religion is valid unless "the practice . . . provides direct benefits to a religion in a manner that threatens the establishment of an official church [or] it compels persons to participate in a religious exercise contrary to their consciences."

The Supreme Court disagreed with the Bush administration's position, which, in effect, was in conflict with previous decisions against government-sponsored school prayer. The Court held that "the prayer exercises in this case are especially improper because the State has in every practical sense compelled attendance and participation in an explicit religious exercise at an event of singular importance to every student." Instead of using the *Lemon* case, the Court argued that "at a minimum the Constitution guarantees the government may not coerce anyone to support or participate in religion or its exercise." It concluded that, in this case, "the State, in a school setting, in effect required participation in a religious exercise." Writing in dissent, Justice Antonin Scalia argued that graduation exercises were optional for students and that nonsectarian prayers in such occasions tended to reduce religious friction and unify the public. The majority of the justices disagreed. Although the prayer was brief, the Court stated that its inroad into religious conscience "was both real and, in the context of a secondary school, a violation of the objectors' rights." The Court decided that because the graduation prayer ceremony induced students to conform, it violated the Establishment Clause. Once again, the Supreme Court had struck down school-sponsored prayer.

After *Lee*, several school districts throughout the country, mainly in the South, tried to skirt a number of Supreme Court decisions against school-sponsored prayer. The main case in this regard is *Santa Fe Independent School District v. Doe* (2000).

Santa Fe Independent School District v. Doe. The *Lee* case struck down prayer by clergy at school graduation exercises. It left open whether student-initiated and student-led prayer at graduation (e.g., by a class valedictorian) was permissible. Also left undecided was whether student-led prayers at school football games are constitutional.

The Court based its *Santa Fe* decision in 2000 largely on the precedent of *Lee*. This new case involved student-led prayers before high school football games. Before 1995, a student elected as the high school's student council chaplain offered a prayer over the public address system before each home varsity football game. Several Mormon and Catholic students, mothers, and/or alumni sued, charging that this practice violated the Establishment Clause of the First Amendment. Before this suit could be decided, the school district decided to implement a different policy that called for two student elections. The first election would decide whether public "invocations" should be delivered at games; and if the vote were yes, the second would select a student to deliver them. This case proceeded anonymously to avoid any possible retribution against the plaintiffs.

Justice John Paul Stevens, writing for the majority, who included Justices O'Connor, Kennedy, Souter, Ginsburg, and Breyer, argued that the district's policy violated the Establishment Clause because it endorsed religion by calling for invocations; the purpose of the invocations was "to solemnize the event," which meant an official endorsement of religion; the history of this district policy was "to preserve the practice of prayer before football games"; the policy caused harmful divisions between majority "insiders" who favored the policy and minority "outsiders" who were opposed; student-led prayer under this policy was not protected as "private" speech; and attendance at high school football games is in effect coercive, not truly voluntary because of social pressure ("The Constitution demands that schools not force on students the difficult choice between whether to attend these games or to risk facing a personally offensive religious ritual."); and in essence violated the three-pronged test of the *Lemon* decision. In *Santa Fe*, the Court found that the main purpose of the district policy was to promote and encourage prayer at football games.

Chief Justice William Rehnquist, joined by Justices Antonin Scalia and Clarence Thomas, dissented. Their main arguments included: the district policy was not on the face of it a violation of the Establishment Clause; the twofold election process did not necessarily lead to student-led prayer, as "the policy itself has plausible secular purposes" (i.e., a religious message is not necessarily "the most obvious means of solemnizing an event" as the majority opinion claimed); the *Santa Fe* case differed from *Lee*, where the main issue was government speech rather than student speech; and finally, that no student had been harmed by the policy, which had not yet gone into effect and been tested.

Controversy over the Role of High School Football Coaches in Pregame Team Prayers

According to Grant Teaff, executive director of the American Football Coaches Association, over 50 percent of high school football coaches across the United States participate in team prayer. But is this constitutional? This question was addressed in *Borden v. East Brunswick School District* (July 25, 2006), a case that is expected to have national repercussions.

For the twenty-four years Marcus Borden had served as coach, East Brunswick's high school football team had continued a tradition of praying twice before every game. There would be a student-led grace at a pasta dinner in the cafeteria, and then again just before game time, when every player bowed his head and took a knee. Coach Borden joined his players in this practice, defending his participation in distinctly nonreligious terms. He said he wasn't a "religious freak" or a "member of the fellowship of Christian athletes." Instead, he claimed he was "just an average Joe. I'm not a spiritual guy. I'm, not preachy . . . . I'm a high school football coach that has certain beliefs . . . . And I believe strongly in certain things. Tradition and honor."

The constitutional question was not whether Coach Borden and his team had the right to pray, but whether a reasonable and objective person would consider the coach's "head bowing" and "taking a knee" during his team-initiated nonsectarian pregame prayer to be symbolic government promotion of religion. A New Jersey federal district court dismissed the school district's argument that this practice amounted to school endorsement of religion that also coerced some players into participation. It then ruled that the coach's actions do not violate the Establishment Clause of the First Amendment. Moreover, the Court held that the school district's prohibition of Coach Borden's actions after a complaint by a parent had violated his First and Fourteenth Amendment rights to free speech, free association, and academic freedom.

Reaction to the *Borden* decision understandably was mixed. Ronald J. Riccio, Borden's attorney and constitutional law expert at Seton Hall Law School's Center for Social Justice, hailed the decision: "It reaffirms that government can't be hostile to religion," he stated, and "that they have to remain neutral and that not all things that partake of religion are impermissible or in violation of the establishment clause." But Barry Lynn, executive director of Americans United for the Separation of Church and State, vehemently disagreed with the verdict, stating: "I just think it's wrong because it misconstrues existing law and it fails to recognize the long tainted history of this coach's effort to promote prayer in public school." He concluded that Coach Borden's actions clearly were an endorsement of religion. Lynn then added: "Anybody who knows anything about high school athletics knows that if you get on the wrong side of the coach—if you don't in this case participate in religious activities—you're going to fear that you're going to get less playing time, and that's going to hurt your chances both on the team and in the future if you want to play collegiate sports. It's destructive to students for a coach to participate in promotion of religion. We think the school is right and the appeal will vindicate the school."

The school district's attorney, Martin Pachman, filed an appeal on constitutional grounds, arguing: "When he [Coach Borden] bows his head or takes a knee, that is clearly participation in prayer, and for him to argue that is a gesture of respect is disingenuous." The appeal, which may be heard by the Supreme Court, will add another wrinkle to the already complex web of Court decisions and federal laws. The Court may also be facing another controversy over school prayer, this one involving two words in the Pledge of Allegiance.

Controversy over the Pledge of Allegiance

While the country was digesting court decisions regarding prayer before and during high school football games, another issue that had been percolating in lower courts for some time rose to the fore: whether recitation by schoolchildren of the phrase "under God" in the Pledge of Allegiance violates the Establishment Clause of the First Amendment. The key case was *Elk Grove Unified School District et al. v. Newdow et al.* (2004).

The Elk Grove Unified School District required each elementary school class to recite daily the Pledge of Allegiance. Roger Newdow, an atheist, objected to his daughter's being asked to recite the Pledge, which includes the words "under God." The original Pledge, which was written in 1892, did not mention God or religion. Congress added these words in 1954 in an attempt to immunize American schoolchildren against atheistic communism.

Newdow claimed that the district policy, which in effect endorsed religion, violated both the Establishment and Free Exercise Clauses of the First Amendment. The child's mother, Sandra Banning, filed a motion to dismiss. As the sole legal custodial parent, Banning claimed that Newdow's suit was not in the best interest of her child.

On June 26, 2002, the U.S. Court of Appeals for the Ninth Circuit agreed with Newdow that the Pledge's words "under God" violate the Establishment Clause. This case was then taken up by the Supreme Court, which handed down its ruling in June 2004. The Court ruled that Newdow lacked "prudential standing to challenge the school district's policy in federal court." However, it did address some of the substantive arguments related to the Pledge that give at least a hint of the issues over which this case might be eventually decided: The flag was seen "as a symbol of our Nation's indivisibility and commitment to the concept of liberty"; parental viewpoints on possible religious effects of a district policy on the Pledge on children must be taken into account; the burden of showing injury to a child that can be remedied by the Court falls on the parents; the Court customarily is reluctant to intervene in domestic relations when parents disagree on this issue; references to God occur in other venues, such as our country's motto agreed upon by Congress in 1956 ("In God We Trust"); and there was reference to President

Abraham Lincoln's inclusion of "under God" in his Gettysburg Address and his second inaugural address (March 4, 1865), which concluded: "With malice toward none, with charity for all, with firmness in the right as God gives us to see the right, ..." Was Lincoln in this address acknowledging the role that God and religion have played in our nation's history or endorsing religion?

Federal Guidelines on School Prayer

Finally, which patriotic exercises, if any, would mean government endorsement of religion? For example, a teacher may now require students to memorize and recite the opening paragraph of the Declaration of Independence, which includes these references to God on which natural rights are based: "We hold these truths to be self-evident, that all men are created equal, endowed by their *Creator* [our emphasis] with certain inalienable rights. Among these are life, liberty, and the pursuit of happiness." Are these lines mainly theological in intent? And which constitutional cases would serve as precedent for the Court's decision? After *West Virginia v. Barnette* (1943), the Court ruled that students did not have to participate in patriotic exercises with a possible religious bent (in this case, compelling students who were Jehovah's Witnesses to salute the American flag); and in *Lee*, the Court focused on "formal religious exercises" which the Pledge does not do. Answers by the Court to the above issues related to the Pledge are uncertain. Whether and when the Court may decide the Pledge case on its merits is unclear.

In 2003 the U.S. Department of Education drew up guidelines on school prayer that take into account both Court decisions and laws such as the No Child Left Behind Act. (NCLB) signed by President Bush in 2002. In essence the new guidelines reflect those issued by the Clinton administration in 1995 and 1999:

1. *Constitutionally guaranteed religious rights of public schoolchildren*: individual private prayer, saying grace at lunchtime, group prayer by students on school grounds but outside the classroom, bringing a Bible or other religious texts to school and reading them during free time, writing a report on a religious work, and announcements by religious clubs on school bulletin boards or public address systems.
2. *Impermissible practices under the Constitution*: teacher-led prayers in classrooms, attempts to convert students from one belief or faith to another, promotion of religion in any way, and requirements that children stay in classes where lessons that are taught are inconsistent with their religious beliefs.

The similarity between the Clinton and Bush school guidelines notwithstanding, there were two important differences—in both content and emphasis. First, there was no penalty for noncompliance under the Clinton guidelines but there is under NCLB, whereby school districts need to certify compliance or risk loss of federal funds; second, under NCLB a school also risked losing federal funding if it had a policy that restricted a student's right to "religious expression" as provided for in the guidelines. This provision applied especially to graduation exercises. Although school officials still cannot initiate prayer or religious speech, under the Bush administration guidelines "the speech of students who choose to express themselves through religious means such as prayer is not attributable to the state, and therefore may not be restricted because of its religious content."

Given the array of complex Court decisions and federal guidelines, school systems have had a hard time knowing just what they can and cannot do regarding prayer. Many superintendents, principals, and teachers either don't know the guidelines or don't know how to interpret them. Nevertheless, at the end of the day they must decide to follow one or more courses of action.

Policy Options

The American people and their governments—on all levels—have struggled over the issue of prayer in the public schools. They have looked to several options, including the following:

1. *Compliance with the Supreme Court decisions.* As decided in the free speech controversy in *Tinker v. Des Moines School District* (1963), students do not leave their First Amendment rights at the school door. There are many constitutionally acceptable ways for students to pray in school. Students have the right to private prayer. For example, they can pray on their own and read their Bibles or other scriptures as long as they do not do so during instructional time or otherwise disrupt the orderly running of the school. Also acceptable is an official moment of silence, as long as its purpose is not government promotion of prayer. Students can use this moment to pray silently, meditate, contemplate, study, or think about whatever they wish. What is prohibited is school-organized or school-sponsored prayer.
2. *Evasion of the Supreme Court decisions.* Some school systems, mainly in the South, simply ignored Supreme Court decisions on school prayer. For example, teachers continued to read prayers or biblical passages at the start of the school day. They did this because they believed that the Supreme Court's decisions wrongly interpreted the First Amendment and thus violated their rights. Other school systems adopted a teacher discretion policy on school prayer that would continue until legally challenged.
3. *A constitutional amendment allowing government-sponsored school prayer.* Many groups and public officials have proposed an amendment to the Constitution that would allow organized school prayer by overriding the First Amendment. After his election in 1980, President Reagan proclaimed that "God should never have been expelled from the classrooms." In 1982, he proposed the following amendment for passage by Congress: "Nothing in this Constitution shall be construed to prohibit individual or group prayer in public schools or other public institutions. No person shall be required by the United States or any state to participate in school prayer."

    Amending the Constitution was intentionally made very difficult. Congress defeated Reagan's amendment and numerous others introduced since the *Engel* decision. One of the latest defeats came in June 1998, when the House defeated an amendment proposed by Representative Ernest J. Istook (R-OK) that would allow government-sponsored prayer in the public schools. Amendment proposals have received both widespread support and condemnation. For example, political conservatives and evangelical Christians strongly support prayer amendments, but other religious groups, such as the Washington, D.C.-based Christian Legal Society, and political interest groups, such as the Coalition for the Separation of Church and State and the American Civil Liberties Union (ACLU), strongly oppose them.
4. *Enactment of federal laws.* Congress has enacted several statutes that have widened the possibility of school prayer. The major ones are the Equal Access Act (1984), the Educate America Act (1994), and NCLB. The Equal Access Act, as previously discussed, provided that public secondary schools that receive federal funds must permit all noncurriculum-related groups, including religious groups, equal access to meet on school premises. Under the Educate America Act, Congress barred state and local education agencies from using funds

under this act to adopt policies that would "prevent voluntary prayer and meditation in public schools." And NCLB reiterated guidelines that stipulated when school prayer is allowed. School districts that did not comply with federal laws risked losing federal funds.

Attempts by Congress to limit federal court jurisdiction over school prayer have failed. Beginning in 1974, several different times Congress has rejected a proposal that would have done this. One reason is the doubtful constitutionality of such laws. Congress has also hesitated to give the states the right to decide on school prayer.

Conclusion

The issue of school prayer continues to be an important public controversy involving fundamental civil liberties. This is a classic case of an issue on which reasonable people disagree. Supreme Court justices have disagreed, for example, on the intent of the Founding Fathers on religion. Certainly, phrases in the First Amendment such as "establishment" and "free exercise" are ambiguous, perhaps deliberately so. There is no question of voluntary prayer in school, as long as this does not conflict with instruction or is not disruptive. However, the Supreme Court has consistently ruled—albeit only since the *Engel* decision in 1962—that prayer which is officially organized or sponsored is unconstitutional. Many people disagree with the school prayer decisions. They say that the Supreme Court has misinterpreted the Establishment Clause and that schools should have the right to sponsor prayer. Among other things, critics of the Court have tried to allow school-sponsored prayer by evading the Court's decisions, trying to pass a constitutional amendment, or passing laws. Others have maintained that the Court's policy of government neutrality on school prayer has been right and insist on absolute compliance with its decisions.

Discussion Questions

1. What do you think was the original intent of the Founding Fathers on the separation of church and state? How does your opinion relate to school prayer?
2. What would you do if you disagreed with the Supreme Court's decisions on school prayer?
3. Can organized prayers be harmful in any way to students, even if those prayers are voluntary and nonsectarian?
4. Some say the United States has suffered moral decay over the past few decades. Do you agree? If so, to what extent, if any, do you believe that Supreme Court decisions on school prayer have contributed to this decline?
5. Do you pray in school? If so, under what conditions?
6. Would you support a policy that allowed each community to decide for itself whether to have organized school prayer?

Class Activities

1. Students role play several of the Founding Fathers (e.g., Jefferson and Madison) regarding their intent on the separation of church and state and prayer in the public schools.

2. The class divides into three groups. One group favors Roger Newdow's argument to eliminate the phase "under God" from the Pledge of Allegiance and prepares an *amicus curiae*. The second group opposes Newdow's argument and prepares an *amicus curiae*. Each group then selects one or more lawyers to argue its position before the third group that plays the role of U.S. Supreme Court justices. At the end of the role playing, the justices decide the case, issuing one or more written opinions.

Suggestions for Further Reading

Alley, Robert S. *School Prayer: The Court, the Congress, and the First Amendment.* Buffalo, NY: Prometheus Books, 1994.

Chemerinsky, Erwin. "Tiptoeing around 'Under God.'" *Christian Science Monitor,* June 18, 2004, 09.

Congressional Digest. "Prayer in Public Schools." *Congressional Digest* 74, no. 1 (January 1995): 3–32.

DelFattore, Joan. *The Fourth R: Conflicts over Religion in America's Public Schools.* New Haven, CT: Yale University Press, 2004.

Ettorre, John. "How Religious Did They Expect Us to Be?" *Christian Science Monitor,* April 11, 2006, 13.

Feiler, Bruce. "Teach, Don't Preach, the Bible." *New York Times,* December 21, 2005, A39.

Fenwick, Lynda Beck. *Should the Children Pray? A Historical, Judicial, and Political Examination of Public School Prayer.* Waco, TX: Markham Press Fund, 1989.

Newdow, Michael. "Pledging Allegiance to My Daughter." *New York Times,* June 21, 2004, A19.

Ravitch, Frank S. *School Prayer and Discrimination: The Civil Rights of Religious Minorities and Dissenters.* Boston: Northeastern University Press, 2004.

Richey, Warren. "Can Students Mix Prayer and Football?" *Christian Science Monitor,* March 29, 2000, 1.

Richey, Warren. "Schools Bow Heads in Defiance." *Christian Science Monitor,* August 28, 2000, 1.

Smith, Rodney K. *Public Prayer and the Constitution: A Case Study in Constitutional Interpretation.* Wilmington, DE: Scholarly Resources, 1987.

Wood, Daniel B. "Many Kids Don't See Pledge as Religious." *Christian Science Monitor,* March 24, 2004, 3.

Helpful Websites

www.aclu.org/religiousliberty. The American Civil Liberties Union is a watchdog organization against government intrusion into religious liberties.

www.au.org. Americans United for Separation of Church and State is an advocate against school prayer and related issues.

www.ffre.org. The Freedom from Religion Foundation publishes material arguing to keep church and state separate.

www.religioustolerance.org. Information is offered on both sides of the school prayer controversy.

4

Civil Rights

Case 4
Race-Based Affirmative Action in College Admissions: Keep it, Mend it, or End it?

Case Snapshot

A FFIRMATIVE ACTION IS DESIGNED TO INCREASE opportunities for minorities and women by considering the importance of race and gender in two main areas: the workplace and institutions of higher education. Affirmative action was an outgrowth of the civil rights movement of the 1960s. To ensure compliance with the Civil Rights Act of 1964, the next year President Lyndon B. Johnson issued an executive order requiring federal contractors to take affirmative action to recruit, hire, and promote more minorities. In a second executive order in 1967 the president extended coverage of affirmative action to women. In this new political climate, colleges and universities decided to adopt a variety of affirmative action policies in admissions policy that included aggressive recruitment of minority students, race-based financial assistance, and use of race in admissions. The focus of this case is the quandary over race-based preferences in college admissions. Colleges have given three main justifications for affirmative action policies that would aid certain minority applicants, especially African Americans and Hispanics: to compensate for long-standing practices of discrimination; to achieve diversity of the student body; and to overcome "underrepresentation" of historically disadvantaged groups. The landmark U.S. Supreme Court decision of *Regents of the University of California v. Bakke* in 1978 yielded mixed results. The Court rejected quotas and ordered the admission of Bakke, a white male, to medical school, but it also ruled that colleges could seek diversity of the student body by considering race as a factor in admissions. Race-based college admissions policies soon came under attack from many quarters, especially angry white males who complained that they were victims of "reverse discrimination." The debate was over competing rights, philosophy, fairness, and remedies to overcome injustice. In the mid and late 1990s, major blows were dealt to race-based college admissions. In the case of *Hopwood v. State of Texas* in 1996, the U.S. Court of Appeals for the Fifth Circuit ruled that the affirmative action system at the University of Texas Law School in Austin was unconstitutional; in California in 1995, the Board of Regents decided to stop race-based admissions, and the next year voters passed Proposition 209, which ended racial preferences in all public-sector state programs including college admissions; and laws were soon enacted in Washington State and Florida prohibiting state universities from using race-based admissions policies. In 2003, the Supreme Court in split decisions ruled on two cases challenging the constitutionality of the race issue in college admissions at the University of Michigan. In *Gratz v. Bollinger*, the Court invalidated the university's undergraduate affirmative action admissions policy because it used a "mechanistic" point system based in part on race. Yet in *Grutter v. Bollinger*, the Court upheld the affirmative action admissions policy of the law school that considered race in a more holistic evaluation of individual applicants but did not utilize quotas or points.

The University of Michigan's admissions policies were called into question when in November 2006 voters in the state approved a referendum banning affirmative action in college admissions. Affirmative action policies of elite urban secondary schools which require a special examination for admission, like Boston Latin School, have also been scrutinized by the courts. And in an important related issue, in December 2006 the Supreme Court heard arguments on whether public school systems in Seattle and Louisville could utilize race as a factor in school placements. The Court's decision, expected in late 2007, will have an important impact on admission of minorities for college admission, for where one goes to elementary and secondary school often correlates closely with preparedness for college. Thus, in a number of different ways race continues to be an important factor in college admissions. What should be the fate of race-based affirmative action in colleges? You decide!

Major Case Controversies

1. *Supporters of racial preference in college admission argue that:*
   - Without affirmative action, past discrimination will never disappear.
   - College admissions committees historically have favored well-to-do white students.
   - Merit is a complicated issue that should not be assessed mainly on objective academic criteria such as high school grades and standardized scores of college entrance exams.
   - Admissions decisions were never solely merit-based anyway, for colleges had long considered nonacademic preferences for acceptance, such as geographic distribution, athletic prowess, special talent, children of alumni, pedigree, or just plain ability to pay.
   - Without affirmative action there will be a severe shortage of minority professionals to serve as role models in African American and Hispanic neighborhoods.
   - Affirmative action admissions policies at academically elite colleges have been "a remarkable success story" in training the leaders of tomorrow and enhancing the educational experience for all students—at least according to a 1998 study by William Bowen, former president of Princeton University, and Derek Bok, former president of Harvard University.
2. *Critics of racial preference in college admission argue that:*
   - The U.S. Constitution, especially the Fourteenth Amendment, protects individuals, not groups.
   - The Constitution calls for equal protection under law, and so should our laws.
   - College admissions should be based mainly on merit as determined by grade point average and standardized test scores.

- Affirmative action penalizes applicants who themselves were never guilty of discrimination.
- Colleges at various times discriminated against unprotected groups such as Jews and Asians.
- By opening college doors wider to historically disadvantaged and underrepresented groups, other groups, especially white males and more recently Asian Americans, are discriminated against.
- Affirmative action benefits immigrant groups that have not been seriously discriminated against in this country.
- Affirmative action programs that are designed to be temporary remedies for injustice seek to achieve "equality as a result," a phenomenon that seems to be continuing indefinitely.
- Affirmative action in admissions often promotes racial friction and discord rather than harmony and understanding.

3. *There is disagreement whether student body diversity in itself provides greater educational benefit for all students.*

4. *College admissions policies that rely on race-based preferences call for "strict scrutiny" by the judicial system.* Under this standard, policies based on preference of an immutable characteristic such as race are inherently suspect. Consequently, colleges have to demonstrate that their policies serve a compelling institutional interest, that they are narrowly tailored to further this interest, and that there is no other way to achieve their goal.

5. *Racial and ethnic designations are not always clear-cut.* For example, one college applicant of mixed African American and Mexican descent called herself a "blaxican." The heritage of President Bill Clinton is also illustrative. In a televised panel discussion on race in July 1998, Clinton announced that he is part Cherokee, for his grandmother was one-quarter Indian. Thus, this former president is genetically one-sixteenth Native American, but does this ancestry also make him ethnically Native American? Complicating this situation is the fact that some Native Americans tend to consider attitude and a feeling of belongingness more important for tribal membership than percentage of blood.

6. *Many colleges accept more students of color from outside this country than those born and raised in the United States.* For example, a 2004 study of Harvard University minorities found that 8 percent of the undergraduates were black, but as many as two-thirds were West Indian and African immigrants or their children, or children of biracial parents. If Harvard (and other colleges) selected minorities mainly to correct past injustices perpetrated in the United States, the results do not match the intentions.

7. *There is debate over the constitutionality and advisability of whether some scholarships that are reserved for racial minorities should be made available to all students.*

8. *There is a question whether the same admission criteria used in undergraduate admissions should be applied without distinction to graduate school admissions.*

9. *There is debate over the fairness of admissions policies of elite city high schools that rely on a special, difficult examination for acceptance* (because of the disparity in quality of academic preparation in elementary schools serving predominantly minority students).

10. *Use of race in assignment of students to public elementary and secondary schools has been challenged in court.*

11. *Racial minorities are divided over affirmative action.* Some argue that it helps mainly the upper echelon of minorities, not those near or at the bottom who need help the most. They maintain that compensatory programs should focus on the earliest years of education

and on preparing students to compete on academic achievement. In addition, some minority students welcome the advantages of affirmative action; yet others feel stigmatized by affirmative action, believing they were admitted on the basis of their group status, not individual achievement or ability. These students often consider themselves second-class students, and feel other students see them in the same light.

Background of the Case

Affirmative action was born during the heyday of the civil rights movement of the 1960s. It dates back to March 6, 1961, when President John F. Kennedy signed an executive order requiring all federal contractors not just to avoid discrimination but to "take affirmative action to ensure that applicants are employed, and that employees are treated during employment without regard to race, creed, color or national origin."

After Kennedy's assassination, President Lyndon B. Johnson continued to push for affirmative action to help African Americans. In a commencement speech at Howard University on June 4, 1965, the president offered this rationale for affirmative action: "You do not take a person who for years has been hobbled by chance and liberate him, bring him up to the starting line of a race, and then say, 'You are free to compete with all the others,' and still justly believe that you have been completely fair. Thus, it is not enough just to open the gates of opportunity; all our citizens must have the ability to walk through those gates." Johnson was not confident that the Civil Rights Act of 1964 by itself would lead to the end of job discrimination based on "race, color, sex, or national origin." In the aftermath of the shocking five-day riot in the Watts neighborhood of Los Angeles in August 1965, he decided that something more than legislation was needed to break the chain of poverty and despair among African Americans. He thus issued an executive order that essentially reinforced Kennedy's. Two years later, in 1967, the president included women under affirmative action. Soon thereafter, the affirmative action umbrella was widened to include other minorities, mainly Hispanics, Asian Americans, and Native Americans.

Colleges and universities, as recipients of federal aid, fell under Washington's affirmative action policies. Many decided on their own to adopt affirmative action admission policies. Race and gender were thus being considered in two key areas: hiring and college admissions. The two went hand-in-hand, for a poor education virtually condemned its recipients to low-paying jobs or unemployment. Yet a good education was the key to a better future.

Attempts to Reverse the Legacy of Unequal Opportunity in Higher Education

Affirmative action programs were initially designed to help African Americans overcome their unique legacy of slavery and segregation. After the Civil War, Jim Crow laws segregated the races and essentially guaranteed that African Americans would not receive equal educational opportunity. The Supreme Court's "separate but equal" decision in *Plessy v. Ferguson* (1896) in reality meant that education for blacks would be separate but hardly equal. Southern states spent much more money on schools for whites, and white schools had better facilities and more up-to-date books and curricula. Moreover, doors to major state colleges and universities in the South were closed to blacks, who could attend only black colleges that had far more limited resources.

After World War II, segregation started to weaken. In Major League Baseball, for example, Jackie Robinson broke the color barrier in 1947 when he played for the Brooklyn Dodgers. The federal government also started to break down segregation. In 1948, President Harry Truman abolished segregation in the armed forces. The early civil rights movement, however, targeted education, for this was seen as the key to economic opportunity.

In 1954, after a series of Supreme Court decisions that chipped away at segregation, the landmark decision in *Brown v. Board of Education of Topeka, Kansas* reversed *Plessy v. Ferguson.* The Court decided that separate schools for African Americans could never be equal and thus they violated the Equal Protection Clause of the Fourteenth Amendment. The Court's goal was to achieve integrated primary and secondary schools "with all deliberate speed." At first, many public school systems in both the North and the South resisted the *Brown* decision. In the South, more white parents sent their children to private schools, and in the North, school systems such as one in Boston, Massachusetts, practiced de facto segregation by gerrymandering school districts. Starting in the late 1960s, both public and private colleges and universities began affirmative action programs in admissions.

Affirmative Action in College Admissions

Affirmative action policies in college admissions initially targeted African Americans as a way of making up for years of racial discrimination. However, these policies soon included women and other minorities, especially Hispanics and Native Americans. Two additional justifications were offered: The country had to overcome underrepresentation of historically disadvantaged groups, and colleges needed to seek a more diverse student body. The supposition was that more minorities on campus would be beneficial to *all* students.

Opposition to affirmative action admission policies was almost immediate. In the 1970s, two white males, Marco DeFunis and Allan Bakke, challenged racially discriminatory graduate school admissions policies in court. Both men complained that they were denied admission on the basis of race. DeFunis protested against a law school's affirmative action policy and Bakke against a medical school's. The Supreme Court decided to hear both cases. DeFunis and Bakke won admission, but the *DeFunis* case became moot when he was admitted before his case was heard. Thus, the *Bakke* case, decided in 1978, became the landmark decision.

Regents of the University of California v. Bakke (1978)

In 1973, Allan Bakke, a thirty-three-year-old white male of Norwegian ancestry, who was an excellent student and a Vietnam War veteran, was denied admission to the University of California at Davis Medical School. Bakke reapplied the following year but he was again rejected. The university's affirmative action policy, adopted in 1968, was to reserve sixteen out of one hundred places in its entering class for African Americans, Chicanos, Asians, and Native Americans. These groups, to be judged under separate criteria, had been underrepresented at the medical school before the special admissions program.

In 1977, Bakke sued the school on two grounds. First, he claimed that by reserving places for "disadvantaged" minorities who would be judged differently, the university had instituted a quota system that violated his rights under the Equal Protection Clause of the Fourteenth Amendment and the Civil Rights Act of 1964. Title VI of this Act held that "no person . . . shall, on the ground of race, color, or national origin, be excluded from participation in, be denied the benefits of, or be subject to discrimination under any program or activity receiving federal financial assistance." Most colleges fell under Title VI because they received federal funds. Second, Bakke claimed that the university had discriminated against him on account of his race because he had better credentials (as measured by college grades and standardized test scores) than some of the successful minority applicants in the set-aside quota pool.

In 1978, the Supreme Court ruled in Bakke's favor and ordered him admitted. In a 5–4 decision, it declared the university's two-track quota system illegal but permitted colleges to "take race into account" in admitting students. However, the justices disagreed on why race should be a factor in admissions. The four justices who accepted the university's admission plan (William Brennan, Byron White, Thurgood Marshall, and Harry Blackmun) said that it was necessary under the Equal Protection Clause of the Fourteenth Amendment to remedy "society discrimination" and to overcome "minority underrepresentation." They cited a report of the Carnegie Commission on Higher Education for 1970 that held that "the greatest single handicap [minorities face] is their underrepresentation in the professions." Marshall, the only African American on the Court, added: "The experience of [blacks] in America has been different in kind, not just in degree, from that of other ethnic groups."

Four other justices (Potter Stewart, Warren Burger, William Rehnquist, and John Paul Stevens) rejected the university's two-track admissions policy as a violation of Title VI of the Civil Rights Act. They did not consider it necessary to address constitutional issues. Justice Lewis Powell Jr. cast the deciding vote, concluding that the university's admission system was both illegal and unconstitutional. His following comments caught national attention:

> Racial and ethnic classifications of any sort are inherently suspect and call for the most exacting judicial scrutiny. While the goal of achieving a diverse student body is sufficiently compelling to justify race in admissions decisions under some circumstances, petitioner's special admissions program, which forecloses consideration to persons like respondent, is unnecessary to the achievement of this compelling goal, and therefore invalid under the Equal Protection Clause.

However, Powell then argued that affirmative action was necessary to achieve "educational diversity." Because diversity "was of constitutional origin [through] the First Amendment and its promise of broad traffic in ideas," it was an acceptable goal of an affirmative action admissions policy. If race were to be taken into account in a single admissions system, then schools would not have to exclude any candidate on the basis of race alone. In such a system, every candidate would receive "competitive" scrutiny. Race, seemingly, could be one "factor" in admissions. Powell's opinion, controversial as it was, led to even more debate as it applied without distinction to both undergraduate and graduate schools.

Backlash against Bakke

Most colleges interpreted the complex *Bakke* decision as giving a green light to race-based affirmative action admissions policies as long as there were no quotas involved. However, they used the *Bakke* decision both to set "diversity" as a goal and to elevate race to a major factor in admissions. Some critics of affirmative action, such as conservative publisher Terry Eastland, argued that Powell was deceiving himself. "To license race 'as a factor,'" he wrote, was "to license its use as the deciding factor."

Soon race-based affirmative action admissions policies led to a backlash, especially in Texas and California, two states with especially large numbers of minorities. Both these states, in different ways, ended racial preferences in admissions. In the case of *Cheryl Hopwood v. State of Texas* (1996) the University of Texas Law School was ordered not to use race as a factor in admissions decisions, and in California the Board of Regents ended race-based admissions. Soon thereafter the state's voters affirmed this decision by passing Proposition 209.

The Hopwood Case

In 1992, Cheryl Hopwood, a white woman with outstanding academic credentials, was denied admission to the University of Texas at Austin Law School. Hopwood clearly was an economically disadvantaged student. She had been admitted to Princeton University but did not attend for financial reasons. Having been raised by a single mother and having had to support herself since she was nineteen, she had to pay for her own education. Hopwood attended several community colleges in Pennsylvania before moving to California. She graduated from California State University at Sacramento with a 3.8 grade point average—an outstanding academic accomplishment, especially considering the fact that while she went to college she worked twenty to thirty hours a week, was active in the Big Brothers/Big Sisters program, became a certified public accountant, and took care of her severely handicapped baby daughter. She applied to law school in Texas because her husband, who was in the military, was stationed there.

When Hopwood was denied admission, she sued when she learned that the school had reserved 15 percent of the approximately five hundred openings in the first-year class for African Americans and Mexican Americans. This percentage of "underrepresented minorities" was based on the same percentages of these two groups who were graduating annually from the state's colleges and universities. Thus, the Texas law school was trying to achieve a form of proportional representation in its classes. These applicants would be judged by a separate admissions subcommittee and admitted under different and lower academic standards than all other applicants. This fact was the key point of the lawsuit.

Although Hopwood's Law School Admission Test (LSAT) scores were high enough to place her in the top echelon of candidates and guarantee her admission, she was put into a lower category of applicants because she had not graduated from what the university's admissions committee considered a highly competitive academic college. Hopwood argued that her race was the main reason she was rejected. In this instance, Hopwood contended, race was not just one factor in admissions but the deciding factor in a system that violated Justice Powell's rejection of a two-tier admissions system. Candidates were being judged in separate racial pools, not all against one another. Hopwood was also challenging the university's use of race to admit a diverse group of students.

The university defended its admissions preference regarding African Americans and Mexican Americans on grounds that it achieved the goals of racial diversity and compensation for past discrimination. In 1994, under the gun of the *Hopwood* suit, the law school abolished its separate admissions system. In court, Judge Sam Parks cited Powell's decision in *Bakke*. Parks concluded that the law school's admission policy was unconstitutional because it "fails to afford each individual applicant a comparison with the entire pool of applicants, not just those of the applicant's own race." Having stated this, Judge Parks said the law school could admit by race as long as its policy followed Justice Powell's opinion in the *Bakke* case. The Supreme Court had ordered the University of California to admit Bakke, but Judge Parks merely allowed Hopwood the right to reapply for admission and one dollar in damages. His reasoning was that the law school had not "intended to discriminate." The judge cited the long history of racial discrimination in Texas that had "left residual effects that persist into the present" and that could be seen "in the diminished educational attainment of the present generation" of African American and Mexican American minorities in the state.

The Court rejected the first defense of the university, maintaining that since it was too hard to determine the magnitude and present effects of past discrimination an appropriate remedy could not be determined. Moreover, the law school's preferential admissions policy benefited equally students from schools inside and outside Texas, both public and private. It rejected the second defense by arguing that it was not possible to measure or rationally estimate the present effects of previous racial discrimination practiced by the law school. Thus, it was not possible to determine whether preferential admissions made up for this odious past. The Court rejected the third defense by pointing out that since the 1960s the law school had a fine record of recruiting minorities, that most faculty and staff were not responsible for previous discrimination, and that any hostile relations among races on the campus clearly could not be blamed on previous discrimination by the school. The Court concluded that the law school had "failed to show a compelling state interest in remedying the present effect of past discrimination sufficient to maintain the use of race in its admissions system."

The Court also rejected diversity as a justification for preferences approved by Justice Powell in the *Bakke* case. In fact, the Court argued, "classification of persons on the basis of race for the purposes of diversity frustrates, rather than facilitates the goals of equal protection." The Court added: "The diversity interest will not satisfy strict scrutiny. Use of race in admissions for diversity in higher education contradicts, rather than furthers, the aims of equal protection. Diversity fosters, rather than minimizes, the use of race. It treats minorities as a group, rather than as individuals . . . . It may promote improper racial stereotypes, thus fueling racial hostility." In addition, racial classifications also "stigmatize" and "promote notions of racial inferiority and lead to politics of racial hostility." And, "finally, the use of race to achieve diversity undercuts the ultimate goal of the Fourteenth Amendment: the end of racially motivated state action."

The *Hopwood* decision dealt a devastating blow to affirmative action admissions policies in the states covered by the Fifth District: Texas, Louisiana, and Mississippi. Both sides appealed the decision, with inconclusive results. The Supreme Court did not take the case because the admissions program that Hopwood challenged had already been scrapped. Nevertheless, her case was to have a significant impact all around the country until it was superseded in 2003 by the Supreme Court's two decisions on affirmative action policies by the University of Michigan, which will be discussed below.

California Takes Steps to Eliminate Affirmative Action in College Admissions

On July 20, 1995, as chair of the state Board of Regents that oversees the country's largest state university system, California Governor Pete Wilson called on the board to end the universities' affirmative action admissions policies: "We cannot tolerate university policies or practices that violate fundamental fairness, trampling individual rights to create and give preference to group rights." He then added: "Race has played a central role in the admissions practice at many University of California campuses. Indeed, some students who don't meet minimum academic requirements are admitted solely on the basis of race. Are we going to continue to divide California by race?" The Board of Regents decided to replace its affirmative action policy on admissions with a "color-blind" policy that made allowances for students with disadvantaged backgrounds. Governor Wilson gambled that he could ride the backlash to California's affirmative action policies to the Republican presidential nomination and then right into the White House. His bid for the presidency failed, but not his campaign against affirmative action.

In the November 1996 election, 54 percent of California voters approved Proposition 209, which stated: "The state shall not discriminate against or grant preferential treatment to any individual or group on the basis of race, sex, color, ethnicity, or national origin in the operation of public employment, public education or public contracting." In essence, this meant the abolition of affirmative action in state programs and policies.

Leading the fight for passage of Proposition 209 was Ward Connerly, a black businessman from Sacramento who was a member of the University of California Board of Regents. Connerly's answer to affirmative action was "Nix it, don't fix it." This was a play on the quip on affirmative action made by President Bill Clinton, who said, "Mend it, not end it." According to Connerly: "There is no public policy which has greater potential to rip the fabric of American democracy than affirmative action as it has evolved. Every citizen should have an equal chance at the starting line of life's race. But there should not be a guaranteed outcome in the race. If you discriminate for someone, you discriminate against someone else."

Almost immediately, there was a legal challenge to the proposition that called for review of its constitutionality. It was put on hold when Federal District Court Judge Thelton E. Henderson issued an injunction that blocked implementation. Then, in April 1997 the U.S. Court of Appeals overturned this injunction, rejecting the judge's argument that the ballot initiative violated the Equal Protection Clause of the Fourteenth Amendment because it eliminated only those programs that benefited women and minorities while leaving intact other preferences, such as for veterans. Instead, the Court of Appeals ruled that Proposition 209 treated race and sex "in a neutral fashion."

Connerly praised the Court's decision: "It's a nail, it's a spike, it's a dagger in the coffin of preferences. I and those who fought so hard on behalf of 209 are ecstatic about it." In the losing battle to overturn the proposition, attorney Mark Rosenbaum argued that the decision went against "decades of mainstream Supreme Court law." He then quipped: "It doesn't just force women and minorities to the back of the bus. It boots them off altogether." The constitutionality of Proposition 209 seemed to be settled, although the battle over the state's affirmative action programs was far from over.

After passage of Proposition 209, Connerly and other opponents of affirmative action formed the American Civil Rights Institute to argue "aggressively" that other states, as well as Congress, should abolish all race and sex preferences in college admissions and hiring. Significant challenges to racial preferences in college admissions policies were undertaken in several other states, most notably Washington and Michigan.

In Washington, opponents of affirmative action placed the controversial issue on the ballot in the November 1998 elections. Modeled after California's Proposition 209, voter approval of Washington's Initiative 200 by a 58 percent margin—despite strong opposition by powerful political figures such as Washington Democratic governor Gary Locke, Vice President Al Gore, and the Reverend Jesse Jackson—signaled an end to most if not all state affirmative action programs. Understandably, supporters of the Initiative were elated. As conservative talk-show host John Carlson proclaimed: "With a victory that outstrips the most optimistic predictions, the message is clear: the era of race-based affirmative action is over." But the legal wrangling over affirmative action in Washington was far from over. In *Smith v. University of Washington Law School* (2000), the U.S. Court of Appeals for the Ninth Circuit let stand the school's affirmative action admissions policy, arguing that diversity in education was a compelling state interest.

The battle over affirmative action was also being fought in other states, especially Georgia and Michigan. In *Johnson v. Regents of the University of Georgia* (2001), a federal appeals court let stand a decision that struck down the university's undergraduate affirmative action admissions policy because it gave minority applicants a fixed numerical bonus. The more important affirmative action cases, decided by the U.S. Supreme Court in 2003, dealt with two admissions policies of the University of Michigan: one (*Gratz v. Bollinger*) at the undergraduate College of Literature, Science, and the Arts; and the other (*Grutter v. Bollinger*) at the law school. Both class-action cases were filed by the Center for Individual Rights (CIR), a public policy law firm determined to weaken and eventually eliminate affirmative action programs nationwide.

The Michigan Affirmative Action Cases

Gratz v. Bollinger. In the fall of 1997, two white students, Jennifer Gratz and Patrick Hamacher, who were denied admission to the undergraduate college of the University of Michigan, filed a class-action suit lawsuit charging that the university had discriminated against them by using different standards to admit students of different races, in effect keeping out white students with excellent high school records and College Board entrance exam scores. Gratz, from a working-class suburb of Detroit, was placed on the waiting list for the flagship campus at Ann Arbor even though she had graduated among the top 5 percent of her high school class of about three hundred. She finally decided to attend the University of Michigan, Dearborn campus, from which she later graduated with a math degree. The *Bakke* decision had prohibited a "dual system" for admitting students of different races. The students bringing this suit were represented by the Center for Individual Rights, a nonprofit law group that had helped bring the *Hopwood* suit against the University of Texas Law School.

The *Gratz* suit differed from the *Hopwood* suit in that it targeted undergraduate admissions policy and would hold individual college administrators responsible for the alleged civil rights violations. The university defended its policy by underscoring the diversity argument put forth by Justice Powell in the *Bakke* case and by emphasizing that it used race as a "plus factor" in admissions along with other key factors such as high school grades. It cited what it considered convincing statistics on admission that should have indicated there was no unconstitutional discrimination against Gratz: the year Gratz was wait-listed, 1,400 white and Asian students with lower grades and test scores were admitted and 2,000 whites and Asians with higher test scores were not admitted. Critics, however, charged that in reality the university admissions policy placed an inordinately high premium on race. Faced by criticism and under pressure from this lawsuit, the university revised its undergraduate admissions policy guidelines. Presumably, the system would be simplified although weight given to race would not change.

On June 23, 2003, in a 6–3 decision, the Supreme Court rejected the undergraduate affirmative action program at the University of Michigan. Chief Justice William Rehnquist wrote the majority opinion, with Justices Stephen Breyer, Anthony Kennedy, Sandra Day O'Connor, Antonin Scalia, and Clarence Thomas concurring. The main reason for the rejection of the undergraduate affirmative action admissions program was that it used a point system which in effect was a quota system banned by the *Bakke* decision. Furthermore, this admissions program was considered too "mechanistic," as it did not give enough attention to individual applicants. Thus the Court found that the undergraduate admissions policy was "not narrowly tailored to achieve the interest in educational diversity" which supposedly was the university's main justification for racial preference.

Justices Ruth Bader Ginsburg, David Souter, and John Paul Stevens dissented, issuing varied opinions. Justice Ginsburg found no constitutional issue since only "qualified applicants" were admitted. Justice Souter considered Michigan's admission system constitutional as it differed sufficiently from that decided in *Bakke*; and Justice Stevens argued that the plaintiffs lacked standing since they were already enrolled in other colleges.

Grutter v. Bollinger. In this case, Barbara Grutter, a white woman who was rejected by the University of Michigan Law School in 1997, sued the university. She wanted the Supreme Court to overturn a ruling by the U.S. Court of Appeals in May 2002 that ruled the law school's admission policy was constitutional. In a 5–4 decision, the Supreme Court upheld this decision. The Court decided that the law school's policy, abiding by *Bakke*, was constitutional on two grounds: it gave each applicant a modicum of individual attention, using race as one of many factors in admission; and it was necessary to bring about racial diversity on campus.

Justice O'Connor, who cast the key vote in both Michigan decisions, explained the difference in the two rulings of the Court: "The law school considers the various diversity qualifications of each applicant, including race, on a case-by-case basis." But "the Office of Undergraduate Admissions relies on the selection index to assign every underrepresented minority applicant the same, automatic 20-point bonus without consideration of the particular background, experience, and qualities of each individual applicant." O'Connor added that this mechanized selection index score "automatically determines the admissions decisions for each applicant . . . [which] precludes admissions counselors from conducting the type of individualized consideration the court's opinion in [the law school case] requires."

The four dissenting justices in *Grutter* (Kennedy, Thomas, Scalia, and Chief Justice Rehnquist), however, charged that this case "involves a straightforward instance of radical discrimination by a state institution" which cloaked an unofficial quota system. These justices focused their opinions on different issues. For example, Justice Thomas, the only black on the Court who himself had benefited from affirmative action, nevertheless opposed the law school's admissions policy since he believed it left a stigma on blacks who were admitted. And Justice Kennedy, agreeing with his dissenting colleagues, considered the law school's admission policy "antithetical to strict scrutiny" since it focused unduly on the institution's goal of achieving a "critical mass" of diverse students rather than on individualized assessment of each applicant.

In effect, what the Supreme Court was saying in the two cases involving the University of Michigan was that affirmative action policies seeking to create educational diversity are constitutional if they do not use a rigid quota system (in essence, overruling the 1996 *Hopwood* decision) and that the constitutionality of undergraduate and graduate affirmative action policies should be seen through the same lens. Finally, the Court did not expect affirmative action college admission policies to be around forever. As Justice O'Connor said in the *Grutter* decision: "We expect that 25 years from now, the use of racial preferences will no longer be necessary to further the interest approved today."

Soon after the Court's decisions on Michigan's controversial admissions policies, Gratz switched her focus in challenging affirmative action to the political arena. As executive director of the Michigan Civil Rights Initiative, she spearheaded a state ballot initiative to bar affirmative action from university admissions and government hiring and contracts. She received financial support and encouragement from Ward Connerly, who had spurred similar initiatives in California and Washington. In November 2006, Michigan became the third state in the country to ban racial preferences in college admissions by passing a referendum (Proposition 2). Almost immediately, the Coalition to Defend Affirmative Action, Integration and Immigration Rights, and Fight for Equality by Any Means Necessary filed a lawsuit challenging the constitutionality of the referendum decision. The group argued that the voters' decision violated the Equal Protection Clause of the Fourteenth Amendment because college admissions (and other government) practices covered by the referendum would be discriminatory without affirmative action. This appeal was rejected in federal court.

At about the same time, the University of Michigan, together with Michigan State University and Wayne State University, sought a six-month delay in implementation of the referendum decision on the grounds that they were in the midst of their admissions cycle. On December 29, 2006, a federal appeals court ordered immediate compliance. Then in early February 2007, the University of Michigan settled its lawsuit with Jennifer Gratz and Patrick Hamacher, agreeing to pay $10,000 damages to each of these leading plaintiffs on condition they would drop all class action suit claims against the university.

Controversial Affirmative Action Admissions Policies of Public Schools

Affirmative action admissions policies by colleges should also be seen in the broader context of two major issues involving admission to public schools: selection to competitive city secondary examination schools, such as Boston Latin School; and the use of race in student assignments to schools throughout a city. Clearly in many instances, where students go to high school has a significant impact on where or even whether they go to college. This is especially the case with Boston Latin School, which historically has provided a hard-earned opportunity for city students to go to college.

Affirmative Action Admissions at Boston Latin School

Supporters of affirmative action in school admissions received a major setback in November 1998 when a three-judge panel of the Court of Appeals for the First Circuit struck down racial preferences for admission to Boston Latin School, the oldest public high school in the country (founded in 1635) and one of the three elite Boston high schools that require entrance exams (*Wessman v. Gittens*). Before this ruling, Boston School Committee policy required the school to reserve 35 percent of its entering seventh-grade class for black and Hispanic students. A federal court had ordered this desegregation policy in 1974 after finding that the Boston School Committee had unlawfully segregated the city schools. The 1998 Court ruling (binding in Maine, Massachusetts, New Hampshire, Rhode Island, and Puerto Rico) struck down a district court ruling that had found the school's admissions policy constitutional on grounds of the school system's compelling interest in diversity and in "overcoming the vestiges of past discrimination and avoiding the re-segregation of the Boston Public Schools." In 1996, when a white student who was denied admission successfully challenged this policy on the grounds that it violated the Equal Protection Clause of the Fourteenth Amendment, the school decided to change its admissions policy. The suit against it was then dropped. The new school policy admitted 50 percent of applicants based only on test scores and grade point averages and the other 50 percent based on "flexible racial/ethnic guidelines" that required selection of students in proportion to their representation in the qualified applicant pool.

The 1998 Court ruling was in response to a legal challenge of this new policy on equal protection grounds by Sarah Wessman, a white applicant, whose test scores and GPA were higher than those of minority candidates who were admitted. The Court held that the Boston Latin School's admissions policy in effect was "racial balancing," that it was not narrowly tailored, and that the school committee had not provided proof of the educational value of diversity though this was recognized as a compelling state interest. After this ruling, Boston Latin School was ordered to admit students solely on entrance exam scores and elementary school grades, each weighed equally.

The Boston School Committee at first planned to appeal the ruling to the Supreme Court, making two familiar arguments: that the use of race is justified in admissions because of past discrimination and that diversity has a genuine educational value for all students. However, the school committee, fearing a negative decision and the nationwide impact this would have, in February 1999 unanimously decided not to appeal.

According to Terence Pell, senior counsel at the Center for Individual Rights in Washington, D.C., which supported Hopwood's case in Texas, the Boston decision put "a further stake in the heart of the diversity rationale." He then added: "People might have thought that if the diversity rationale would survive at all, it would be in the elementary and secondary school context, but the Court said, no, the legal standard is the same." However, critics of the Boston decision such as Jeff Simmering, director of legislation at the Council of the Great City Schools, were "very concerned that it could lead to racial isolation, re-segregation, and less educational opportunity for minority children." The problems of unequal elementary school education in Boston and the differences in academic preparation between graduates of private and public schools in the city also led to charges that the appeals court's decision was unfair to racial minorities. If racial minorities faced what in effect were insurmountable difficulties in winning acceptance to elite public high schools, they certainly would have a much harder time getting admitted to college. Thus, college admissions officers would be left with even less academically prepared racial minority applicants.

For several years after the Court ruling, minority enrollment at Boston Latin School plummeted. But school officials soon started to work hard at minority recruitment. School representatives began visiting more of the city's elementary schools, hosting events to acquaint parents of minority students with the school's admissions requirements, offering a free summer program to prepare students for the fall entrance exam to the school, providing interpreters for students speaking Spanish, Haitian Creole, and other foreign languages, and contacting parents of minority students who passed the entrance exam to encourage them to actually enroll. These aggressive recruitment efforts soon began paying off in significantly higher percentages of minority student enrollment. To many observers, this method of increasing minority student enrollment was seen as preferable to the previous system of affirmative action in admissions.

Use of Race in Student Assignments to Public Schools

After the Michigan cases, it looked like the Supreme Court would not accept further affirmative action cases in education for quite some time. However, in December 2006 the Court heard two cases involving public school district policies that would have an impact on affirmative action college admissions programs.

Parents Involved in Community Schools v. Seattle School District *and* **Meredith v. Jefferson County Board of Education.** These two cases involved the issue of race-conscious assignment of students to public schools. This was the first time the Court addressed affirmative action affecting the country's K–12 students. In December 2005 (and again in July 2006) the Court had declined to hear a case involving the race-conscious plan of Lynn, Massachusetts (*Comfort v. Lynn School Committee*). But the newly constituted Court with its two Bush-appointed justices, Chief Justice John G. Roberts Jr. and Associate Justice Samuel A. Alito Jr. agreed to hear cases from Seattle, Washington, and Louisville, Kentucky.

Both the Seattle and Louisville cases involved challenges to plans known as "managed choice" or "open choice." Both plans, upheld by lower courts, were being appealed. The key question was whether school officials could promote diversity by using racial balance in enrollment at public K–12 schools without violating the Equal Protection Clause of the Fourteenth Amendment. The Court had to decide whether the "diversity" plans of both school districts should be considered a sufficiently compelling government interest to justify race-conscious school assignments. From a related standpoint, the Court also had to decide whether the accepted rationale for law schools to achieve racial diversity in *Gratz v. Bollinger* applied to public school districts.

In the Seattle case, where there was no history of official segregation in the schools, an appeals court upheld the district's system that let students choose their school but relied on race as the final "integration tiebreaker" when their decisions resulted in a racially imbalanced school: a school that differed by more than 15 percent from the racial composition of the Seattle public schools as a whole. The basic goal was to create a racial enrollment balance of about 40 percent white and 60 percent nonwhite at all the city's high schools.

In October 2005, the U.S. Court of Appeals for the Ninth Circuit upheld the Seattle plan, citing Justice O'Connor's goal of educational diversity as a compelling state interest for law schools and colleges. One judge also noted that the Seattle plan differed from the original rationale of affirmative action policies in college admissions in that it did not "seek to give one racial group an edge over another."

The Kentucky school assignment plan required that most schools in a district maintain a black enrollment of between 15 percent and 50 percent. The plan, which involved the metropolitan Louisville district, differed from the Seattle plan in that Louisville had been under a federal court order to desegregate its schools until 2000. Louisville implemented its race-conscious school assignment plan after the desegregation order was lifted to ensure the district's schools would be diverse.

Crystal Meredith, a white parent, had appealed a decision by the school district that forbade her son Joshua McDonald first from attending his neighborhood school and then from transferring to another elementary school because those schools already had filled their quotas for white students. According to the complaint, Joshua was expected to travel to a school that was an hour's drive away in heavy morning traffic and where the teaching "was not fit for him." According to the plaintiff's lawyer Teddy Gordon, race did not enter into the complaint. Did the Louisville district's decision violate Joshua's Equal Protection rights under the Fourteenth Amendment? The district argued that no harm was done since all its schools offered equal educational opportunity and all students would benefit equally from integrated schools. But attorney Gordon argued that the district should focus on the quality of schools rather than their racial composition.

In a brief filed with these two cases, the Bush administration took an extreme color-blind position against the constitutionality of utilizing "race-conscious measures" that addressed "racial imbalance in communities or student bodies." The president's brother, Governor Jeb Bush of Florida, also filed briefs against both cities' race-balancing plans, arguing that in the public schools there is no persuasive evidence linking racial diversity and educational achievement. The Supreme Court is expected to make a decision on these cases in late 2007. These decisions will have an important impact on both the number and quality of academic preparation of minority students in these two districts and elsewhere around the country. Consequently, they will also impact affirmative action programs of colleges and universities.

Given the wide range of issues and arguments regarding affirmative action in Supreme Court decisions and voter referenda, what options involving race should college admissions officers consider that would be most beneficial?

Policy Options

1. *Follow the Bakke and Grutter decisions.* Actively recruit minorities and consider race as one factor in admissions, but do not use separate admissions categories or quotas and base admissions decisions on the argument that all students benefit from more diversity on campus.
2. *Use affirmative action to overcome "underrepresentation" of minorities.* Attempt to create a student body whose composition reflects the proportion of minorities that graduate from

the state's high schools or colleges. Some critics of this position, such as conservative author Dinesh D'Souza, argue that "the only way for colleges to achieve proportionalism is to downplay or abandon merit criteria, and to accept students from typically underrepresented groups such as African American, Hispanics, and American Indians over better qualified students among Asian and white groups." In other words, according to D'Souza, this option means that colleges would have to lower both their admissions and their academic performance standards.

3. *Employ affirmative action based on student income.* This would treat all racial applicants equally. Both white and nonwhite applicants would be judged according to the same criterion of ability to pay. Under this option, presumably Cheryl Hopwood would have been admitted to the University of Texas Law School.

4. *Actively recruit minorities, but let them compete on an equal footing with other applicants.* This means that race in itself would not be a factor in admissions. Rather, admissions decisions would be based on merit, as determined mainly by grade point average and standardized test scores. Other criteria for admission, such as geographic distribution, athletic prowess, extracurricular activities, and special talent would be left intact.

5. *Consider only grades in secondary school courses and college entrance examinations.* Among other things, this would eliminate athletic scholarships. Critics of this option argue that athletic scholarships depend not on race but on athletic ability. Perhaps more important, this option disregards the wide disparity in educational opportunities afforded poor minority students in various urban and rural areas.

6. *Use race-normed tests for admission.* For a variety of reasons, minorities score lower than white Americans on most standardized intelligence and College Board tests. Some say that the tests themselves are culturally biased; others argue that minorities have lower scores because they have not had equal educational opportunity as a result of poor urban school systems, poverty, and cultural deprivation. With race norming, all applicants would take the same tests for admission, but the scores of minorities would be adjusted. In other words, there would be separate norms for minorities, whose test results would be considered separately from the others. Alternatively, minorities might get extra points for their status (e.g., veterans preference) or given other special consideration. Critics of this option point out that all college applicants should be considered on individual achievement, not group membership, and that this practice also unfairly discriminates against whites and others not given special consideration.

7. *Admit to undergraduate state colleges the top academic 10 percent of graduating high school seniors in the state.* This option was adopted by the State of Texas in the aftermath of the *Hopwood* decision. In early 1999, the California legislature adopted a similar policy that admitted the top 4 percent from each high school to state universities; and starting in fall 2000, the Talented 20 Program in Florida started admitting the top qualified 20 percent of public high school graduates to the state university system, though not guaranteeing admission to the institution of choice. Supporters praise this option for treating all college applicants equally. Yet critics point to segregated high schools, from which 90 percent or more of the minorities would be admitted. They also point out that high schools differ significantly in quality and academic rigor, so a student below the top designated percent in one school might be academically more qualified than a top student in a less academically strong school.

8. *Use different standards for consideration of race for admission to undergraduate and graduate schools.* Arguments for affirmative action in colleges, such as diversity, do not necessarily

apply to graduate schools—the *Grutter* decision notwithstanding. Underrepresentation of minorities, especially black males, in areas such as medicine and law is a serious national problem that can be addressed at least in part by affirmative action plans in graduate school admissions. Consider, too, that if colleges do not graduate more minorities there will be fewer minority graduate school applicants. In the fall of 1997, the University of California at Berkeley Law School, in the wake of a worrisome decline in minority admissions, decided to stop treating applicants from elite colleges better than those from lower-level ones. In the future, admissions officers could consider the undergraduate school of applicants but not automatically use upgrading or downgrading according to arbitrary categorization of quality. This change allows more minorities, who tend not to graduate from elite schools, to compete more equally.

9. *Improve the academic preparedness of all students.* This means improving K–12 education, especially in poor inner-city and rural schools, and examining nonacademic root causes of disadvantage beyond race, such as poverty, drugs, dysfunctional families, and poor academic motivation. This might be the best option for the long term but would do little to help disadvantaged children at the present time.

Conclusion

Racial preference policies in college admissions grew out of the civil rights movement of the 1960s. The original intent was that giving preference to blacks and other minorities would help rectify historical injustices. In the *Bakke* case, the Supreme Court decided that colleges could not use quotas but could consider race as a factor in admissions decisions. Supreme Court Justice Powell added the justification of "diversity," which he believed would benefit all students. Soon colleges included other justifications, such as making up for historical "underrepresentation" of minorities. In the 1990s, resistance against race-based admissions policies grew. In the *Hopwood* case in Texas, the Court of Appeals for the Fifth Circuit rejected all the arguments used by the University of Texas at Austin Law School for its race-based admissions policy. In California, the Board of Regents ended the preferential use of race in admission to the state's colleges and universities. California voters also decided to end race-based admissions by passing Proposition 209. Shortly thereafter, voters in Washington State ended race-based affirmative action admissions decisions by passing Initiative 200. Both applications and admission of minorities to colleges in these states, especially at the elite institutions, dropped precipitously in the first year after these decisions. However, the next year, after some reworking of admissions criteria, there was a spike in minority enrollment. Nevertheless, many civil rights advocates charged that ending affirmative action would result in the resegregation of college campuses. In 2003, the Supreme Court in two separate but related decisions regarding admission policies at the University of Michigan upheld the practice of affirmative action. Yet the Court, in striking down the undergraduate admissions policy but upholding the law school's, said that race must not be used in a formulaic or mechanistic way that did not allow for a broader consideration of each applicant. Finally, in December 2006 the Supreme Court heard oral arguments regarding *Parents v. Seattle* and *Meredith v. Jefferson County*, two cases involving the constitutionality of race-conscious public school assignment policies in Seattle and Louisville that focused on educational quality and equity. It is quite possible that the Court's decision, expected in 2007, will have a significant impact on the number of qualified minority candidates for college admission in the years ahead.

Discussion Questions

1. To what extent, if any, should race be a factor in college admissions? What are the main arguments for and against a color-blind admissions policy?
2. Should race as a factor in admissions be considered differently in undergraduate and graduate schools?
3. Are there effective alternative methods to deal with minority access to college other than explicit racial preferences?
4. Should race be considered the same as other nonacademic factors (e.g., geographic distribution, athletic ability, and special talent) that colleges traditionally have used in admissions decisions?
5. Are grades in high school and scores on College Board entrance exams generally the best predictors of success in college and later in life?
6. Should colleges and universities adopt an open-admissions policy to students with a high school degree? Have open-admissions policies generally been successful? How do you define successful?
7. How important is racial diversity on college campuses? Consider faculty and staff as well as students.
8. Do you favor an affirmative action policy based on a student's family income rather than race?
9. Would you support a lottery to accept all students above a certain academic threshold? If so, what threshold would you recommend? Would it be the same for all colleges, or would it vary from college to college? Why?
10. Does diversity in K–12 public school education have less, more, or the same importance as it does in college? Is there a different standard that could be applied to public school education? If so, what would it be, and why?
11. Students in New York City must pass a difficult test to enter its three most elite public high schools (Stuyvesant High School, the Bronx School of Science, and Brooklyn Technical High School). The number of black and Hispanic students entering these schools has dropped over the past ten years, despite the availability of a special institute established by the city to prepare minority students to pass this test. Should New York City's elite public high schools be allowed to accept students on the basis of elementary school grades and recommendations rather than just a special exam?
12. Should school districts be allowed to utilize race-conscious policies in school assignments?
13. Do you think that there will no longer be a need for racial preferences in college admissions policies in about twenty to twenty-five years, as anticipated by Justice O'Connor in her *Grutter* opinion?

Class Activity

Simulate decision making by a public college or university admissions committee. The class makes up admissions folders for several racial minority and white students, each with different strengths and weaknesses and coming from varied economic and social backgrounds. Candidates present their qualifications and state their interest in the college to the admissions committee, which interviews them. The committee then meets to decide on admissions. When the committee makes its decision, it must justify those decisions to the candidates for admission and the rest of the class.

Suggestions for Further Reading

Anderson, Elizabeth S. "Integration, Affirmative Action, and Strict Scrutiny." *New York University Law Review* 77 (November 2002): 1195–271.

Arenson, Karen W. "CUNY Seeing Fewer Blacks at Top Schools." *New York Times*, August 10, 2006, B1.

Arnold, N. Scott, "Affirmative Action and the Demands of Justice." *Social Philosophy and Policy* 15 (Summer 1998): 133–75.

Beckwith, Francis J., and Todd E. Jones, eds. *Affirmative Action: Social Justice or Reverse Discrimination?* Amherst, NY: Prometheus Books, 1997.

Berger, Joseph. "Adjusting a Formula Devised for Diversity." *New York Times*, December 13, 2006, A31.

Bowen, William, and Derek Bok. *The Shape of the River: Long-Term Consequences of Considering Race in College and University Admissions*. Princeton, NJ: Princeton University Press, 1998.

Braveman, Dan. "Affirmative Action is Essential to Education; End its Erosion." *Rochester Democrat and Chronicle*, November 9, 2006, 13A.

Carter, Stephen. *Reflections of an Affirmative Action Baby*. New York: Basic, 1991.

Dreyfuss, Joel, and Charles Lawrence III. *The Bakke Case: The Politics of Inequality*. New York: Harcourt Brace Jovanich, 1979.

Eastland, Terry. *Ending Affirmative Action: The Case for Colorblind Justice*. New York: Basic, 1996.

Fullinwider, Robert K., and Judith Lichtenberg. *Levelling the Playing Field: Justice, Politics, and College Admissions*. Lanham, MD: Rowman & Littlefield, 2004.

Glazer, Nathan. "In Defense of Preference." *The New Republic*, April 6, 1998: 18–25.

Gootman, Elissa. "Despite New York's Efforts Black and Hispanic Students in Its Elite Schools Decline." *New York Times*, August 18, 2006, A16.

Guinier, Lani, and Susan Sturm. *Who's Qualified?* Boston: Beacon, 2001.

Lewin, Tamar. "Campaign to End Race Preferences Splits Michigan," *New York Times*, October 31, 2006, A19.

McWhorter, John H. "Who Should Get into College?" *City Journal*, Spring 2003, 60–67.

Orfield, Gary, Patricia Marin, and Catherine L. Horn, eds. *Higher Education and the Color Line*. Cambridge, MA: Harvard Education Press, 2005.

Orfield, Gary, and Edward Miller, eds. *Chilling Admissions: The Affirmative Action Crisis and the Search for Alternatives*. Cambridge: Harvard Education Press, 1998.

Traub, James. "The Class of Proposition 209." *New York Times Magazine*, May 2, 1999: 44–51, 76–79.

Zernike, Kate. "Educators Perplexed at How to Seek Diversity Minus Race." *Boston Globe*, November 21, 1998, A1.

Helpful Websites

www.acri.org. The American Civil Rights Institute, founded by Ward Connerly, is a national civil rights organization created to educate the public about racial and gender preferences.

www.affirmativeaction.org. The American Association for Affirmative Action is a national nonprofit association of professions working in the areas of affirmative action, equal opportunity, and diversity. This is a comprehensive site with information on a wide range of affirmative action issues.

www.civilrights.org. The Civil Rights Project at Harvard University has published several important research studies on affirmative action in college admissions (e.g., *Reaffirming Diversity: A Legal Analysis of the University of Michigan Affirmative Action Cases*, 2003).

www.lib.umich.edu/govdocs/affirm.html. This website on affirmative action in college admissions is run by the University of Michigan.

5

Political Socialization and Culture

Case 5
Are Bilingual Programs the Best Way to Teach Students with Limited English Proficiency?

Case Snapshot

LANGUAGE HAS BECOME ONE OF THE MOST important and contentious problems in the United States. A major reason is that it is interlaced with a number of other highly controversial issues such as politics, immigration, civil rights, citizenship, equality of educational opportunity, and American culture and national identity. Arguably, even more than the American flag and national anthem, it is the English language that holds together diverse races, ethnicities, and cultures in this country and communicates its common values and heritage. Historically, the public schools have been the great Americanizing force, with the teaching of English their major tool. There are approximately five million students with limited English proficiency (LEP) in the public schools, comprising over 10 percent of the entire student population. LEP students, sometimes referred to as English language learners (ELLs), are those whose first language is not English and who are unable to perform regular school work in English. Although many of these students are American-born citizens, most of their parents are immigrants, a number of whom are illegal. The continuing arrival of more and more immigrant children who do not speak or understand English presents a difficult challenge to the public schools. There is widespread agreement that the ability to understand and speak English reasonably well is essential for success, but there is contentious debate over the best way to achieve this goal. Is bilingual education or some form of English immersion the way to go? Should schools try to assimilate these children into the traditional American "melting pot" as fast as possible, or should they strive for multilingual and multicultural diversity by preserving and perhaps even developing the students' native language and culture? Over the years, supporters and critics of bilingual education have clashed over its philosophy, effectiveness, costs, methods, and goals. Research results on the best way to teach LEP students have been inconclusive, with each side citing studies that support its position. In the 1980s and 1990s, the public and government support for bilingual education that had built up in the 1960s began to erode. In June 1998, California voters scrapped bilingual education in favor of English immersion. Passage of this referendum reverberated around the country as other states considered similar referenda. Voters first in Arizona and then Massachusetts passed antibilingual measures. In 2002 President George W. Bush signed the No Child Left Behind Act, which favored English immersion instruction over bilingual education. As the debate over rapidly growing illegal immigration has intensified, the language issue has also flared up outside the classroom. While Congress debated an immigration reform bill in 2006, highly emotional conflicts over language broke out around the country. People clashed over whether the national anthem could be sung in Spanish; whether employers could impose an on-the-job "English-speaking only" policy; whether private businesses like restaurants could be allowed to serve only customers who ordered food in English; whether public libraries on limited budgets should order books in Spanish and other languages; whether voters should continue to have access to multilingual ballots; and finally whether English should receive special status—perhaps as the country's official, national, or common language. Though government action in these areas is important, in the long run decisions on how schools should teach students with LEP will have a much greater impact on American society and democracy. Are bilingual programs the best way to teach students with limited English proficiency? You decide!

Major Case Controversies

1. *There is a civil rights issue over whether bilingual education is an appropriate compensatory response to ensure that LEP students have equal educational opportunity.*
2. *It is unclear whether bilingual education is worth the extra cost.* It requires texts in foreign languages and teachers skilled in teaching various languages.
3. *Educators debate over how long students should stay in bilingual classes.* Supporters of bilingual education maintain that the transition should not be rushed (five to seven years on average needed for proficiency in English) and the focus should be on achieving long-term investment results. Critics point out that students often stay in bilingual classes far too long, preserving their comfort level but delaying and retarding their progress in English.
4. *There is controversy about the goals of bilingual education beyond the learning of English.* Bilingual education is caught in the debate over whether American society should be seen more as an assimilating melting pot or as a pluralistic patchwork quilt. Should the goal be to "Americanize" immigrants in schools while leaving it to ethnic groups to preserve their native language and culture at home and in their neighborhoods? Or should schools themselves try to preserve native languages and cultures and thereby promote a more multilingual and multicultural society? Proponents of this position argue that Americans have been too insular, too satisfied with monolingualism, and too unaware of the growing importance of foreign languages in a globalized world. Traditionalists counter that the U.S. will be stronger at home when everyone speaks English, and that English is fast becoming the main language of the rest of the world.
5. *There is disagreement about whether bilingual education promotes a better attitude of immigrants toward school and boosts their self-esteem.* Too often, it is said, immigrants with LEP believe that that their own language and culture are inferior and that they are stupid and failures in school because they can't understand instruction in English. For this reason, many become school dropouts. Critics of bilingual education argue that it tends to coddle LEP students by letting them stay in bilingual classes far too long.

6. *There are arguments over pedagogy.* The biggest question is whether bilingual education helps or interferes with a student's ability to learn English as fast as possible. Critics of bilingual education point out that often there is not enough English in bilingual class-rooms. Some say that bilingual education needs only to be reformed. One answer might be better bilingual instruction, which would mean hiring more skilled bilingual teachers who are proficient in both their native language and English and their content area(s). Others want to abolish bilingual education altogether as an unsound and unworkable concept. They look to alternative programs such as English as a second language (ESL) and full immersion in English after a very short (often one year) transitional period of bilingual instruction.

7. *Research on the effectiveness of bilingual education programs is inconclusive.* Do bilingual or immersion programs work better? Each side points to studies that support its position.

8. *Schools usually agree upon a single approach to teach students with LEP, but experts say success in teaching English cannot come from a "one size fits all" program.* In addition to variations in motivation and ability, there are too many variables in both the students' home environments and neighborhoods. Individualized instruction would probably yield much better results, but the cost is prohibitive.

9. *Bilingual education has become entangled in the debate over whether English should be declared the official, common, or national language of the United States.* After the November 2006 elections, Arizona became the twenty-eighth state that required official government business to be conducted only in English; other states considered similar legislation. Moreover, in 2006 several towns (e.g., Hazleton, PA; Taneytown, MD; and Farmers Branch, TX) passed ordinances making English their official language, though similar proposals had been rejected in other towns. In May 2006, the Senate passed an amendment that called for English to become this country's national language. Supporters of official English argue that this policy would provide additional incentives for immigrants to learn English, strengthen the unity of the country, and save money, since government would not have to pay for such things as multilingual ballots, notices, and documents. Critics of the official English position argue that it is discriminatory against largely Hispanic people and unnecessary because most immigrants want to learn English anyway. Instead, they argue, the goal should be to produce a diverse culture with English as the one common language.

10. *Critics ask whether it is advisable to isolate and segregate students with LEP when the goal should be to teach them English as fast as possible.*

11. *There is a problem of how learning-disabled students with LEP should be taught.* A related concern is that some students with LEP who have difficulty in regular classes are mistakenly placed in special education classes.

12. *There is a question of the locus of decision making.* Should it be made by government, and if so, at what level? Should voters decide through a referendum? Should parents of students with LEP decide?

13. *There is debate over the cost of educating students with LEP.* Should there be a fixed amount per pupil, and if so, how much? Where should the money come from?

14. *The issue of teaching LEP students is enmeshed in an ongoing debate over assimilation of immigrants.* Some argue for the traditional "melting pot"; some seek bilingual/bicultural assimilation; others contend that we have entered a new "postnational" period where migrants keep ties and allegiance to their country of origin while traveling to and from their new one and retain their native language and heritage rather than assimilate.

Background of the Case

The Rise and Fall of Early Bilingual Education Programs

Bilingual education is a complex and ambiguous term, representing a number of different programs that deal with diverse students and goals. Many Americans believe that, historically, immigrants successfully learned English in the public schools through immersion in regular classrooms. However, the historical record is varied: Some immigrants sat in regular English-only classrooms, with mixed results; others participated in bilingual programs, also with mixed results.

Bilingual educational programs in the United States began in the early 1800s. Because of their large numbers, early on German immigrant children became the focus of attention of local school districts. The first bilingual school in New York City was established for German immigrants in 1837. Its official policy was that after students were taught in German for twelve months, they would transfer to an English-speaking school. Yet the German teachers balked at this rule, arguing that their students needed more time to prepare for regular English-only instruction. Ohio became the first state to enact bilingual education legislation, offering bilingual German-English instruction at parental request. In Pennsylvania, German Lutheran churches began educating German-speaking children in parochial schools when this instruction was not available in public schools. And in Cincinnati public schools before the Civil War, students were taught in both English and German, with half-day instruction in each language. The German half of the day was devoted to instruction in the German language rather than the teaching of other subjects. German-English schools also sprouted in other cities with large German immigrant groups, such as Indianapolis, St. Louis, and Baltimore. French-English programs started in Louisiana in 1847, and the next year Spanish-English programs began in the Territory of New Mexico. There were similar programs in other languages such as Dutch, Norwegian, Italian, and Polish in areas where there were large numbers of these immigrant groups.

Toward the end of the nineteenth century, many of these bilingual programs were dropped to appease anti-immigrant groups, such as the American Protective Association and the Immigration Restriction League. Furthermore, anti-German feeling was fed by growing anti-Catholic sentiment. Within this nativist climate, school districts turned to English-only classes in which they assumed immigrant children could rapidly assimilate as "Americans." President Theodore Roosevelt became a leading force in the Americanization movement, calling for immigrants to be assimilated as fast as possible. In 1917, when the U.S. was fighting Germany during World War I, Roosevelt wrote in *The Foes of Our Homeland*: "There is no room in this country for hyphenated Americanism . . . . Any man who comes here . . . must adopt the language which is now the language of our people, . . . and that language is English."

During the war, anti-German feeling (and antiforeignism in general) swept the country. This led to the abolition of most bilingual education programs and to state adoption of English-only policies. For example, in 1918 a Texas law made teaching Spanish a crime. And in early 1920 the Ohio legislature, pressured by Governor James Cox, who stated that German was "a distinct menace to Americanism," banned that language from the state's elementary schools. By 1923, thirty-four states had banned native language instruction.

In 1923, the Supreme Court struck down a Nebraska law that banned teaching foreign languages in public, private, and parochial schools (*Meyer v. Nebraska*). The Court held that states that had this ban violated the Due Process Clause of the Fourteenth Amendment: Parents were being unduly deprived of their liberty to send their children to schools of their choice; and teachers were being unduly deprived of property by losing their jobs. This Court decision notwithstanding, bilingual education programs continued their sharp decline. There was some reappearance of bilingual education in the 1920s, but for the most part it remained very limited until the 1960s. During this period, immersion of immigrant children in an all-English curriculum was the norm; some succeeded but others did not.

Congress Supports Bilingual Education

In the early 1960s, a chance event—the arrival in southern Florida of large numbers of Cuban refugees who fled Fidel Castro's revolution after 1959—led to increased interest in bilingual education. In 1963, Coral Way Elementary School in Dade County (Miami) adopted a bilingual program in the first three grades. The goal of this program, sponsored by the Ford Foundation, was for native speakers of *both* English and Spanish to become bilingual. The large influx of Cubans and increasing numbers of Hispanic students who came from Mexico to the Southwest sparked a national debate on the merits of bilingual education. The success of the Coral Way program was important in paving the way for subsequent congressional support of bilingual education. Part of the impetus for federal action was the burgeoning civil rights movement. In addition to the more highly publicized struggle for voting and housing rights, civil rights advocates wanted the federal government to address educational, social, and emotional problems faced by LEP students, who often were being branded by schools as mentally retarded or "slow."

Congress soon acted to improve the educational opportunities of these immigrant children. Title VI of the Civil Rights Act of 1964 prohibited denial of educational opportunity "on the ground of race, color, or national origin in any program or activity receiving federal assistance." For students whose native language was not English, it mandated that "districts take affirmative steps to rectify the language deficiency in order to open [their] instructional program to these students." Federal funds could be withheld from schools that did not comply.

The 1965 Immigration Act, which ended the 1924 national origin quota system, led to a significant increase in immigrants from Asia and Latin America. Earlier that year, Congress had passed the Voting Rights Act which, among other things, ruled a New York law requiring English literacy to vote was unconstitutional because it violated the Due Process Clause of the Fourteenth Amendment. The following year, the Supreme Court upheld the Voting Rights Act (*Katzenbach v. Morgan*) citing the right of Congress to pass appropriate legislation to implement the Fourteenth Amendment.

In 1967, Texas Senator Ralph Yarborough and six other senators sponsored the Bilingual Education Act. They were concerned over the learning problems faced by increasing numbers of poor Mexican American pupils in the public schools who were not doing well academically. They also hoped that bilingual instruction would curb the high dropout rate of these children. Supporting witnesses argued that bilingual education was necessary to redress several other problems faced by LEP children. They maintained that English-only instruction was causing them academic retardation, psychological and emotional harm, and the loss of potential bilingualism; bilingual education would help deal with these problems and also encourage Spanish-speaking parents to become more involved with their children's education. These witnesses also pointed to the success of pilot programs both in Coral Way and in cities in Arizona, Colorado, New Mexico, and Texas.

In 1968, President Lyndon B. Johnson signed the Bilingual Education Act (BEA). Officially, this was Title VII of the amended Elementary and Secondary Education Act of 1965. It provided funds to "local educational agencies to develop and carry on programs . . . to meet the needs of children from low-income families (below $3,000 per year) with limited English (speaking) ability." Although originally intended by Senator Yarborough to help Spanish-speaking children, the Act made funds available to all language minority (LM) programs.

The BEA was an offshoot of President Johnson's War on Poverty and plans for the Great Society. It was designed to help poor students who were "educationally disadvantaged," presumably because of their inability to understand classroom instruction in English. However, the Act was vague and subject to wide interpretation. The BEA did not require bilingual programs, but it made funds available to school districts that wanted to establish them. Moreover, it did not advocate a specific bilingual program; rather its intent was to enhance the prospects of equal educational opportunity in public school classrooms by stopping discrimination based on language. It would thus reinforce the Equal Protection Clause of the Fourteenth Amendment. But there was almost immediate concern that bilingual education in the long run could lead to cultural fragmentation and disunity of American society if new immigrants clung more to their native language and culture.

The administration of President Richard M. Nixon supported the BEA and continued federal efforts to reduce discrimination against LEP students. In 1970, the Department of Health, Education, and Welfare (HEW) established guidelines for school districts that stressed the necessity to provide equal educational opportunity for all students. Among the guidelines was the need to send notices to LM parents in their native language. By 1974, education amendments to the BEA expanded the federal bilingual program by providing additional funds for state-sponsored technical assistance, training programs, and a national clearinghouse for the collection, analysis, and dissemination of information on bilingual programs. It also made two other important changes. Henceforth, the BEA eliminated poverty as a requirement for bilingual funding; it also limited the objectives of bilingual programs by focusing on advancing students in English-language development and opposing native language development.

Court Decisions Bolster Bilingual Education

Lau v. Nichols (1974)

In this case, Chinese parents complained that about two-thirds (18,000) of their children in San Francisco public schools were placed in all-English classes. They argued that unlike English-speaking students, their children could not understand what was being said in class. Pointing out that the BEA did not require schools to establish bilingual programs, they claimed that their children were being denied "a meaningful opportunity to participate in the public educational program."

Because the Constitution is silent on language, the justices relied on inference and federal civil rights laws. Justice William O. Douglas decided that "students who do not understand English are effectively foreclosed from any meaningful education. . . . We know that those who do not understand English are certain to find their classroom experiences wholly incomprehensible and in no way meaningful." He concluded: "It seems obvious that the Chinese-speaking minority receive fewer benefits than the English-speaking majority from respondents' school system which denies them a meaningful opportunity to participate in the educational program—all earmarks of the discrimination banned by the [Title VI] regulations."

The Court found that by not taking positive action to help these students, the school district violated Title VI of the Civil Rights Act that prohibits discrimination "on the ground of race, color, or national origin" in federally funded programs. It decided that "no specific remedy is urged upon us. Teaching English to the students of Chinese ancestry who do not speak the language is one choice. Giving instruction to this group in Chinese [i.e., bilingual education] is another. There may be others." Thus, like Congress, the Court recognized the problem of unequal treatment for LEP pupils and required some remedy, but it did not mandate bilingual education. The Court's recommendation was flexibility. School districts and local courts had to come up with their own solutions to this vexing problem. Almost immediately after the *Lau* decision, Congress passed the Equal Educational Opportunities Act (EEOA) that affirmed *Lau* and widened its jurisdiction "to apply to all public school districts, not just those receiving federal financial assistance."

The Lau Remedies

In August 1975, the U.S. Office of Civil Rights (OCR) issued a report regarding enforcement of the *Lau* decision and resulting in widespread implementation of various bilingual education programs. Some regional directors of HEW inferred from this report that the federal government should order local school districts to establish bilingual programs. This caused an uproar in some districts that did not believe there was a federal mandate. Consequently, on April 6, 1976, the OCR issued the so-called *Lau Remedies*, which were intended as "guidelines only." These remedies told school districts they had to take positive steps to help LEP students, including providing more ESL programs. Schools also had to use the native language of students in their bilingual programs of one sort or another. They could set up transitional bilingual programs that provided native-language instruction until pupils could learn in English, bilingual/bicultural programs designed to develop fluency in both languages, or multilingual/multicultural programs designed to develop proficiency in three or more languages.

From 1975 to 1980, the administrations of Presidents Gerald Ford and Jimmy Carter enforced the *Lau Remedies*. In the 1975 Voting Rights Act, bilingual ballots had to be provided if the primary language of more than 5 percent of the voters in a given district was not English. This meant that in some election districts like Los Angeles, ballots had to be provided in several languages, including Spanish, Chinese, Japanese, Korean, Tagalog, and Vietnamese. There was concern not only over the considerable cost involved, but also over whether Americans should be allowed to vote in languages other than English. The Education Amendment of 1978, trying to avoid segregation of students by national origin, authorized inclusion of up to 40 percent of native-English-speaking students in bilingual education programs. The main objective still was to help LEP children improve their English-language skills.

The decision in *Castaneda v. Pickard* (1981) further bolstered bilingual education. A school district in Raymondville, Texas, was charged with violating the civil rights of LEP students under the EEOA. The U.S. Fifth Circuit Court of Appeals, agreeing there was a violation, issued a three-pronged test to determine whether a school district was abiding by this Act and the *Lau* decision. According to the Court a program for LEP students was acceptable if it:

1. Was based on sound educational theory;
2. Had adequate resources and personnel to transform theory into practice; and
3. Produced successful results that showed that LEP students were making progress in both English and major content areas.

The Reagan Administration's Assault on Bilingual Education

Although President Jimmy Carter strongly advocated bilingual education, Ronald Reagan, his successor, firmly opposed it. As governor of California, in 1967 Reagan had signed into law the state's first bilingual education program. However, as president he sought to reduce both federal support of bilingual education and the federal role in education in general. In fact, he tried unsuccessfully to abolish the Department of Education. The Reagan administration soon stopped enforcing the *Lau Remedies* and even slashed the budget for bilingual education. Opposing the use of native language in the classroom, the president encouraged local school districts to develop other programs to meet the needs of LEP students.

In 1984, the BEA came up for renewal. It was an election year and the issue of bilingual education was hotly contested. President Reagan advocated English-only immersion and ESL programs. In Congress, arguments were heard from supporters of bilingual education, such as the National Association of Bilingual Education (NABE), and its opponents, such as the newly organized English Only movement led by Senator H. I. Hayakawa of California. Congress decided on a compromise that in effect strengthened the BEA: 75 percent of the BEA's budget would go to programs using the pupils' native languages; the rest would go for Special Alternative Instruction Programs (SAIP) that would include mostly English immersion programs. Congress also decided that the goals of the BEA should be "to achieve competency in the English language . . . [and] to meet grade-promotion and graduation standards."

The new legislation authorized two types of bilingual programs: transitional bilingual education (TBE), designed to teach LEP students academic subjects in their native language only until they developed English proficiency; and developmental bilingual education (DBE), designed to achieve bilingual fluency. The DBE programs would enroll approximately equal numbers of LEP pupils and pupils whose first language was English in programs that would "help develop our national linguistic resources." As things turned out, however, these modifications of the BEA intensified rather than resolved the conflict over bilingual education.

President Reagan's newly appointed secretary of education, William J. Bennett, led a strong campaign against bilingual education. In a September 1985 speech, he called federal bilingual policy a "failure" that had "lost sight of the goal of learning English as the key to equal educational opportunity." He added that "a sense of cultural pride cannot come at the price of proficiency in English, our common language." He argued that bilingual education had not kept Hispanics from dropping out of school or performing poorly in their schoolwork.

The conservative Reagan administration tried to steer funds toward monolingual English programs. It also aimed to stimulate foreign language instruction to meet the political, economic, and cultural needs of the Cold War and globalization. Reagan thus shifted the debate from an emphasis on native-language instruction as a civil right protected by the Fourteenth Amendment to the development of bilingual or multilingual youngsters as an important national resource. At the same time, many people were worried that language might become a dangerously divisive issue among the American people, as it had in neighboring Quebec, where in 1995 voters would come within a whisker of deciding to secede from Canada.

The BEA came up for its fifth reauthorization in 1988. This time Congress tried to eliminate the vagueness and flexibility of the original law. The new focus was on funding TBE programs. However, Congress also allocated up to 25 percent of bilingual education funding for alternative programs such as ESL and English only. In addition, with certain exceptions students were prohibited from staying in bilingual programs more than three years. This provision was aimed at the practice of school districts that tended to keep some LEP students in "transitional" programs for a much longer time. As Ray Domanico of the New York Public Education Association said, "We support bilingual education, but it is becoming an institutionalized ghetto." The 1988 revised law also established within the Department of Education the Office of Bilingual Education and Minority Affairs, whose task was to monitor bilingual education programs.

The administration of George H. W. Bush did not focus on bilingual education. The centerpiece of its education policy was "America 2000," a program that dealt with a host of school-reform measures and school-choice plans. Renewed support for bilingual education programs came from the administration of President Bill Clinton, who sought to improve bilingual education.

Growing Opposition to Bilingual Education Programs

Growing anti-immigrant sentiment across the country in the 1990s, notably in California, and the election of President George W. Bush in 2000 put proponents of bilingual education on the defensive. Critics pointed out that the varied goals of bilingual education were often in conflict: learning English; developing a bilingual or multilingual society (with perhaps biculturalism and multiculturalism); building the self-esteem and self-confidence of LEP students; reducing school dropout rates; providing equal educational opportunity through equal access to educational programs; and helping to reduce poverty. Furthermore, critics charged that the TBE programs were misguided in their goals and methods, unworkable, damaging, and unnecessarily costly and wasteful. They argued that they actually did serious harm to Hispanics, the presumed major beneficiaries. One reason, in their opinion, was that students were kept far too long in these programs, delaying their learning of English and hurting their chances for success in school and the workplace. Moreover, realization of one of the goals of this approach—establishing a multilingual country—would deprive the United States of a national language. Thus, divisive language problems could lead to the country's becoming "a Babel brought up-to-date."

Proponents of English as the official language of the United States also sought to kill what they considered failed bilingual education. As one official-English-movement leader argued, "Bilingual education has failed at the one thing Congress has asked it to do: Teach English."

There was growing criticism of bilingual education not only in the K–12 classroom but also in high-stakes testing. There are a variety of approaches and accommodations for bilingualism in exams for the federally sponsored General Education Development (GED), the College Board, and state-required high school graduation. Supporters of linguistic test accommodations for LEP students argued that this was a good idea because it gave immigrants an opportunity to demonstrate their true academic ability. Critics, however, charged that this was the wrong approach for two main reasons: The policy was discriminatory because it put thousands of immigrants who speak languages where there were no test accommodations at a disadvantage; and it undercut the incentive of immigrant students to learn English. Other issues complicated the test problem. For example, whereas states were under pressure to hold all students to higher standards under the No Child Left Behind Act, LEP students spent significant school time learning English while English-speaking students could focus more on subject matter. In addition, many high school teachers simply lacked the training to help students with LEP. The result, according to a 2005 study by the Washington, D.C.–based Center on Education Policy, was a serious "performance gap": Students with LEP passed graduation exams on their first try approximately 30 to 40 percentage points less often than other students.

Although the majority of bilingual education programs were designed to help Hispanic children, many Hispanic parents disapproved of this approach. Some even filed suit to remove their children from bilingual programs, complaining that bilingual classes segregated their children and delayed their learning of English. There were also complaints of forced placement of students with Spanish names into bilingual classes regardless of their proficiency in English. Moreover, sometimes academically "slow" students and learning-disabled students were misplaced into bilingual programs. Some LEP students, on the other hand, were misdiagnosed as learning-disabled.

Proposition 227 in California

The biggest blow to bilingual education came when the question was put on the ballot in several states. Led by businessman Ron Unz, in June 1998 California voters resoundingly decided to scrap the state's bilingual programs in favor of English immersion by passing Proposition 227. This was especially remarkable, considering that this referendum was opposed by President Clinton, all four candidates for governor, and the editorial pages of some of the state's largest newspapers.

When Proposition 227 came up for a vote in June 1998, there were approximately 1.4 million schoolchildren attending bilingual classes in California (nearly half the LEP students in the country). This initiative gave school officials sixty days to replace hundreds of bilingual programs with intensive one-year English immersion classes. Students would then enter regular classes. Parents of LEP students could still opt for bilingual classes if they wished.

After Governor Reagan signed the 1967 legislation mandating bilingual education instead of English-only instruction, for the next thirty-one years the state's school districts tried a variety of approaches to satisfy this new requirement. But voters gradually became disillusioned with bilingual education. This was so even among many Hispanic parents, whose children were supposed to benefit most from bilingual programs.

The idea for Proposition 227 began in 1997 when Mexican American parents in a poor section of Los Angeles insisted that their children be taught in English. When the school refused, the parents took their children out of class. These parents prevailed two weeks later when the school agreed to their request, but at the same time many other Hispanic parents believed that bilingual education was best for their children.

The split in the Hispanic community over bilingual education was seen in voting tallies for Proposition 227. The initiative passed by a convincing 61–39 percent margin. The breakdown of support by race or ethnic group is important: 67 percent of white voters; 57 percent of Asian voters; 48 percent of black voters; and 37 percent of Hispanic voters. Clearly, most Hispanic parents, though perhaps recognizing deficiencies in existing bilingual programs, were reluctant to give them up, but over one-third thought otherwise.

After the vote, some 1,500 teachers signed a petition to oppose or ignore the requirement to dismantle the state's bilingual programs. At the same time, minority rights advocates filed suit to prevent implementation of the initiative. They charged that the proposition violated the Equal Protection Clause of the Fourteenth Amendment, as well as various federal education and civil rights laws. However, on July 15, 1998, a federal judge refused to block enforcement of the proposition. This cleared the way for implementation of the new policy on bilingualism at the beginning of the school year in September. Nevertheless, some teachers resisted compliance. They believed that the bilingual classroom was still the best way to teach certain children with little or no English-language proficiency.

The California vote caused mixed reactions among the nation's educational leaders and politicians. Some states with large immigrant children populations, including New York, New Jersey, and Connecticut, struck back in the opposite direction by deciding to keep and even strengthen their bilingual programs. But buoyed by the outcome of the California referendum, Unz spearheaded the movement to get similar amendments on the ballot in other states. Although Colorado voters (in 2002) defeated a referendum that would have eliminated its bilingual programs, voters in Arizona (in 2000) and Massachusetts (in 2002) abolished bilingual programs by passing referenda similar to California's. In Arizona, the ongoing landmark case of *Flores v. Arizona*, which started in 1992, has forced the state to reform and increase funds for teaching students with LEP. And in Massachusetts, there are mixed feelings about how well English immersion has been working. It has been very hard to tell the reasons for failure or success of either bilingual or immersion programs because there are so many variables inside and outside the classroom, including funding, quality of teaching, home environment, neighborhood environment, student motivation, and length of time in a program. Therefore, the debate over how best to teach children with LEP continues unabated—with one's political ideology often the determining factor for support of one side or another. Even immigrants themselves are divided over this issue, which continues to get heavy national attention because the stakes are so high.

Political Options: Who Should Make Decisions on Bilingual Education?

1. *The federal government decides, using control over state and local spending of Washington's money as clout.* Examples are the Bilingual Education Act of 1968 and the No Child Left Behind Act of 2002.
2. *State legislatures decide.* Some states require bilingual programs, providing funds for districts to set them up.
3. *Local school districts decide.* This option allows local school districts to decide for themselves whether to have bilingual programs, though they could request financial assistance from any level of government.
4. *Voters decide by statewide referendum.* Referenda in California, Colorado, Arizona, and Massachusetts are examples. Other states are considering putting bilingual education on the ballot.
5. *Parental choice.* School districts can make decisions on bilingual education only by parental choice. In some states that have passed referenda abolishing bilingual education, parents can opt to keep their children away from English-immersion programs for longer than one year. Although many immigrant parents may choose to do this, others want their children in English-immersion classes as soon as possible.

Main Bilingual Education Options

1. *Transitional bilingual education.* Students spend some time each day on learning English. Students are taught all or most of their academic subjects in their native language until they know enough English to have instruction in English-only classes. The idea is that such programs are temporary. Students should stay in them only as long as it takes to learn English well enough to attend English-only classes. In California, Arizona, and Massachusetts (three states that passed referenda), students must move on to classes offered only in English after just one year.
2. *Dual language/dual culture education.* This is designed to achieve bilingual fluency for all students. For example, Spanish-speaking students learn English while English-speaking

students learn Spanish. The Coral Way Elementary School, which in 1963 became the first bilingual school in the United States, is now one of five such neighborhood schools in Miami whose goal is for all students to become proficient in English and Spanish. The push behind this program is the Miami business community, which needs bilingual employees. By spring 2007, there were an estimated 320 dual language/dual culture programs in the United States. Three of the better known programs are in Oyster Bilingual Elementary School in Washington, D.C., Key Elementary School in Arlington, Virginia, and Kemp Hill Elementary School in Silver Spring, Maryland. Supporters of this type of program, like former Secretary of Education Richard W. Riley in the Clinton administration, consider it an excellent way for students to achieve highly valued bilingualism. However, critics such as the English First organization deem it a mistake as it detracts from the learning of English by new immigrants which, among other things, will retard their assimilation into American culture.

3. *Bilingual/bicultural education.* The aim is to teach LEP students both English and their native history and culture. The assumption is that it is important to teach these students to be proud of their native heritage. Presumably, they would also develop a more positive self-image and better self-esteem. This approach might also encourage parents to take a more active role in their children's education.

Main Nonbilingual Education Options

1. *English as a second language (ESL).* This approach calls for instruction of English by special techniques. Courses are offered in different levels and skill areas. Emphasis is on English grammar, writing, reading, and pronunciation. Usually, students who speak a variety of native languages are in the same class. Often, songs and games are used to ease the transition to English. Instruction in ESL is used to supplement other classes in which instruction is in English. Orientation to American culture is part of most ESL programs. Proponents argue that this approach is better than bilingual education for two main reasons: It helps LEP students learn English faster, and it is more cost-effective because one ESL class handles students with any number of different native languages.

2. *Sheltered English.* These programs vary. Usually, they entail learning English in two years or less. Instruction is in English, but with the use of many visual aids.

3. *English Immersion (aka "sink or swim").* This approach calls for full or nearly full immersion in English (usually in simplified form at first) either right away or as soon as possible. In California, Arizona, and Massachusetts (the three states where voters opted for immersion programs) LEP students generally have to move into all-English classes after one year of bilingual education. The assumption is that full exposure to English inside and outside the classroom is the best way to learn English. However, this approach contradicts the basic assumption of bilingual education laws—that the primary means of learning is through building upon a child's native language and cultural heritage.

Conclusion

In the 1960s, the federal government supplied money to school districts to develop bilingual programs. These would address the needs of increasing numbers of non-English-speaking immigrant children. Originally designed as a spin-off of President Johnson's War on Poverty program to help poor Mexican American youngsters in the Southwest, bilingual programs became enmeshed in the civil rights movement of that period. With passage of the BEA in 1968, Congress determined that providing special services for LEP students was necessary to ensure equal protection of the law. In 1974, the Supreme Court reaffirmed this right in *Lau v. Nichols*. Subsequently, federal support for bilingual education programs has varied from administration to administration. For example, Presidents Carter and Clinton strongly endorsed bilingual education whereas Presidents Reagan and George W. Bush strongly opposed it. States are also divided over this issue, evidenced by voters in three states (California, Arizona, and Massachusetts) passing referenda abolishing bilingual education in favor of programs in English immersion, but voters in Colorado deciding to keep bilingual education. This issue is being debated in almost all states, especially where illegal immigration is a hot topic. Supporters of bilingual education programs contend that non-English-speaking children do not have an equal educational opportunity to learn academic subjects taught in English. Thus, they need compensatory bilingual programs in one form or another. Although the major goal of bilingual programs has been learning English as fast as possible, other goals such as developing bilingual fluency, building self-esteem, and reducing school dropout rates complicate the picture. Critics charge that bilingual programs are misguided in their goals and methods, have failed utterly, and actually impede student success in school and the workplace. Research results on bilingual education are inconclusive. Overhanging this largely pedagogical controversy is the debate over English as the glue of American society and key to civic participation in a democracy. Thus, how to teach LEP students not only is a provocative issue among education leaders, but also among politicians and others who realize the critical consequences involved.

Discussion Questions

1. How can public schools best meet the needs of LEP students?
2. If you support bilingual education, which program do you believe is best? Why?
3. Should College Board exams be both in English and in the native language of the test taker?
4. Should states that require proficiency exams for high school graduation allow LEP students to take these exams in their native languages? If not, should LEP students who take the same exam as all other students be allowed special accommodations, such as extra time and the use of bilingual dictionaries? Do you have the same opinion on GED and College Board exams?
5. Do you agree with the amendment to the Voting Rights Act of 1975 that mandated the "bilingual ballot" for LEP voters that comprise 5 percent or more in a voting district?
6. Should English be recognized as the official language of the United States?
7. Should the United States strive to be a monolingual, bilingual, or multilingual country? Why?

Class Activities

1. Debate the following resolution: The "sink or swim" approach is the best method for LEP students to learn English.

2. Debate the following resolution: English should be the official language of the United States.

Suggestions for Further Reading

Amselle, Jorge. "The Bilingual Blunder." *New York Times,* May 6, 1998, A23.

Aratani, Lori. "Espanol, English Mingling in Md. Classroom." *Washington Post,* November 12, 2006, C06.

Arias, M. Beatriz, and Ursula Casanova. *Bilingual Education: Politics, Practice, and Research.* Chicago: University of Chicago Press, 1993.

Christian Science Monitor, "With Liberty and English for All," June 15, 2006, 08.

Crawford, James. *Bilingual Education: History, Politics, and Theory and Practice.* 5th ed. Los Angeles: Bilingual Education Services, 2004.

Enriquez, Juan. *The Untied States of America: Polarization, Fracturing, and Our Future.* New York: Crown, 2005.

Hakuta, Kenji. *Mirror of Language: The Debate on Bilingualism.* New York: Basic, 1986.

Harlan, Judith. *Bilingualism in the United States: Conflict and Controversy.* New York: Franklin Watts, 1991.

Hendricks, Tyche. "No Benefit Found in English-Only Instruction." *San Francisco Chronicle,* February 22, 2006, A1.

Herszenhorn, David M. "More Students in New York Will Take Regular English Test." *New York Times,* August 5, 2006, B2.

Krashen, Steven. *Condemned without a Trial: Bogus Arguments against Bilingual Education.* Portsmouth, NH: Heineman, 1999.

Lang, Paul. *The English Language Debate: One Nation, One Language?* Springfield, NJ: Enslow, 1995.

Llana, Sara Miller, and Amanda Paulson. "Bilingualism Issue Rises Again." *Christian Science Monitor,* June 13, 2006, 01.

Ovando, Carlos J. "Bilingual Education in the United States: Historical Development and Current Issues." *Bilingual Research Journal* 27, no.1 (Spring 2003): 1–24.

Porter, Rosalie Pedalino. "The Case against Bilingual Education." *Atlantic Monthly* 281 (May 1998): 28–30, 38–39.

Ravich, Diane. "First Teach Them English." *New York Times,* September 5, 1997, A35.

Rhor, Monica. "English Immersion Hits Home: Spanish Speakers Fear Erosion of Culture." *Boston Globe,* March 21, 2004, A1.

Sachetti, Maria, and Jan Tracy. "Bilingual Law Fails First Test: Most Students Not Learning English Quickly." *Boston Globe,* May 21, 2006, A1.

Stern, Seth. "Conversion to Immersion." *Christian Science Monitor,* November 5, 2002, 12.

Teicher, Stacy A. " 'English language learners' succeed in St. Paul, Minn." *Christian Science Monitor,* December 21, 2006, 14.

Wright, Wayne E. "English Language Learners Left Behind in Arizona: The Nullification of Accommodations in the Intersection of Federal and State Policies." *Bilingual Research Journal* 1 (Spring 2005): 1–29.

Helpful Websites

www.nabe.org. The National Association for Bilingual Education covers a wide variety of pedagogical and other issues related to bilingual education.

www.usenglish.org. U.S. English is a group that promotes English as the official language of the United States.

6

The Media

Case 6

Should the U.S. Media Have Shown the Cartoons of the Prophet Muhammad Originally Published by a Danish Newspaper?

Case Snapshot

ON SEPTEMBER 30, 2005, THE DANISH NEWSPAPER *Jyllands-Posten* published twelve cartoons of the Prophet Muhammad along with an explanatory text. The paper's culture editor, Flemming Rose, wrote that the cartoons were meant to be a statement about the "slippery slope" of self-censorship he believed was occurring in his country. His paper was printing the cartoons in the wake of continued refusal by Danish illustrators to draw depictions of Muhammad for inclusion in a children's book on Islam. Reaction to the cartoons at first was limited, with a few protests mainly in Denmark and the Middle East. However, by early 2006, reaction among Muslims throughout the world heated up. Many Muslims, already feeling disrespected and abused in Europe, believed publication of the cartoons was another deliberate attempt to denigrate and humiliate their religion. There was little initial reaction, but when a group of Muslim clerics in Denmark complained about the cartoons and then brought them to the attention of Muslim governments there were protests, acts of violence, threats, and boycotts against the Danish paper and the Danish government. In time, over one hundred newspapers in over sixty countries around the world published one or more of the cartoons; some even published new ones. The cartoon controversy reflected the intersection of religion, domestic and international law, politics, history, and ethics. For most Muslims, any depiction of Muhammad is forbidden as blasphemous; what made matters worse is that they saw the topics of some of these cartoons (e.g., Muhammad on a cloud telling dead male suicide bombers that he was sorry, "we have run out of virgins"—presumably to be offered as a reward for martyrdom) as insulting and humiliating. The cartoons presented the U.S. media with a difficult dilemma. The overwhelming number of media outlets decided not to show them, choosing instead to cover the story only with words. Editors recognized their right to show the cartoons, but they reasoned that since Muslims would consider publication of the cartoons offensive, good judgment dictated they should not be published. Critics considered this decision dangerous self-censorship. Some charged that the stated explanation for not showing the cartoons was actually a rationalization, as the real reason was fear of violent reprisal from radical Islamists. Complicating this issue further was the fact that the Danish cartoons could be found all over the Internet. Should the U.S. media have shown the cartoons? You decide!

Major Controversies

1. *Few people questioned the right of the media to show the Danish cartoons.* However, there was a question whether their showing was an appropriate exercise of freedom of expression, because many Muslims saw them as blasphemous, insulting, offensive, and humiliating.
2. *Showing the cartoons may have been equivalent to falsely shouting "fire" in a crowded theater.* Until recently, only the domestic impact of this limitation to free speech by Oliver Wendell Holmes has been a consideration. However, the Danish cartoon controversy reflects the globalization of this caveat. If all news is now global, is the whole world now a crowded theater?
3. *Muslims are divided over whether showing images of Muhammad is idolatry, which is believed to be condemned in the Koran and in some hadith* (Islamic traditions based on recorded words and deeds of Muhammad). In general, Shiite Muslims accept the practice of showing Muhammad whereas Sunni Muslims (about 90 percent of all Muslims) oppose the use of visual images to depict Muhammad (referred to as "aniconism.") Furthermore, some Muslims (both Sunni and Shiite) objected not so much to the showing of Muhammad but to what they considered the insulting manner of his portrayal, especially his association with terrorism.
4. *Decisions not to show the cartoons in the U.S. media may have been motivated by an exaggerated sense of "political correctness."*
5. *American editors who did not run the cartoons were called cowards for having caved to threats of violent reprisals by radical Islamists, labeled by President George W. Bush and others as "Islamic fascists."* This meant that the media had bowed to a "heckler's veto" due to fear of violent reprisal.
6. *Those opposed to showing the cartoons argued that they were hate speech, violations of human rights, and even racist.*
7. *Some say that the answer to offensive free speech is more speech, or in the case of the Danish cartoons, more cartoons.*
8. *Several American editors argued that the public could understand the story well enough without showing the pictures.* Others like Professor Alan Dershowitz of Harvard Law School said no, that "a picture is worth a thousand words," and that by not showing the cartoons the media were actually depriving the public of its right to fully understand the controversy.
9. *There is a question of how college newspapers in the U.S. should have dealt with the cartoon controversy.* Some argued that college newspapers, with a different audience and purpose from the mainstream media, should have shown the cartoons to spark discussion and debate on campus. Opponents of this view contended that good sense and responsibility dictated against publication of the cartoons.

10. *A related controversy is how professors should have handled the cartoons.* One view is that professors, exercising their academic freedom, should have had the right to show them. Yet at least at one college—Century College in Minnesota—Professor Karen Murdock's attempts to post the cartoons on a hallway bulletin board were repeatedly thwarted by the administration. Understandably, such acts of censorship caused some students to worry that not publishing the cartoons could have a chilling effect on their classroom freedom. As one student wondered: "How long before Salvador Dali's 'blasphemous' caricature of Mohammed is expunged from art history classes?"

11. *The cartoons were available all over the Internet.* In fact, some U.S. newspapers like the Denver *Rocky Mountain News* and *Philadelphia Inquirer* provided links to websites showing the cartoons. In this way, editors could conclude that they did not have to actually publish the cartoons for their news stories, as they could leave viewing them to the discretion of their readers.

12. *In the aftermath of the cartoon controversy, some people called for regulation of the Internet, including blogs.* But who would regulate the Internet, and according to what principles or criteria? Does an unbridled Internet, as some claim, actually promote rage, anger, and hate, which poison reasoned debate? However, others insisted that the Internet should remain unregulated and issues should be sorted out in "the marketplace of ideas." The Electronic Frontier Foundation (EFF), an organization dedicated to protecting freedom of speech on the Internet, may play an increasingly important role in this debate. Based in San Francisco, this privately funded organization works to protect First Amendment rights—largely by lobbying government officials and educating the public at large.

13. *The uproar over the cartoons may reflect what Harvard University professor Samuel Huntington has called "the clash of civilizations."* Freedom of expression, which is a long-standing, hard-earned right in Western Europe and the United States, is largely absent in Muslim-majority countries. However, some people argued that it was a minority of Muslim fanatics that stirred the pot rather than a "clash of civilizations," and that the cartoon controversy more accurately reflected growing conflicts raging within Islam: between radicals and moderates, and between Shiites and Sunnis.

14. *There is a question of what role the U.S. government should have played in the cartoon controversy.* One view was that the cartoons constituted "fighting words" that the government should have banned. Another view held that the government should have stayed out of the controversy altogether, allowing the media free reign. A third view argued that for national security purposes—in this case fear of inflaming the Muslim world—the government should have tried to pressure the media not to show the cartoons. Finally, some wanted the U.S. government to issue a strong defense of the media in showing the cartoons that would have demonstrated this country's commitment to freedom of expression. Moreover, they claimed that self-censorship even worsened anti-Americanism, as this indicated the U.S. would not stand up for the freedoms it claims are a cornerstone of democracy.

15. *Pope Benedict XVI, while decrying the acts of intolerance and violence of some protesting Muslims, criticized publication of the cartoons.* The pope stated, "It is necessary and urgent that religions and their symbols are respected, and that believers are not the object of provocations that harm their progress and their religious feelings." Muslims generally welcomed the pope's words. This was in stark contrast to the negative Muslim reaction to his September 2006 speech at his college alma mater in Regensburg, Germany. Muslim leaders criticized the pope for quoting and seemingly supporting the view of a

fourteenth-century ruler who sharply criticized Islam. "Show me just what Muhammad brought that was new," the pope quoted the Byzantine emperor Manuel II Palaeologus, "and there you will find things only evil and inhuman, such as his command to spread by the sword the faith he preached." The pope's speech angered many Muslims, with some accusing him of Islamophobia. He then apologized several times for unintentionally offending Muslims, quieting at least for the time being the furor he had caused.

16. *There was a question of the media's consistency in showing images considered offensive to various religions.* For example, most U.S. media outlets released the horrific pictures of prisoner abuse at Abu Ghraib in Iraq that, among other things, showed American soldiers humiliating Muslims. Furthermore, in previous years the U.S. media had published unflattering pictures relating to Christianity, such as a crucifix sitting in a jar of urine (known popularly as the "Piss Christ"), a shot taken in 1987 by the American photographer Andres Serrano that had been funded by the National Endowment for the Arts. Although this picture angered many Christians, most major newspapers published it so the public could see for itself what the fuss was about. On the other hand, the media in the U.S. and Europe arguably have been reluctant to publish material that Jews might consider anti-Semitic. Indeed, just before the cartoon controversy, David Irving, the notorious Holocaust denier, was sentenced to prison in Austria for hate speech. Some Muslim critics, like writer Ziauddin Sardar, compared the Danish cartoons to stereotypical anti-Semitic cartoons published in Nazi Germany. The Danish cartoons, according to Sardar, were equally hurtful to Muslims because they reinforced European stereotypes of Muslims as violent, backward, and fanatical.

17. *There was inconsistency in how various Muslim governments treated the cartoon issue.* For example, Saudi Arabia allowed (some say even encouraged) public demonstrations against the cartoons although it has not allowed women to demonstrate for their rights. Moreover, the government-controlled media in Arab countries that criticized the cartoons regularly publish anti-Semitic cartoons; in fact, Egyptian television in 2004 aired a dramatic series based on the infamous and widely discredited *Protocols of the Elders of Zion,* a publication fabricated by the Tsarist secret police in Russia that claims that Jews plan to take over the world.

18. *Some writers argued that American newspapers should have published the cartoons, like many European newspapers did, to show solidarity with their Danish colleagues in defense of freedom of expression.* As *Boston Globe* commentator Jeff Jacoby wrote: "The freedom of speech we take for granted is under attack, and it will vanish if not bravely defended. Today the censors may be coming for some unfunny Mohammed cartoons, but tomorrow it is your words and ideas they will silence. Like it or not, we are all Danes now."

19. *Editors faced a difficult ethical choice in deciding whether to publish the cartoons.* Should they have exercised ethical restraint in not publishing the cartoons? As ethics expert Bob Steele noted: "This is one of those cases where there can be multiple, justifiable ethical right answers . . . . The ethical decisions editors and broadcast executives face [in the post-9-11 era] are tougher than ever."

20. *There was debate over the difference between self-censorship and editing.* For a variety of reasons, including not wanting to unnecessarily offend their audience, all news media edit materials before publication—even declining to publish what they believe might be particularly offensive and harmful—like pornography. But when and under what circumstances does editing become self-censorship?

21. *Editors in the U.S. had to consider the foreign policy ramifications of publishing the Danish cartoons.* The image of the U.S. in the Muslim world was already at a low point, given among other things the U.S. prosecution of the wars in Iraq and Afghanistan, the revelation of prisoner abuse at Abu Ghraib and the U.S. Naval Base at Guantanamo Bay, Cuba, and continued U.S. support for Israel in conflicts with its Arab neighbors.

Background of the Controversy

Publication of Danish Cartoons of the Prophet Muhammad Sparks Controversy

On September 17, 2005, the Danish newspaper *Politiken* published an article entitled "Dyb angst for kritik af islam" ("Profound fear of criticism of Islam"). This article was in response to the difficulty writer Kare Bluitgen had in finding an illustrator for his children's book on Muhammad (*The Koran and the Prophet Muhammad's Life*). In its discussion of Bluitgen's fear of reprisal from radical Muslims, it noted that three artists had declined his offer before one finally accepted, but only on condition of anonymity. Bluitgen explained that in declining his offer one artist cited the murder in Amsterdam of Theo van Gogh, a Dutch film director whose movie was critical of Islam's treatment of women; another had declined, referring to an attack on a lecturer at the Niebuhr Institute at the University of Copenhagen by five assailants who objected to the professor's reading of the Koran to non-Muslims in one of his lectures. Moreover, the artists probably all remembered the fatwa (religious edict) issued by Iran's Ayatollah Khomeini in the 1980s urging Muslims around the world to kill noted author Salman Rushdie for writing his "blasphemous" book, *Satanic Verses*.

On September 30, the Danish daily newspaper *Jyllands-Posten* published an article titled "Muhammeds ansigt" ("The Face of Muhammad"). For his article, Flemming Rose, the paper's culture editor, had invited about forty artists in the Danish editorial cartoonists' union to "draw Muhammad as they see him." Rose's article included twelve cartoons on Islam and the prophet Muhammad, the publication of which many Muslims considered blasphemous and insulting. For example, one cartoon depicted the artist's fear of Islamic reprisal (he was nervously looking over his shoulder while hesitatingly drawing the Prophet); another poked fun at the subordination of women under Islam. Two cartoons were considered particularly offensive: one jibed at an Islamic conception of martyrdom (with Muhammad sitting on a cloud apologizing to martyrs that "we have run out of virgins"); and the other showed Muhammad with a lit fuse sticking out of a bomb in his turban.

These cartoons were accompanied by an explanation from Rose, who expressed concern that cartoonists were self-censoring their work for fear of violent reprisal from Islamic radicals. He was worried that reluctance of artists to participate in open discussion and debate on issues related to Islam was "a slippery slope where no one can tell how the self-censorship will end." Rose commented on what he considered the special treatment Muslims demanded because of their "own religious feelings." He concluded that to be part of "contemporary democracy and freedom of speech" one must also be prepared for insults. Rose further explained his decision to publish the cartoons in an op-ed column in the *Washington Post* on February 19, 2006. He wrote that the inclusion of Islam by the Danish media, which often publishes offensive satirical portrayals of other religious figures, should be seen as a mark of progress of the integration of Islam into Western society.

Muslims in Denmark and around the world complained about the cartoons and sought an apology from both the paper and the Danish government. On January 30, Carsten Juste, editor-in-chief of the *Jyllands-Posten*, did eventually issue a formal apology to the Muslim world for printing the cartoons: "In our opinion, the 12 drawings were sober. They were not intended to be offensive, nor were they at variance with Danish law, but they have indisputably offended many Muslims for which we apologize." But Rose would not bend, stating: "We do not apologize for printing the cartoons. It was our right to do so." The Danish government refused to apologize, citing freedom of the press and the fact that newspapers in the country were not controlled by the government. It should be noted that the cartoons were published during a time when much of Europe was experiencing increased tension between its native population and a growing number of Muslim immigrants. Europeans were engaged in a difficult struggle to strike a balance between handling new customs and maintaining traditions. However, rather than promoting dialogue, the cartoon controversy caused many on both sides to dig in their heels: many Muslims showed a "thin skin" to criticism, whereas many non-Muslims felt the need to reassert traditional Western values.

International Reaction to the Danish Cartoons

Publication of the cartoons at first received little international attention. However, through a globalized media and vigorous campaigning by various Muslim groups, international awareness of the cartoons grew. Soon reactions in many countries—especially in Europe and the Middle East—included violent protests, arrests, diplomatic tension, boycotts, and acrimonious debate about the scope of freedom of expression.

On October 14, *Jyllands-Posten* reported that two of its illustrators who had received death threats were advised to go into hiding. On October 17, Egyptian newspaper *El Fagr* published six of the cartoons on its front page during the Muslim holy month of Ramadan. These cartoons sparked little controversy, yet the paper's editor was dismissed—even though his accompanying editorial was critical of the original publication of the cartoons. On October 20, ambassadors from eleven Muslim-majority countries complained to Danish Prime Minister Anders Fogh Rasmussen, demanding that the Danish government denounce publication of the cartoons. Rasmussen refused to meet with the ambassadors, arguing that his government could not infringe on freedom of the press.

On October 28, several Muslim organizations complained to the Danish police that *Jyllands-Posten* had violated a section of the Danish Criminal Code that prohibits public ridiculing or insulting any religious community in the country; another section of the code criminalizes the dissemination of statements or other information that would threaten, insult, or degrade a group because of their religion. On January 6, 2006, the Danish police stopped its investigation, claiming publication of the cartoons was permissible under the country's right to free speech.

During this time of investigation, there were several important reactions to the Danish cartoons. For example, on November 3, the German newspaper *Frankfurter Allgemeine Zeitung* published one of the cartoons. The decision by a group of Muslim clerics in Denmark to bring their grievances to Muslim governments, organizations, and the global media was a key development in fueling international awareness and reaction. Dissatisfied with the response of the Danish government to their initial complaints, they drew up a forty-three-page dossier to present their case.

This dossier contained several letters from Muslim organizations to the Danish government, a number of clippings from *Jyllands-Posten* and *Weekend Avisen*, a Danish paper that published "even more offending" cartoons, and three images that had been sent anonymously by mail to Muslims participating in an online debate about the original Danish cartoons, one of which was an image of a man in a pig mask. This image offended many Muslims, who consider pork an unfit food. It was discovered later that the image in question was actually taken at a French pig-squealing contest that had nothing to do with Islam. The main point of the dossier was that Muslims in Europe were subjected to "ridicule" and that the cartoons had been presented "in a disgusting and outrageous way." The clerics planned to contact politicians and embassies in the Islamic world "to inform them about the true situation" so they could take appropriate action; the dossier also called upon Muslim leaders to contact local and global media, "especially since they've ignored the issue so far."

On December 3, the Danish Muslim clerics started sending delegations to Muslim-majority countries. The first delegation went to Egypt on December 3, and the next went to Lebanon on December 17. On December 6, the Organization of Islamic Countries (OIC), which represented fifty-seven Muslim states, met in Mecca to discuss the cartoon controversy. Reacting angrily, the OIC resolved to pressure international institutions to criminalize insults to Islam and Muhammad. Its resolution had an immediate effect: On December 7, the UN High Commissioner for Human Rights announced the UN was investigating whether racism was involved in the publication of the cartoons; on December 19, twenty-two former Danish ambassadors criticized the Danish Prime Minister for not meeting with the Islamic ambassadors in October; on December 21, the Council of Europe, established in 1950 as a watchdog on human rights protection, criticized the Danish government for unwisely relying on "freedom of the press" in its decision not to do anything regarding the "insulting" cartoons; on December 29, the Arab League also criticized the Danish government for inaction on the cartoons; and on February 9, 2006, the European Union (EU) called for a voluntary code of conduct to refrain from offending Muslims, and UN Secretary —General Kofi Annan affirmed an OIC proposal calling upon the UN Human Rights Council to "prevent . . . intolerance discrimination [and] incitement of hatred and violence . . . against religions, prophets and beliefs."

The Cartoon Controversy Heats Up in 2006

One of the strongest government reactions to the cartoons came from Iranian president Mahmoud Ahmadinejad. On February 2, 2006, he ordered cancellation of contracts with countries where the media carried the "repulsive" cartoons and the establishment of an official body to respond to the cartoons. Iran then recalled its ambassador from Denmark and banned Danish journalists from reporting from Iran. Moreover, Iran's supreme leader, the Ayatollah Ali Khamenei, blamed the lack of reaction against publication of the cartoons by Western states on a "Zionist conspiracy." Iran's *Hamashahri* newspaper even organized a contest for cartoons denying the Holocaust. Organizer Masoud Shojai said: "You see they allow the Prophet to be insulted. But when we talk about the Holocaust, they consider it so holy that they punish people for questioning it." This cartoon contest sparked a sharp response from a spokesman of Yad Vashem, the Holocaust memorial in Israel, who said the display in "Iran, a nation that aspires to nuclear capabilities, and whose president had made genocidal statements against Israel, is a flashing red light signaling danger not only to Israel, but to all enlightened nations." Previously, Iran's president had said the Holocaust was a "myth" and that Israel should be "wiped off the face of the earth."

Starting in January 2006, various newspapers around the world printed the Danish cartoons. In total, at least one hundred eighteen newspapers and magazines in sixty-three countries republished some or all of them; some newspapers even published new cartoons. Several editors from such diverse places as France and Jordan were fired for their decision; some newspapers were shut down, such as in Russia and Yemen. Most of these printings were in Europe (e.g., in Norway and Belgium), but some were in the Middle East (e.g., in Jordan, Egypt, and Yemen). On January 24, the government of Saudi Arabia condemned the cartoons and urged its citizens to boycott Danish goods. Another boycott began on January 27 in Kuwait. Within the next few weeks several other newspapers in Europe published the cartoons; some governments of Islamic-majority states condemned the cartoons and recalled their ambassadors from Denmark while others closed the Danish embassies in their own countries; there were numerous boycotts of Danish goods and continued demands by several Islamic nations for the Danish government to issue an apology, punish the cartoonists, and "ensure that it doesn't happen again." There were also scattered incidents of violence, such as the storming and burning of the Danish General Consulate in Beirut.

Reaction of U.S. Media Outlets to the Cartoon Controversy

Television Networks

Most national networks decided not to show the Danish cartoons. NBC aired a picture showing part of a cartoon. According to its spokeswoman Allison Gollust, "We felt that in order to convey the essence of the story, it was not necessary to show the entire cartoon."

CBS News chose not to show any of the cartoons after a long internal debate. According to spokeswoman Sandra Genelius, "The feeling was that we were able to tell the story without actually showing it."

ABC News showed the cartoons briefly on "World News Tonight" and "Nightline" on February 2, 2006. According to spokesman Jeffrey Schneider, "We felt you couldn't really explain to the audience what the controversy was without showing what the controversy was." Immediately afterward, however, ABC decided it would no longer show the cartoons because it concluded that it could report the story "without continually needing to show the offending image."

CNN issued this terse statement: "CNN has chosen not to show the cartoons out of respect for Islam . . . . We always weigh the value of the journalistic impact against the impact that publication might have as far as insulting or hurting certain groups." According to CNN spokeswoman Laurie Goldberg, "CNN's role is to cover the controversy surrounding the publication of the cartoon and not to unnecessarily fan the flames." CNN had been showing a picture of a cartoon with the face of Muhammad blurred out in both its U.S. and international shows.

Fox News Sunday aired one of the most provocative cartoons, a depiction of Muhammad with a lit bomb in his turban. Chris Wallace, a Fox News anchor, commented on the meaning behind this decision: "My feeling was, if we're going to tell the story about people rioting and burning down embassies, it's part of the story to know what it is that has caused such outrage."

However, the often irreverent Comedy Central, which usually pulls no punches in the use of satire, backed off from showing the cartoons. Understandably, though, it had a unique "take" on the topic. Its popular show "South Park" addressed the cartoon controversy during Easter week in April 2006. The show's creators Trey Parker and Matt Stone were told several weeks earlier that they could not show an image of Muhammad. During the two-part episode called "Cartoon Wars," just when the Prophet Muhammad was expected to make his entrance this message appeared on the screen: "Comedy Central has refused to broadcast an image of Mohammed on their network." Some viewers thought this was a joke, but it was not. The network then explained that its decision "was based solely on concern for public safety in light of recent world events. Much as we wish it weren't the case, times have changed and, as witnessed by the intense and deadly reaction to the publication of the Danish cartoons, decisions cannot be made in a vacuum without considering what impact they may have on innocent individuals around the globe."

Some praised the networks' decision not to show the cartoons out of respect for Muslim sensitivity on the issue. However, others charged the networks with cowardice for having caved in to the fear of violent reprisal from extremist Muslim groups. One viewer was especially angry at Comedy Central and its parent company MTV: "You guys are gutless [expletive] . . . don't console yourself thinking how 'cutting edge' you are . . . . You got tested and you failed, [expletive]. Thanks for letting down your fellow Americans."

Finally, National Public Radio (NPR) also declined to show the cartoons on its website. According to Bill Marimow, NPR's vice president for news, "I believe that our audience can, through our reports—on radio and the Web—get a very detailed sense of what's depicted in the cartoon. By not posting it on the Web, we demonstrate a respect for deeply held religious beliefs."

U.S. Newspapers

Only a small handful of U.S. newspapers, almost half associated with colleges and universities, published the cartoons; a few newspapers published new cartoons of their own. On November 11, 2005, the *Valley Mirror* of Sacramento, California, became the first newspaper in the U.S. to republish a cartoon, printing two of them in its twice-weekly publication. In early February 2006 *The Austin-American Statesman*, Denver's *Rocky Mountain News*, *The New York Sun*, and *The Philadelphia Inquirer* published one or more of the cartoons.

Almost immediately there were protests against publication of the cartoons, yet the editors of these papers stood firm in their conviction that they made the right decision. For example, editor Rich Oppel of *The Austin-American Statesman* said: "It is one thing to respect other people's faith and religion, but it goes beyond where I would go to accept their taboos in the context of our freedoms and our society." And Amanda Bennett, the *Inquirer's* editor, said that the cartoons were "being published 'discreetly' with a note explaining the rationale" [that read]: "The *Inquirer* intends no disrespect to the religious beliefs of any of its readers. But when a use of religious imagery that many find offensive becomes a major news story, we believe it is important for readers to be able to judge the content of the image for themselves." Bennett added: "This is the kind of work that newspapers are in business to do. We're running this in order to give people a perspective of what the controversy's about, not to titillate, and we have done that with a whole wide range of images throughout our history." Reaction to the *Inquirer's* decision in some Muslim circles was harsh. For example, Mahdi Bray, executive director of the Muslim American Society (MAS) Freedom Foundation, stated: "This has nothing to do with free speech; it's pure sensationalism that reeks of religious disrespect. What *The Philadelphia Inquirer* has done is irresponsible, provocative, and reckless."

Bennett also criticized the Associated Press (AP) wire service for its decision not to make the cartoons available to its affiliated papers. According to AP executive editor Kathleen Carroll: "We don't distribute content that is known to be offensive, with rare exceptions. This is not one of those exceptions. We made the decision in December [2005] and have looked at the issue again this week and reaffirmed that decision not to distribute." Thus, some newspapers that might have at least considered publishing the cartoons were precluded from doing so by the

AP's policy. Still others, not sure what to do, may have decided to "play it safe" by siding with the AP with its greater power and influence in the media.

The fact that most newspapers in the U.S. shied away from printing the cartoons was in stark contrast with Europe, where many newspapers published some or all the cartoons in solidarity with their journalist colleagues in Denmark and as a demonstration of freedom of expression. This difference in handling the cartoon controversy was somewhat surprising. In general Europeans tend to focus more on the potential impact of free speech on societal cohesion and stability, whereas the tradition of free speech in the U.S. is based more on a libertarian protection of individual rights. However, there are differences among European countries themselves toward hate speech. For example, Denmark and the United Kingdom tend to be more tolerant of hate speech than France, which shortly before the cartoon controversy had fined the former actress Bridget Bardot for anti-Arab and anti-Islamic statements.

Here is a sampling of the reasons some national and limited market newspapers in the U.S. gave for not publishing the cartoons:

New York Times.   Editor Bill Keller wrote that his paper concluded after a "long and vigorous debate" that publishing the cartoons would be "perceived as a particularly deliberate insult" by Muslims. He added: "Like any decision to withhold elements of a story, this was neither easy nor entirely satisfying, but it feels like the right thing to do."

The Christian Science Monitor.   In an editorial published on February 7, 2006, the paper stated that the Danish editor Flemming Rose "could have found a less in-your-face way" of making his point against self-censorship of Islamic-related issues. It added: "His plethora of illustrations was a cultural assault akin to staging a neo-Nazi rally in a Jewish neighborhood. It bordered on yelling 'fire' in a crowded theater—not a matter for censorship but judgment . . . . With freedom [of expression] comes the responsibility to use it wisely."

The Miami Herald.   In an editorial posted on its website on February 7, 2006, the paper stated: Publication of the cartoons "now seems like a calculated offense against Islam. We support the right of editors to decide what to publish in their publications. But editors everywhere, including at this paper, must take great care not to offend . . . . However, this should not be an excuse to insult an entire culture and then hide behind 'freedom of thought' as a blanket defense." The paper then compared the cartoon situation to the refusal of most newspapers to publish photos of Janet Jackson's "wardrobe malfunction" at the Super Bowl: "It wasn't necessary to see an explicit photo for readers to understand what the scandal was all about. Similarly, it is not necessary to reprint the offending cartoons for U.S. readers to understand the issue. A religious taboo was violated, and those involved knew full well what they were doing."

The Boston Globe.   In an editorial, the paper stated: "No devotee of democratic pluralism should accept any infringement on freedom of the press." However, "the original purpose of printing the cartoons . . . was plainly to be provocative." The editorial then concluded: "publishing the cartoons reflects an obtuse refusal to accept the profound meaning for a billion Muslims of Islam's prohibition against any pictorial representation of the prophet. Depicting Mohammed wearing a turban in the form of a bomb with a sputtering fuse is no less hurtful to most Muslims than Nazi caricatures of Jews or Ku Klux Klan caricatures of blacks are to those victims of intolerance. That is why the Danish cartoons will not be reproduced on these pages."

USA Today.   According to deputy world editor Jim Michaels, "We concluded that we could cover the issue comprehensively without republishing the cartoon, something clearly offensive to many Muslims. It's not censorship, self or otherwise."

Los Angeles Times.   In an editorial, the paper explained why it decided not to publish the "insensitive images." And in a statement to *Editor & Publisher*, a journal that covers the newspaper industry, the paper added: "Our newsroom and op-ed page editors, independently of each other, determined that the caricatures could be deemed offensive to some readers and that there were effective ways to cover the controversy without running the images themselves."

The Boston Phoenix.   This is one of the few papers that admitted it made its decision not to publish the cartoons for nonjournalistic reasons. Instead, the paper said its decision was made "out of fear of retaliation from the international brotherhood of radical and bloodthirsty Islamists who seek to impose their will on those who do not believe as they do . . . . Simply stated, we are being terrorized, and as deeply as we believe in the principles of free speech and a free press, we could not in good conscience place the men and women who work at the *Phoenix* and its related companies in physical jeopardy. As we feel forced, literally, to bend to maniacal pressure, this may be the darkest moment in our 40-year publishing history." However, within a few days the paper's editor wrote that he had second thoughts about his paper's position after speaking with a number of Muslims: "When I became convinced they were deeply disturbing to virtually every practicing Muslim—and that the media could still report the story without literally displaying the cartoons—it seemed a matter of basic decency and respect not to show them. A First Amendment right doesn't mean it's always right to exercise it. The news media engage in plenty of self-censorship on a variety of issues for a variety of reasons." We can see, therefore, that the range of issues considered at the *Phoenix* reflects the agonizing decision most papers faced over publishing the cartoons.

Muslim WakeUp! *(calling itself "The World's Most Popular Muslim Online Magazine").* This publication published a statement on the cartoon controversy issued by the Progressive Muslim Union of North America (PMU): "Many of the cartoons are deeply offensive, not so much because they portrayed the Prophet Mohammed, but because they are hateful, slanderous, and inflammatory to the point of verging on racism . . . . These cartoons pander to the basest prejudices, defaming the Prophet's character with gross stereotypes of Arab culture, equating the mistakes of his followers with his personage."

The Jewish Week *(serving the Jewish community of Greater New York).*   Publishing the cartoons "was a blatant and vulgar act of disrespect to Islam. Such insults no doubt contribute to the frightening specter of a clash of civilizations . . . . When you give respect, you get it."

The **New York Press.** The editors of this newspaper resigned en masse on February 7, 2006, when their newspaper refused to print the cartoons. The paper's editor-in-chief Harry Siegel wrote this scathing justification: "New York Press, like so many other publications, has suborned its own professional principles . . . . We have no desire to be free speech martyrs, but it would have been nakedly hypocritical to avoid the same cartoons we'd criticized others for not running . . . . We are not willing to side with the enemies of the values we hold dear, a free press not least among them."

U.S. College and University Newspapers

College newspapers occupy a special niche in the U.S. media market. Their coverage of national and international news targets mainly a student audience that arguably has a higher receptivity to provocative materials than the public at large. Also, their aim is more to educate and stimulate discussion than to entertain. Even so, editors of college papers wrestled with the same issues of free expression, sensitivity, and judgment as their counterparts elsewhere in the media as they debated how to handle the controversy over reprinting the Danish cartoons. Most college papers, like the media in the U.S. in general, decided not to reprint the cartoons. The positions and arguments of their editors, in general, paralleled those of the outside media.

Here is a sampling of the decisions of college papers that decided to reprint some or all of the cartoons, or in some cases to print a cartoon of their own:

Harvard College. The biweekly conservative student newspaper, *The Harvard Salient,* reprinted four of the controversial cartoons in its edition on February 8, 2006, under the headline, "A Pox (Err, Jihad) on Free Expression." In an accompanying editorial, the paper's editors wrote: "Publishing materials that criticize the ways Islam has been usurped worldwide for purposes of violence and expression is a risky, but honest and necessary business." Muslim students at Harvard criticized the paper, claiming that it purposely published materials that were "inflammatory and offensive." However, Travis R. Kavula, the paper's editor, stated that the purpose was to stimulate "meaningful conversation" on campus rather than to show disrespect to Muslims. In the same issue the paper reprinted two "truly vile" anti-Semitic cartoons published in newspapers in Saudi Arabia and Egypt—to show the contrast between world reaction to cartoons offensive to Muslims and to Jews. The main daily Harvard student newspaper, *The Harvard Crimson,* decided not to print the cartoons, though it published an editorial supporting the *Salient's* decision that concluded: "While the Salient is certainly commendable in its bold publication . . . The Crimson instead has chosen to express its position in a discussion of the issue, rather than a reprinting, which at this point in the controversy would neither further inform the public nor the debate."

Northern Illinois University. Editors at *The Northern Star,* the student newspaper, published the cartoons with an accompanying article on the controversy stating that the images were published "on the basis of their news value."

University of Illinois at Urbana-Champaign. Two editors of the student newspaper, *The Daily Illini,* which is an independent publication, were suspended for publishing six of the cartoons. Acton Gorton, editor-in-chief, and opinions-page editor Chuck Prochaska were suspended and then fired by the paper's publisher, Illini Media Company, because they "failed to adequately discuss the publication of the cartoons before they appeared in print Feb. 9." Richard Herman, the chancellor of the university, then wrote a letter criticizing publication of the cartoons, stating: "I believe that the D.I. could have engaged its readers in legitimate debate about the issues surrounding the cartoons' publication in Denmark without publishing them. It is possible, for instance, to editorialize about pornography without publishing pornographic pictures."

Gorton strongly criticized the publisher's decision to oust him as a dangerous blow to free speech on campus: "If I can be fired, what will other students think who maybe want to challenge the status quo? This is a bad precedent." Gorton later complained that "*The Daily Illini* never followed up [my firing] with anything that could have turned this thing into a learning experience for the student body." Referring to an article written by Christine Won in *The Daily Illini* on February 17 titled "Student Papers Print Muhammed Images; Cause Campus Meetings, Demonstrations," Gorton was upset because this article reviewed what other colleges like Harvard did regarding the cartoons but did not even mention what happened at the university when he published the controversial cartoons. In a column published in May 2006 by *The Torch,* the journal of the Foundation for Individual Rights in Education (FIRE), Gorton expressed his chagrin that the publisher and "interim editors" had "removed all traces of the offending cartoons from the Daily Illini website," along with his commentary; they had even "requested that Google remove any related material from their cache, and enacted a prohibition on mentioning anything about the incident in the newspaper." Gorton then concluded: "It's a truly astonishing experience to be summarily fired . . . and then erased from the public's memory for trying to provide one's readers with information pertaining to one of the most newsworthy stories of the year. It's a nauseating pattern that one might have expected to find in the pages of a dystopian novel—but not at a modern American university."

University of South Alabama. The student newspaper, the *Vanguard*, published one cartoon depicting Muhammad holding a curved sword with a black bar over his eyes and flanked by two women wearing burkas. Joseph Steward, the president of the school's Muslim Students Association, asked for an apology from the *Vanguard*, arguing that what it did was "rude" and "offended a lot of people." However, Jeff Poor, the paper's editor-in-chief, said he would not apologize since the paper printed the cartoon in defense of freedom of speech. Its accompanying editorial was titled, "A Truly Free Press Must Not Cower to Extremists." Dean of Students Tim Beard told the *Mobile Register*, which itself published one of the cartoons, that the university would not restrain the paper. According to the dean, "If any place should be a place to discuss philosophy and religion and press, it should be a university."

University of Wisconsin-Madison. On February 13, 2006, the school's paper, *The Badger Herald*, printed one of the cartoons—an image depicting Muhammad wearing a bomb with a lit fuse sticking out of his turban. In an editorial titled "Sacred Images, Sacred Rights," the paper argued that "the cartoons are clearly newsworthy and it is our firm belief that the media ought not to be a gatekeeper guided by prude censorship, but rather a vehicle of facilitation in the grand marketplace of ideas . . . . People have a right to see these drawings and make their own impressions as to whether they are per se offensive." The editorial concluded: "It is the duty of the press to inform, not censor, and when free speech is under fire that responsibility is only heightened."

University of North Carolina at Chapel Hill. On February 9, *The Daily Tar Heel* published an original cartoon drawn by Philip McFee depicting the Prophet Muhammad saying: "They may get me from my bad side . . ." amidst scenes of violence and rioting. Muhammad finishes his sentence, "but they show me from my worst." According to the paper's editor Ryan Tuck, the paper wanted to challenge students to think about the controversy and that despite protests from students who claimed the cartoon was offensive, he would not apologize. Tuck responded, "The point of any cartoon in any newspaper is to challenge belief systems." He then added: "We knew it would offend, but that doesn't make it the explicit goal of the cartoon." In addition, according to Tuck, "Newspapers, and really, editorial cartoonists, have always been discussion sparkplugs. This cartoon filled its purpose." But Margaret Jablonski, vice chancellor for student affairs at the college, though not taking action against the paper, challenged its decision to run the cartoon: "Many of our national media outlets chose not to publish the original pictures or cartoons and we believe our student paper should have used the same editorial judgment."

The University of Arizona at Tucson. The student newspaper *The Arizona Wildcat*, like *The Daily Tar Heel*, decided not to reprint any of the Danish cartoons but instead to publish an original cartoon by Abbey Golden. This cartoon showed Jesus, Buddha, and other religious leaders with Muhammad, with Jesus saying to Muhammad, "You really needa learn how to take a joke, Mohammed." According to Aaron Mackey, the paper's editor-in-chief, his paper made the right decision: "The mainstream media will talk and talk about it, but very few have said, here are the pictures, you decide. I think college papers have a little bit of a niche role and we're definitely trying to exercise our rights and provoke our society into debate and dialogue." Though recognizing that this issue was "sensitive," Mackey noted, "We feel it was right to provide a starting point to free expression, to be able to comment on a situation." But another columnist for the paper, Yusra Tekbali, who disagreed with publication of the cartoon, wrote that "respect and sensitivity should outweigh absolute freedom of speech." Mackey responded that "dialogue is good and challenging things is good," but "it's a big mistake to say that there are some things that are so sacred that you can't talk about them." Thus, at least at the University of Arizona, the cartoon controversy sparked an important debate on campus.

Ohio University. Editors of their campus newspaper *The Post*, wrote they had only "theoretical discussions" about reprinting the cartoons. Evidently they took their lead from AP's decision not to distribute the cartoons. According to Dan Rinderle, associate editor of the paper, "We thought, if AP is making that decision, we weren't going to step on anyone's toes. . . . It was more than we wanted to deal with."

The University of Kansas at Lawrence. The college paper, *The University Daily Kansan*, decided not to publish the cartoons, stating: "Our paper didn't think it was ethical to publish cartoons that show the prophet Mohammed, which by itself is forbidden in the Muslim faith, in such an offensive light."

The Controversial Role of the U.S. Government

The decision of U.S. media outlets to refrain from showing the Danish cartoons was not a First Amendment issue. There was never a question whether editors had a right to show or publish the cartoons, but whether it was the right thing to do. Some argued that the government should have stayed away from this issue, letting the media decide for itself what to do. Others argued that the president should have stepped into the controversy, but on the side of freedom of expression.

The Bush administration tiptoed around the issue. It decided to pressure the media not to show the cartoons, but it did not take any concrete steps to prevent this from happening. Its first official reaction came on February 3, 2006, when State Department spokesman Sean McCormack said that "we certainly understand why Muslims would find these images offensive." He then added that publication of "anti-Muslim images" is just as "unacceptable as that of anti-Semitic images, anti-Christian images, or images attacking any other religious belief." However, this official statement added that the U.S. government was committed to "vigorously defend the right of individuals to express points of view." A few days later, President Bush commented on the controversy when speaking to reporters after meeting with King Abdullah of Jordan. Trying to appear evenhanded, the president supported freedom of the press while noting: "With freedom comes the responsibility to be thoughtful about others." Some interpreted this comment as subtle pressure on the U.S. media not to show the cartoons. Bush went on to reject violence "as a way to express discontent over what is printed in the free press," and called upon governments "to stop the violence, to be respectful, to protect property and to protect the lives of innocent diplomats who are serving their countries overseas."

Given the essentially laissez-faire attitude of the Bush administration, editors were left to decide for themselves what to do. Whatever censorship took place was self-censorship. Some editors refrained from running the cartoons because they believed this was their most responsible choice. Others, however, although their public argument for not running the cartoons was prudence and sensitivity to Islam, chose not to reprint them out of fear of violent reprisal. Still others may have been influenced by the expectation of potentially harmful effects reprinting the cartoons might have had on U.S. foreign policy, given the already tarnished image of the U.S. in the Muslim world.

Recent Court Decisions on Censorship of College Newspapers

Future choices by college newspaper editors whether to publish controversial materials may be influenced by the decision in *Hosty v. Carter* that was made by the U.S. Court of Appeals for the Seventh Circuit on June 20, 2005. The Court said that the Supreme Court's decision in

Hazelwood v. Kuhlmeier (1988), which gave high school principals a wide latitude for censorship of student newspapers, could extend to colleges and universities. On February 21, 2006, the Supreme Court refused to hear an appeal in the *Hosty* decision, in effect ruling that it stands. This decision, which applies directly to Wisconsin, Indiana, and Illinois, will have repercussions nationwide. According to the Court of Appeals, college administrators can censor student-funded newspapers. However, even if administrators do not actually censor material, college editors may feel the pressure for self-censorship. Some critics of *Hosty*, such as the Student Press Law Center, have urged state legislatures to pass "reverse *Hosty*" laws and have asked college administrators to sign declarations protecting freedom of the press on their campuses. Their main argument is that the right of editors to publish controversial material that may offend readers is fundamental to a free society.

The U.S. media handled the Danish cartoon controversy in a variety of ways. Editors of television networks, mainstream and alternative newspapers, and college and university newspapers faced essentially the same dilemma: Their right to show the cartoons was not in question, but was it right to do so? Assuming you were an editor of a college newspaper, what decision would you have made?

Policy Options

1. *Do not run any of the cartoons.* This option was taken by editors of most U.S. media outlets who said they did so out of respect for Muslims. Some also argued that their papers could tell the story of the cartoons well enough by describing them. These editors, who opted to write editorials (e.g., *The Boston Globe* editorial on February 4, 2006, entitled "Forms of Intolerance") that described the cartoons instead of showing them, argued that this was the best way to present the controversy without adding to it. Critics argued that these editors were not upholding journalistic responsibility because they did not present the full story, which necessitated showing the cartoons. Critics also contended that by not showing the cartoons the media were treating Islam differently from other religions that have long been subjected to cartoon satire.

2. *Run one cartoon or a selection of the cartoons.* Some cartoons (e.g., the one with a lit fuse sticking out of the turban of the Prophet Muhammad) were deemed more offensive than others. Some editors chose to print the most offensive cartoon(s) to make their point of freedom of expression; others printed what they considered the least offensive cartoon(s) out of respect for the feelings of Muslims.

3. *Run your own cartoon or other cartoons.* In the U.S., this option was taken by both mainstream media (e.g., the *Akron Beacon Journal* and the *Billings Outpost*) and college newspapers (e.g., *The Daily Tar Heel* and *The Arizona Wildcat*). Done mostly as an act of solidarity with the *Jyllands-Posten* and as a bold demonstration of freedom of expression, this option allowed newspapers to present their own interpretation of the controversy. However, this option may also have been seen as fueling the controversy, as readers could now see even more potentially offensive cartoons.

4. *Do not run any cartoons, or maybe just one or two, but also provide a link to a website that showed all the cartoons. The Rocky Mountain News* is an example of a newspaper that chose this option. The advantage of this option is that readers could decide for themselves whether to view the cartoons. Readers could choose to see the cartoons even without a link in a newspaper, as they were all over the Internet.

5. *Run some or all of the cartoons as an educational opportunity to spark dialogue.* Many college newspapers, like *The Salient* at Harvard and *The Daily Illini*, chose this option. However, publication of the cartoons caused more than debate on campus. In both colleges, Muslim students complained that the cartoons were offensive and the newspapers were insensitive to their religion. In the case of *The Daily Illini*, the publisher fired the two editors responsible for printing the cartoons and then ordered removal of any trace of the cartoons in the paper's archives or Google.

Conclusion

Most editors in U.S. media outlets concluded that not showing the cartoons was the best decision. They were fully cognizant of violent reactions in other countries and feared a similar dangerous reaction in the U.S. Moreover, showing the cartoons would be an unnecessary exercise of freedom of expression that would worsen the already strained relations between Muslims and other Americans inside this country and further damage the image of the U.S. among Muslims worldwide. Some editors saw the cartoons as gratuitously offensive and disrespectful, citing cultural and religious sensitivity to feelings of Muslims in their editorials not to reprint them. They claimed that they could tell their audience the full story of the cartoons by describing them and commenting on them without actually showing them. Moreover, the cartoons were readily accessible on the Internet so they could be viewed by anyone who wanted to see them.

Those editors who favored reprinting the cartoons argued that this would more fully satisfy the public's right to know, that "a picture is worth a thousand words," and that not printing the cartoons was placing the media on a dangerous slope of self-censorship. They added that the media in the U.S. should stand firm on the cornerstone of free expression that could be weakened by caving into a "heckler's veto." Moreover, they pointed out that the reluctance to include Islam as a subject of political satire is reflective of an unwise double standard, as the American media have had a long tradition of lampooning other religions. Some argued that not printing the cartoons was bowing to undue political correctness.

Some also suggested that the cartoon controversy reflects a "clash of civilizations," pitting the Western right of freedom of speech against the right of Muslims not to be offended. The argument here was that the extreme reactions were caused by the inability of the West and Muslims to understand each other: Westerners claimed Muslims did not understand their ideal of free speech, and Muslims argued Westerners did not understand that showing the image of Muhammad—especially in an insulting manner—was sacrilegious and offensive. "Misunderstandings" coincided with the cartoon controversy that seemed to deepen the rift between Muslims and the West. In September 2006, Pope Benedict XVI had to apologize to Muslims for quoting a fourteenth century Byzantine emperor who criticized Muhammad and Islam. And a few weeks later, authorities in Berlin, citing security reasons, canceled a controversial production of *Idomeneo*, a Mozart opera showing the severed heads of Muhammad, Jesus, Buddha, and Poseidon onstage. German Chancellor Angela Merkel called this cancellation "a mistake," adding: "Self-censorship does not help us against people who want to practice violence in the name of Islam. It makes no sense to retreat." This incident also led Flemming Rose to lament: "Here we go again. It's like déjà vu. . . . This is exactly the kind of self-censorship I and my newspaper have been warning against." Rose concluded that this decision is "weakening the moderate Muslims who are our allies in this battle of ideas."

In October 2006, a Danish court dismissed a lawsuit brought by seven Danish Muslim groups against *Jyllands-Posten* that claimed the intent of its publication of the twelve cartoons was to insult the Prophet Muhammad and mock Islam. The court agreed that although some Muslims found the cartoons offensive it could not be assumed that "the purpose of the drawings was to present opinions that can belittle Muslims." The paper's editor Carsten Juste praised the verdict as a victory for freedom of speech and "the media's ability to fulfill its duties in a democratic society." However, the Muslim groups that brought the case planned an appeal, fearing the decision would spark further unrest in the Muslim world. For example, Mohammed Habash, a Syrian legislator who heads the Islamic Studies Center in Damascus, stated that the ruling would "widen the gap between the Western and Islamic world."

The Danish cartoon controversy, among other things, showed that many news stories are no longer just local or even national. Rather, almost immediately they are accessible to anyone in the world with a computer or television (cable or satellite). The Internet especially has created new ways to gather and share information and opinions merely by the click of a mouse. This globalization of the media challenges traditional concepts of censorship, for the caveat against falsely "shouting fire in a crowded theater" now involves the "global theater." Finally, the Danish cartoon controversy sparked a dialogue on both sides of the cultural divide between Muslims and non-Muslims. Hopefully this controversy can be a learning experience for everyone concerned.

Discussion Questions

1. Did media outlets in the U.S. have the right to show the Danish cartoons?
2. Should these outlets have shown the cartoons?
3. Should editors of college newspapers have based their decisions whether to reprint the cartoons on the same criteria as the mainstream media?
4. If you were a college dean or president, would you have interfered in any way in your college newspaper's decision whether to publish the cartoons?
5. Could the American public have fully understood the media's coverage of the cartoon controversy without having seen the actual cartoons?
6. What was the main goal of those U.S. media outlets that showed or printed the Danish cartoons?
7. What was the main goal of those U.S. media outlets that decided not to show or print the cartoons?
8. What First Amendment issues in the U.S. were involved in the Danish cartoon controversy?
9. Were those U.S. media outlets that decided not to show the cartoons unduly influenced by an exaggerated sense of political correctness?
10. Could publication of the cartoons have been considered "hate speech" that called for government regulation?
11. Do you believe that seeing all the Danish cartoons in this case is necessary for your full understanding of the controversy?
12. Discuss these four quotes:
    a. "*The Guardian* [a British newspaper considered on the political left] believes uncompromisingly in freedom of expression, but not in any duty to gratuitously of-

fend. It would be senselessly provocative to reproduce a set of images, of no intrinsic value, which pander to the worst prejudices about Muslims. . . . Their most likely effect will be to encourage Islamic extremism already finding fertile ground in Iraq. The volatile context of this issue, with its echoes of the furor over Salman Rushdie's book, *The Satanic Verses*, cannot be ignored."

b. Oliver Wendell Holmes, Supreme Court Justice: "If there is any principle of the Constitution that more imperatively calls for attachment than any other, it is the principle of free thought—not free thought for those who agree with us, but freedom for the thought that we hate."

c. Doug Marlette, Pulitzer Prize–winning cartoonist for the *Tallahassee Democrat*: "When we withhold information in the name of misguided sensitivity, by default we allow nihilistic street mobs from London to Jakarta to define the debate in this country. In effect, we have capitulated to intimidation and threats and negotiated with terrorists. No need for Zarqawi to behead us. We do it ourselves."

d. Ibn Warraq, author of *Why I am not a Muslim*: Free expression is "sorely lacking in the Islamic world, and without it Islam will remain unassailed in its dogmatic, fanatical, medieval fortress, ossified, totalitarian and intolerant. Without this fundamental freedom, Islam will continue to stifle thought, human rights, individuality, originality, and truth . . . . Freedom of expression is our western heritage and we must defend it or it will die from totalitarian attacks. It is also much needed in the Islamic world. By defending our values, we are teaching the Islamic world a valuable lesson, we are helping them by submitting their cherished traditions to Enlightenment values."

Class Activities

1. Several students, assuming the role of the editorial board of your college newspaper, discuss whether they should publish the Danish cartoons of Muhammad. They then explain their position to the rest of the class which discusses it.
2. Those students in your class that decide to see the cartoons are asked to judge whether they believe they are offensive. They are also asked to decide which cartoons, if any, they would reprint.
3. The class divides into small groups, half in each group role-playing Muslims in the U.S. and half non-Muslims. Each group discusses whether U.S. media outlets should have published the cartoons.

Suggestions for Further Reading

Appelbaum, Anne. "A Cartoon's Portrait of America." *Washington Post*, February 8, 2006, A19.
Badger Herald (University of Wisconsin-Madison), "Sacred Images, Sacred Rights." February 13, 2006.
Bennett, William, and Alan Dershowitz. "A Failure of the Press." *Washington Post*, February 23, 2006, A19.
Bernard, Ariane. "Trial Over Muhammad Cartoons Begins in France." *New York Times*, February 8, 2007, A7.
Bright, Arthur. "U.S., British Media Tread Carefully in Cartoon Furor." *Christian Science Monitor*, February 6, 2006, 01.
Cesari, Jocelyne. *When Islam and Democracy Meet: Muslims in Europe and the U.S.* New York: Palgrave and Macmillan, 2004.

Esposito, John. *Can You Hear Me Now: What a Billion Muslims are Trying to Tell Us.* Princeton, NJ: Gallop Press, 2006.

Hentoff, Nat. "'Free Speech' Cries Ring Hollow on College Campuses and Beyond." *USA Today*, April 18, 2006, 11A.

Higgins, Andrew. "How Muslim Clerics Stirred Arab World Against Denmark." *Wall Street Journal*, February 7, 2006, A1.

Howell, Deborah. "Why Not Publish These Cartoons?" *Washington Post*, February 12, 2006, B06.

Jacoby, Jeff. "We are all Danes Now." *Boston Globe*, February 5, 2006, E11.

Rasmussen, Dan R. "*Salient* Publishes Danish Cartoons." *The Harvard Crimson*, February 14, 2006.

Rose, Flemming. "Why I Published Those Cartoons." *Washington Post*, February 19, 2006, B01.

Village Voice, "The Cartoons Conspiracy," February 28, 2006, 18.

Won, Christine. "Colleges React to Cartoons." *The Daily Illini*, February 17, 2006.

Zimmerman, Jonathan. "Why American Newspapers Should Publish the Cartoons." *Christian Science Monitor*, February 23, 2006, 09.

Helpful Websites

www.eff.org. This official website of the Electronic Frontier Foundation covers issues related to freedom of expression on the Internet.

www.firstamendmentcenter.org. This site is a valuable source for all issues regarding the First Amendment, including freedom of expression.

www.iop.harvard.edu. The Institute of Politics at Harvard University's Kennedy School of Government sponsored a forum, "The Prophet Muhammed Cartoon Controversy," on February 21, 2006. A transcript of this forum, along with a video, is available at this site.

www.thefire.org. The Foundation for Individual Rights in Education covers issues regarding freedom of expression pertaining to education.

www.vdare.com. This site contains articles protesting immigration and multiculturalism. See, for example, Michelle Malkin, "Fight the Bullies of Islam," January 31, 2006.

7

Political Interest Groups

Case 7

Are School Vouchers a Key to Meaningful Educational Reform?

Case Snapshot

USE OF SCHOOL VOUCHERS HAS BEEN ONE of the most controversial and acrimonious public policy issues since the idea was first proposed in the 1950s. Few would deny that improvement of our nation's public schools, especially in poor urban areas, is an urgent necessity. One answer is vouchers, also known as "opportunity scholarships" or "parental choice programs." Most voucher programs target low-income families. A specified amount of government or private money would be given directly to these families so that they can place their children in the schools of their choice. Presumably, students from poor families could then have the same educational opportunity as students from more well-to-do families. Some plans involve choice only within public schools, others include nonreligious private schools, and still others include parochial schools. The main argument for vouchers is that choice would promote competition, which would lead to improved educational services at lower cost. Public schools would have to improve or run the risk of losing students or even closing. Presumably all students would then be better off. Interest groups have battled over school voucher plans. Support for vouchers comes mainly from conservatives (especially libertarians) and business, who want to rely more on the free market than government control of the public schools to produce a better product at the lowest price; religious groups, mainly Catholic and Protestant, that want more religious-based education; and some liberal groups that believe poor minority children are hopelessly trapped in failing urban public schools. Voucher opposition is mainly from the education establishment (especially teachers' unions), who want more government money spent on improving public schools; civil libertarians who argue tax money should not be provided for private schools, especially those religiously based; and African American organizations who want government funds to go to improving public schools for all students, not just the few selected to receive vouchers. Voucher plans have been tried in some areas of the country, notably Milwaukee, Wisconsin; Cleveland, Ohio; Washington, D.C.; and Florida—with mixed results. The same is true for privately funded voucher programs in a number of school districts such as Edgewood, Texas. In the early years of the twenty-first century, there have been two important court cases regarding vouchers—one in support and one in opposition. In *Zelman et al. v. Simmons-Harris et al.* (2002), the Supreme Court ruled that the voucher program in Cleveland does not violate the Establishment Clause of the First Amendment. And in *Bush v. Holmes* (2006), the Florida Supreme Court declared that the state's Opportunity Scholarship Program was unconstitutional, since it violated that state's constitutional mandate of a "uniform" system of public schooling. As significant problems continue in the public schools, the voucher issue will remain a controversial remedy; so too will interest groups continue vying to influence the outcome of this controversy. Are school vouchers a key to meaningful educational reform? You decide!

Major Case Controversies

1. *Voucher plans may or may not improve educational opportunity and academic achievement.* Research studies on existing voucher programs in general show mixed results and are inconclusive.
2. *Most voucher programs can accommodate only a relatively small number of students, leaving most students behind in failing public schools.* African American columnist Carl Rowan calls the voucher plan for the public schools in Washington, D.C., "a wicked little sham that will barely benefit the 2,000 youngsters, if at all, while doing great damage to the 75,111 children who will be left in the district's beleaguered public school system." However, others argue that the voucher program gives parents of poor children in failing schools an opportunity for better education.
3. *Some see vouchers as a major civil rights issue, arguing that parents need choice to fulfill the equality of educational opportunity promise of the landmark Brown school desegregation case of 1954.* Some believe voucher programs would help achieve desegregation of urban public schools where students of color predominate, whereas others believe voucher programs would increase segregation, since the poorest students of color would tend not to participate.
4. *Voucher supporters tend to focus on poor African American students in failing urban schools but do not address the education needs of poor white students in rural areas.*
5. *With passage of the No Child Left Behind Act of 2002, parents should be able to transfer their children out of "failing" public schools.* But what if there are not enough spaces in other public schools in their district? Voucher supporters contend that parents should then have the option to send their children to private schools, including religious schools. In other words, vouchers are seen as a key to meaningful education reform because they expand meaningful options for public school education.
6. *There is a question whether parents are qualified to judge which schools are best.* For example, some might choose schools on the basis of nonacademic criteria such as sports programs. Parents might also choose religious or racially extremist schools which, according to Jonathan Kozol (noted author on race, inequality, and the public schools) "would rip apart the social fabric of already fragile cities . . . [and] would be the last nail in the coffin of public education."

7. *Money for vouchers can usually cover tuition for parochial schools but not elite private schools.* Because parents will have to make up this difference, limited funding might create problems of equity.
8. *There is criticism that voucher money for private schools siphons off money for public schools.*
9. *Vouchers also face the charge of "cherry-picking," or taking the cream of public school applicants, leaving behind the unwanted disabled, lowest achieving, most disruptive students.*
10. *Many local school boards dislike voucher programs, which take away their authority to fund and exercise control over their districts.*
11. *Many believe that by shifting schoolchildren from public to private schools, voucher programs weaken the very important long-standing mission of the public schools of Americanizing immigrants and being the "great equalizer" in assimilating a wide range of racial, ethnic, religious, and socioeconomic groups.*
12. *Using government money to send children to parochial schools must follow strict constitutional guidelines so as not to violate the Establishment Clause of the First Amendment.*
13. *Exclusion of parochial schools from voucher plans might unlawfully discriminate against parents who prefer religious schools and thus violate the Equal Protection Clause of the Fourteenth Amendment.*
14. *Voucher plans do not deal with the root causes of poor education, which are partly societal.* Some argue that the focus of government attention and funding should be on improving public schools.
15. *Because schools are fundamentally different from businesses, what works in the competitive business world might not work in competitive education.* Thus, voucher plans might not induce failing public schools to improve.
16. *There is criticism that there is no accountability for private schools that receive public voucher funding.* Teachers in private schools do not have to be state-certified, nor are their students required to pass state-mandated achievement tests.

Background of the Case

Origins of the Voucher Concept

In 1955, conservative Nobel Prize-winning economist Milton Friedman suggested that the government give every family irrespective of income a tax-financed certificate, or voucher, with the same amount of money for each child of school age. Parents could choose whatever officially approved public or private school they wanted for their children. They could supplement the amount of the voucher, and private schools could establish their own tuition costs and entrance requirements. Friedman assumed that parents, not the government, know what's best for their children, and that free market competition is more likely than a government monopoly to lead to better education. Unlike later voucher enthusiasts who focused on the need to help the most needy low-income minority students in failing urban schools, Friedman argued on ideological grounds that school choice and competition would benefit all students regardless of their income. He was confident that voucher programs would work well partially because of the successful track record of the G.I. Bill, which allowed returning servicemen and women from World War II to use government money for education in any authorized public, private, or religious educational institution.

The first voucher plans were used by white families in the South to circumvent compliance with the *Brown v. Board of Education* (1954) school desegregation case. The State of Virginia provided funds for white students to attend private academies. Although Friedman supported integration, he argued that the right of parents to choose schools for their children was even more fundamental.

Toward the end of Lyndon B. Johnson's presidency in the late 1960s, Harvard University professor Christopher Jencks and his colleagues at the Center for the Study of Public Policy (CSPP) received a grant to devise a plan for vouchers. Their 1970 study, called *Education Vouchers: A Report on Financing Elementary Education by Grants to Parents*, endorsed the voucher concept.

Jencks's voucher proposal received a mixed reception. The administration of President Richard M. Nixon, wanting to reverse the trend toward the Great Society programs initiated by President Johnson, lent its support. The Office of Economic Opportunity, seeking ways to improve education for disadvantaged youth in urban areas without relying on big government, latched onto the idea of vouchers.

Interest Groups Fail to Give Early Support for Vouchers

The voucher idea never caught fire in the 1970s. There was no solid base of support for the plan inside the federal government, nor was there strong support outside Washington. Supporters hoped to gain encouragement from Catholics and the Protestant religious Right, but at that time they preferred other approaches to parochial school aid, such as direct government subsidies. Moreover, local proponents of vouchers, especially libertarians, did not want to include parochial schools in their plans. They were wary that voucher plans involving religious schools might be declared unconstitutional if they were found to have violated U.S. Supreme Court decisions on the separation of church and state. Voucher plans were supposed to appeal especially to disadvantaged minorities in the cities, but they too did not impart strong support. African American organizations were aware that the Nixon administration, which touted vouchers, also opposed busing and endorsed neighborhood schools. Thus, they were suspicious that vouchers might be a way for whites to evade school integration. Other groups, notably teachers' associations, vigorously opposed voucher plans. They feared that by supporting private schools, vouchers would negatively impact the public schools as well as their own unions.

In the 1980s and 1990s, the school voucher idea gained momentum. Secretaries of Education William Bennett and Lamar Alexander, Presidents Ronald Reagan, George H.W. Bush, and Bill Clinton, and 1996 Republican presidential candidate Bob Dole pushed voucher programs of one sort or another.

A Variety of Voucher Programs Take Root in the 1990s and Early Twenty-first Century

Several very important voucher programs started in the 1990s and early twenty-first century. Arguably, the publicly funded programs in Milwaukee, Cleveland, the District of Columbia, and Florida are the most important, widely known, studied, and contested ones in the country—both politically and constitutionally. Programs in Milwaukee, Cleveland, and the District of Columbia are means-tested, targeting poor families. Florida had two statewide programs until they were struck down by the state Supreme Court in January 2006: an educational performance-based program allowing parents to take their children out of failing public schools and send them to better performing public, private, or religious schools; and a program designed for special education students.

The Milwaukee Parental Choice Program

The Milwaukee Parental Choice Program was the first and one of the most important major publicly funded school voucher plans in the country. In 1990, Wisconsin enacted legislation that provided funds to Milwaukee children to attend nonreligious private schools. The plan targets the needs of disadvantaged urban pupils whose family income, on average, is only slightly above the poverty line. Sponsoring this program was Representative Annette "Polly" Williams, an African American Democrat from Milwaukee. Milwaukee's school system, like that of many other urban districts throughout the country, had been failing many of its students for a long time. Williams considered the Milwaukee public school system nearly hopeless. "I will not waste my time trying to change the system," she stated. "This is all about saving children." Improvement was desperately needed; maybe vouchers would be a start.

Scholarly support for Williams' initiative came from a book by John E. Chubb and Terry M. Moe called *Politics, Markets, and America's Schools*. This book embraced Friedman's original argument for vouchers. It contended that public schools cannot improve without first shedding government control, and it called for a market-based competition for schooling.

Children who participate in Milwaukee's Parental Choice Program receive tuition vouchers for a little less than half the per-pupil costs of the city's public schools (initially about $2,500). Parents do not pay supplemental tuition. To qualify, a family has to have an annual income no greater than 1.75 times the poverty level (about $26,000 for a family of four). This meant, however, that only about 1.5 percent of the approximately 100,000 Milwaukee public school students were eligible for this voucher program.

The plan initially was intended to provide for up to 1,000 students. In the first school year (1990–1991), 558 students applied for and 341 enrolled in the ten participating schools. In 1998, about 1,500 students participated in twenty-three private, nonsectarian schools. In the 1993–1994 legislative session, efforts to include parochial schools in the Milwaukee plan failed. In 1995–1996, Republican Governor Tommy Thomson's attempt to include parochial schools also failed. Then in June 1998, the Wisconsin Supreme Court ruled that Milwaukee could spend tax money to send pupils to parochial or other religious schools. Its reasoning was that the program "has a secular purpose" and "will not have the primary effect of advancing religion." Teachers' unions and other interest groups such as Americans United for the Separation of Church and State, claiming a violation of the Establishment Clause of the First Amendment, vowed to appeal this decision to the U.S. Supreme Court.

In November 1998, the U.S. Supreme Court let the Wisconsin ruling stand. Because it put off ruling on what kind of government support for parochial school education is permissible under the Establishment Clause, the Court's decision set no precedent. Supporters of the decision, like Clint Bolick of the Washington-based Institute for Justice that represented the state of Wisconsin in court, praised the Supreme Court's decision. However, critics of the decision like Joseph Conn of Americans United for Separation of Church and State, headquartered in Washington, D.C., said the Court's decision "opens a crack in the wall of separation between church and state."

By the 2005–2006 school year, approximately 15, 000 Milwaukee students were using vouchers in about 125 schools, 70 percent of which were parochial. In addition to government vouchers worth up to $6,500 per year, eligible students (based on whether their families qualified for the federally subsidized school lunch program) could receive a $1,000 scholarship from Partners Advancing Values in Education (PAVE). This nonprofit organization was founded in 1992 as an outgrowth of the Milwaukee Archdiocesan Education Foundation. PAVE became an independent group, though it still retained close ties with the Catholic Church and its parochial schools in Milwaukee.

From the outset, the Milwaukee voucher program received national attention. Endorsement and praise came from sources such as the administration of President George H. W. Bush, the *Wall Street Journal,* the conservative Landmark Legal Center for Civil Rights, and the Bradley Foundation. They saw the experiment in parental choice as a critically important step toward improving public school education.

Opposition to Milwaukee's voucher program came from Wisconsin Superintendent of Public Instruction Herbert Grover, who believed that Polly Williams was being used by conservative business interests. Milwaukee School Board President Mary Bills called vouchers "a smoke-screen for reduced funding of public education." The American Civil Liberties Union (ACLU) strongly condemned efforts to include parochial schools in the voucher program. It also pointed out that the vast majority of Milwaukee's public school students would not have any choice at all. Instead, they would have to stay put in their schools.

Also opposed to Milwaukee's voucher plan was the National Association for the Advancement of Colored People (NAACP). In 1996, the NAACP joined in a lawsuit with the Milwaukee Teachers' Association (MTEA) and the ACLU to seek an injunction to stop expansion of the voucher program to religious schools. However, the NAACP most likely was at odds with the view on vouchers held by a majority of African Americans in the country, as many blacks favored vouchers. In an interesting twist, at its convention held in July 1997, some members of the NAACP argued that school integration had not worked very well and that black youngsters might well receive a better education in mainly black schools. Historically Black Colleges have long provided this type of choice. Whereas integration remains an official goal of public school education, by no means have America's cities even come close to this goal. In fact, according to Kozol's 2006 book *The Shame of the Nation: The Restoration of Apartheid Schooling in America,* this country's urban schools are just as mired in segregation as they were before the *Brown* case in 1954!

The most vigorous opposition to the Milwaukee voucher plan has come from the MTEA, the state's two largest teachers' unions (the Wisconsin Federation of Teachers [WFT] and the Wisconsin Education Association Council [WEAC]), and groups like the People for the American Way (PFAW). In WEAC's 1997–1998 issue paper, the WFT and the WEAC listed several reasons for their opposition: Vouchers do not guarantee a quality educational experience for students; vouchers drain scarce resources needed for public schools by subsidizing private schools; private schools can select the students they want and leave behind minorities and students with special needs; and unlike public schools that receive state funds and are audited by the state, private schools are not accountable to the public.

In March 2006, Wisconsin Governor Jim Doyle (D) signed a bill increasing the cap of Milwaukee students eligible for vouchers to 22,500 beginning the next school year. This bill also required new accountability measures such as accreditation and standardized testing. A main reason for this requirement was that some voucher schools were clearly not doing a good job. Early supporters of vouchers had expected such schools to fold when parents recognized their weaknesses and sent their children elsewhere. But for the most part this was not happening.

Predictably, interest groups squared off immediately over this planned increase. Susan Mitchell, president of the pro-voucher group School Choice Wisconsin, stated elatedly: "This is an educational reform that works." Counteracting this position was Nancy Van Meter, director of the American Federation of Teachers (AFT) Center on Accountability and Privatization, who argued: "You've got to wonder about the wisdom of increasing the program by 50 percent when there's no evidence from Milwaukee and no evidence from places like Cleveland that vouchers have succeeded in raising student achievement." The cost of the Milwaukee program was expected to rise to nearly $94 million a year.

Cleveland's Scholarship and Tutoring Program

A pilot voucher program in Cleveland, Ohio, started in 1996, after being approved by the Ohio state legislature the year before. The state would provide vouchers for up to 90 percent of private school tuition, up to a maximum of $2,250. The child's family would have to provide the balance. This amount was approximately a third of the per-pupil cost of Cleveland public schools ($6,507 in 1997). About 3,000 low-income students (with preference for those below the poverty line) in grades K–3 would participate in a lottery to receive "scholarships." At the outset, about 60 percent of the students were at or below the poverty line. Each year thereafter, the voucher program would expand by adding a new kindergarten class. Twenty-one percent of the scholarships went to students already attending private schools.

The Cleveland program was the first in the country to offer poor urban schoolchildren vouchers that could be used at any participating public or private school, religious or secular, in both Cleveland and adjacent school districts. Parents who decided to stay in the public schools could use vouchers for tutoring assistance. The number of these public school awards had to equal the number of vouchers for private school tuition. This program gained national notoriety when its constitutionality was challenged. The sticky issue was whether the inclusion of religious schools violated the Establishment Clause of the First Amendment.

A group of Ohio taxpayers immediately challenged the Cleveland program in court on the separation of church and state issue, citing violations of both the state and federal constitutions. They were joined by major teacher unions and other interest groups such as the Institute for Church-State Studies at Baylor University in Texas and the Anti-Defamation League, both of which had an interest in the case because of its national implications. In December 2000, a federal appeals court, affirming an earlier ruling of the District Court, decided on a 2–1 vote that the program was unconstitutional because the overwhelming percentage of participants (96 percent) in the 1999–2000 school year used vouchers to attend religiously affiliated schools. Seemingly, there was no real choice of nonreligious schools for parents to send their children to.

Supporters of vouchers appealed to the Supreme Court. In the landmark decision *Zelman, Superintendent of Public Instruction of Ohio et al. v. Simmons-Harris et al.* (2002), the Court held in a 5–4 vote that the Cleveland voucher program is constitutional as it does not violate the Establishment Clause. Writing for the majority, Chief Justice William Rehnquist argued that the Cleveland program was constitutional because it "was enacted for the valid secular purpose of providing educational assistance to poor children in a demonstrably failing public school system." Rehnquist added that the program was "one of true private choice" and thus "neutral in all respects toward religion"; and that the program's "only preference . . . is for low-income families, who receive greater assistance and have priority for admission."

The *Zelman* decision stipulated five constitutional requirements for a voucher program: Programs must have a secular purpose; provide aid directly to parents, not private schools; be available for all students irrespective of religion; be neutral between religious and nonreligious options; and provide sufficient nonreligious educational options.

The major arguments in the dissenting opinions, such as those delivered by Justices David Souter and Stephen Breyer, stressed that the Cleveland program, while clearly designed to help poor children in the city's public schools who were not getting a good education, was unconstitutional because in effect it supported religious schools. According to Justice Souter: "No tax in any amount large or small can be levied to support any religious activities or institutions, whatever they may be called, or whatever form they may adopt to teach or practice religion." And in the view of Justice Breyer, funding for religious schools would be "divisive" and "potentially harmful to the Nation's social fabric."

The *Zelman* decision, as expected, was hailed by interest groups that support vouchers and criticized by those in opposition. For example, Jay Sekulow, chief counsel for the American Center of Law and Justice concurred, arguing that "this is not a situation where this program was established for the purpose of establishing religion. This was a program established because the schools in Cleveland stunk, and they were in trouble . . . . To exclude the religiously affiliated school . . . shows hostility toward religion, which is specifically prohibited by the Establishment Clause."

Opponents, however, warned that the *Zelman* decision was seriously misguided and would have deleterious effects. For example, WEAC President Stan Johnson pointed to additional reasons against vouchers: their lack of pubic accountability and the absence of a proven track record of success. And Elliott Mincberg, general counsel and legal and educational policy director of the PFAW, stressed that Cleveland's vouchers hurt most public schoolchildren because they drained resources from the city's public schools; the participating private schools were not publicly accountable; and there was no real choice because most voucher options were for religiously affiliated schools.

Washington, D.C., School Choice Incentive Program

The first federally funded voucher program was established in Washington, D.C., in 2004 when Congress authorized an annual appropriation of $14 million for a five-year experimental program that would serve at least 1,600 students. Vouchers would be provided to parents of up to $7,500 per child that could be spent for tuition and other education expenses at private or religious schools. These parents would have to meet the household income guidelines of no more than 185 percent of the federal poverty limit (about $36,000 for a family of four). In December 2006, Congress raised the guidelines to 300 percent of the federal poverty level and the corresponding income ceiling to $60,000 a year.

The legislative battle over vouchers was led by the pro-voucher Republican leadership in both houses, as well as by President George W. Bush. Bush wanted vouchers included in the No Child Left Behind Act that he signed in 2002, but Congress rejected this idea and settled instead on a voucher program for Washington, D.C. This voucher program, administered by the Department of Education (DOE), was implemented by the Washington Scholarship Fund (WSF), the nonprofit organization established in 1993 to provide privately funded scholarships for public schoolchildren in the District of Columbia to attend private schools, both religiously affiliated and secular.

Congress stipulated three recipient pools for Opportunity Scholarships in order of priority: (1) disadvantaged low-income schoolchildren attending schools in need of improvement (SINI) as designated by the No Child Left Behind Act of 2002; (2) schoolchildren attending non-SINI public schools; and (3) students already attending private schools.

Sides were drawn almost immediately over the D.C. voucher program. It was strongly supported by the city's African American mayor Anthony A. Williams, a product of Catholic school education, who remarked: "As mayor, if I can't get the city together, people move out. If I can't get the schools together, why should there be a barrier programmatically to people exercising their choice and moving their children out?" Many parents of children receiving vouchers pointed to what they perceived as a better opportunity for their children who were doing poorly in the D.C. public schools, known for their long record of poor performance. For example, April Cole Walton said her eight-year-old daughter Breanna gets up before dawn and takes a long bus ride from "the crime and drugs" of Northeast Washington to attend Rock Creek International School, near Georgetown University. Mrs. Walton, noting that Breanna's school had "broken down," stated, "I refuse to let my child be cheated." And Patricia William, a single mother, stated that the neighborhood school her son attended "was not working." Under the voucher program, he had switched to a Catholic elementary school. There he was doing much better academically. However, as some voucher critics would be quick to point out, he was also learning Catholic prayers—presumably in direct violation of the Constitution.

Critics of the D.C. voucher program, who quickly lined up, included Congressional Delegate Eleanor Holmes Norton (D-DC), most members of the D.C. school board, the country's major teachers' unions, and the PFAW. They argued that the voucher program ignored the needs of most of the city's public schoolchildren; that the program was not serving the needs of the students designated as high-priority (e.g., of the 1,359 students awarded vouchers for the 2004–2005 school year, only seventy-four (less than 6 percent) attended the city schools that were most "in need of improvement" and 208 students already enrolled in private schools received vouchers); that most of the participating schools were religiously affiliated; and that federal law did not prohibit religiously affiliated schools in the voucher program from discriminating against disabled students.

Florida's Voucher Program

In 1999, Florida passed the country's first statewide voucher program. The Opportunity Scholarship Program (OSP) allowed students from failing schools to attend higher-performing public or private schools. The number of students availing themselves of this opportunity—approximately 700—was fairly small. 64 percent of these students were African American, and 30 percent Hispanic. The annual cost was about $3 million. There were also two other voucher programs in Florida: the John M. McKay Scholarships for Students with Disabilities Program, also established in 1999, which served about 14,000 students whose public schools did not meet their special needs; and the state's Corporate Tax Credit Program, established in 2001, which served more than 13,000 low-income students. This program was funded through donations from corporations which receive tax credits. In 2004, about 10,000 students received a scholarship of up to $3,500 to pay for tuition at a qualifying private school (religious or nonreligious) or transportation to a public school across district lines.

Almost immediately after OSP was signed into law by Governor Jeb Bush, anti-voucher groups went on the attack. The lawsuits they filed, consolidated under *Bush v. Holmes*, were led by groups such as the PFAW, the National Education Association (NEA), and the National School Boards Association (NSBA). These anti-voucher organizations at first argued that Opportunity Scholarships violated the Establishment Clause of the U.S. Constitution and the provision in Florida's Constitution that prohibited public aid for religious schools. This provision reflected what is popularly known as the "Blaine Amendment," named after an attempt in 1876 by Republican Congressman James G. Blaine to pass an amendment to the federal Constitution to bar tax money from going to parochial schools, particularly Catholic schools. Although Blaine failed at the federal level, by 1890 twenty-nine states had passed their own Blaine amendments.

After the *Zelman* decision in 2002, the anti-voucher interest groups withdrew their claim that Florida's Opportunity Scholarships violated the Establishment Clause and focused instead on the state's Blaine Amendment constitutional provision. The trial court in August 2002 and the First District Court of Appeals in November 2004 both declared that the Opportunity Scholarships were unconstitutional because they provided state aid to religious schools. In January 2006, the Florida Supreme Court ruled in a 5–2 decision that the OSP violated the state Constitution's promise of a "uniform system of free public schools." The Court ruling cast doubt upon the other two state voucher programs, though it did not directly affect them.

Anti-voucher groups were elated by the decision. For example, Mark Egan, director of federal affairs for the NSBA, said: "For the last five or six years, Florida has really been the center of the school voucher universe . . . . Having been such a flagship, the fact that it is going to lose one—or possibly all—of its voucher programs blows a major hole in the national voucher movement."

Pro-voucher groups blanched at the legal setback, although they resolved to continue their fight. Clark Neily, attorney for the Institute for Justice, noted: "There is no question that this decision will embolden the school choice opponents to throw the uniformity argument against the wall and see if it sticks to other states." But Neily then went on the offensive, adding: "But Wisconsin has already resolved the issue the other way. I would feel comfortable going into any court and reading both decisions. I have no doubt the courts would pick the Wisconsin decision." Voucher supporters began planning to remove the nub of the Court's decision by passing a state constitutional amendment. How successful they will be is uncertain.

Other Government Voucher Programs

During the early years of the twenty-first century, a number of voucher programs have been established, most notably in Utah. In February 2007 that state became the first in the nation to enact a universal school voucher program (Parent Choice in Education Act). This program, reflecting the vision of Milton Friedman, will provide a voucher worth between $500 and $3,000 a year, depending on a family's income, that can be used by nearly every student at any eligible private school. All students in Utah will be eligible for a voucher by 2020. However, attempts in other states to implement voucher programs, like Colorado's, have been blocked in the courts. When Colorado's government program failed to get off the ground, in June 2006 the Archdiocese of Denver announced a new voucher initiative for children of low-income families.

A variety of other government-sponsored voucher programs have also been established because of special circumstances. For example, state programs in Maine and Vermont authorize local school districts in rural areas without their own elementary or secondary schools to provide money to send their children elsewhere. Natural disasters spawned a voucher program in Louisiana and Mississippi. In December 2005, the federal government provided vouchers to parents of 372,000 schoolchildren dislocated by Hurricanes Katrina and Rita for use in any public or private school. Even in this emergency situation, interest groups vigorously lobbied for and against passage of this program. Leading the successful lobbying effort were the Alliance for School Choice and Advocates for School Choice; the main interest group on the losing side of this lobby battle was the NEA. However, this voucher program lasted only one year as an emergency program for hurricane victims. In spring 2006 Congress voted to channel federal aid directly to the public schools through Title V of the Elementary and Secondary Education Act. There are also states, Minnesota and Arizona, with "backdoor" voucher programs that target low-income families with public schoolchildren. Since 1995, Minnesota families have been able to deduct education expenses from their state taxes.

In Arizona, the State Supreme Court has upheld a program that provides tax credits to families who donate to organizations that provide scholarships to send children to private schools, religious and secular. This program has withstood legal challenges from the ACLU in both 2000 and 2005. Reportedly, New Jersey is considering a similar program, spearheaded by Newark's mayor Cory Booker, a member of the national Alliance for School Choice.

Interest Group Competition over Major Voucher Issues

Interest groups have squared off over three major voucher issues: school choice, separation of school and state (i.e., the role of government control over education), and separation of church and state.

Support for vouchers comes mainly from the following groups:

- Certain religious groups, such as the Catholic Church and the Christian Right (e.g., the Christian Coalition and Citizens for Excellence in Education), which see vouchers as a way to bring religious-based education and the teaching of moral values to more children;
- Conservative groups, such as the Heritage Foundation, the Cato Institute, the Institute for Justice, the Center for Education Reform, and the Acton Institute for the Study of Religion and Society; and conservative opinion magazines, such as *National Review* and *Reason*; which see competition and parental choice as effective ways to improve educational quality while reducing government control over schools;
- Business organizations, such as Chambers of Commerce, which, like political libertarians, believe that free competition will produce the best products at the lowest price; and
- Liberal groups, such as the Urban Institute, which see vouchers as a way to improve educational opportunities for disadvantaged minority children in poor inner cities.

Opposition to vouchers comes mainly from the following groups:

- The education establishment, including the NSBA and the nation's largest teachers' unions, the NEA and the AFT, which argue vouchers undermine public schools by siphoning off precious resources and higher-achieving students to private schools;
- Civil libertarians, especially the ACLU, who want to maintain what they consider the integrity of the Establishment Clause by keeping government money from subsidizing religious schools;
- Church/state separatists, like the Americans United for Separation of Church and State and PFAW, which object to the prospects of providing government money to religious schools. PFAW also opposes vouchers on grounds of equity and effectiveness.
- Religious organizations, such as the Texas Faith Network, which fear government control over parochial schools through government funding; and
- Establishment African American groups, like the NAACP, which argue that while vouchers may help some students, government money should be spent on improving the education for all students in failing urban public school systems.

The activities of these interest groups include intense government lobbying, offering legal advice and serving as parties in lawsuits, publishing informational literature, public speaking, conducting public forums, appearing on radio and television, and providing information on the Internet. Their goal is to educate and persuade. Both sides have been engaged in a continuing battle to win government and popular support.

Research Results on Vouchers

Research results on the major voucher programs are mixed. Here are some important sample findings from research on the Milwaukee and Cleveland programs:

The Milwaukee Parental Choice Program (MPCP)

The first major study, conducted by Professor John Witte in 1995, concluded that after two years the academic performance of voucher students was not significantly better than that of public school students. A subsequent study by voucher advocates Jay P. Greene and Paul Peterson contradicted Witte's findings. After examining students' tests scores over a four-year period, Greene and Peterson found that voucher school students scored significantly higher than public school students on reading and math tests. A later analysis of the MPCP by Princeton University professor Cecelia Rouse in 1998 found no effect from vouchers in reading and a small gain in math for students who had remained in the program for four years. Finally, two studies by Harvard professors Caroline Hoxby and Rajashri Chakrabarti concluded that as the MPCP grew, test scores rose significantly at the public schools with large numbers of eligible voucher pupils. But Duke University professor Helen Ladd found that voucher programs had "no positive effects on public school achievement."

The Cleveland Scholarship and Tutoring Program (CSTP)

According to findings released in October 2004 by Kim Metcalf of Indiana, who led a team of researchers contracted to research the CSTP, there was no difference in overall achievement between voucher students and regular public school students. Moreover, as the AFT was quick to point out, overall the achievement of public school students was greater than that of voucher students from grades one through five. However, a 1997 evaluation of Cleveland's voucher program by Jay Greene, William Howell, and Paul Peterson of Harvard University, issued by Harvard's Program on Education Policy and Governance, found generally favorable results as regards parental satisfaction, test score results in math and reading, and student retention in voucher schools.

Because the research on vouchers is so inconsistent and inconclusive, it does not offer a reliable guide to policy makers. Consequently, policy options have developed based more on what educators and interest groups believe are best.

Policy Options

Parents have a variety of choices for the education of their children, some of which include vouchers.

Voucher Plans

1. *Government vouchers for public schools only.* This concept focuses on improving public schools. Variations of this plan include "alternative" schools within the same school, "district-wide" choice (choice within the home district only), and "inter-district" choice (allowing choice across district lines).

2. *Government vouchers for public and private schools, excluding parochial schools.* This plan breaks the public school monopoly and promotes wider competition than if parental choice were limited to public schools only.

3. *Government vouchers for public and private schools, including parochial schools.* This option provides the widest latitude for choice and competition, but it continually raises questions of separation of church and state.

4. *Privately financed voucher plans.* Parents can send their children to any school, public or private, including parochial schools. There are a number of private school programs in the country. The argument is that private funding (e.g., from businesses and foundations) should be spent less on reforming the public schools and more on providing parents with school choice. Sometimes private money supplements government vouchers, such as with PAVE in Milwaukee. Other times, private money alone provides vouchers. For example, in May 1998 Robert Aguirre, director of the Children's Educational Opportunities Foundation (CEO), made a bold offer: full-tuition vouchers for each one of the 14,000 students in the poor, largely Hispanic Edgewood neighborhood of the public schools of San Antonio, Texas, to attend a private school of their choice in their district. They would receive slightly less money if they attended a private school outside their district. CEO made a massive commitment of $5 million a year for a ten-year period. The teacher unions opposed this private voucher initiative, arguing that it would worsen educational opportunities for most students who remained in the public schools.

Choices without Vouchers

Here are several rapidly growing alternatives to the traditional system of public school education:

1. *Charter schools.* These are public schools supported by tax money that are set up outside the bureaucracy. They usually are established by "out-of-the-loop" groups, such as community members, neighborhood associations, and parents. They generally are free from the control of unions, school boards, and state laws and regulations. Instead, a charter school operates under its own charter, which outlines its specific goals, educational philosophy, and teaching methodology. This setup allows considerably more freedom for innovation than is allowed in regular public schools. Charter schools must meet certain state standards. Because students are not obligated to attend them, they must compete for students, and thus to remain open, presumably they have to be better than traditional public schools. They can operate on less money because they have less bureaucracy and thus can use money saved on administration to provide innovative or improved programs. Because of competition, charter schools can also provide an incentive for traditional public schools to improve. This option avoids the problem of using tax money to subsidize private schools. It also eliminates the issue of separation of church and state.

2. *Virtual charter schools.* With more widespread computer use, some parents are choosing to educate their children through online schools. In April 2006, there were 147 online-only charter schools in eighteen states, with a total of 65,354 students. This option is especially attractive for students in rural areas and for parents who may prefer home-schooling but have neither the resources nor time for it.

3. *Homeschooling.* Increasing numbers of parents are choosing this option, since it offers an opportunity to inculcate strong religious beliefs, instill values, implement liberal educational philosophies, and provide individual attention in a safe environment. Possible drawbacks include less opportunity to develop social skills, participate in organized school sports, and utilize laboratory equipment. States generally accept this option as long as the teaching meets certain government requirements. This option gives parents the widest latitude over their children's education.

Conclusion

Public schools in the United States have failed many of their students. Especially hurt are disadvantaged minority youth in urban areas. One proposal to improve and revitalize schools is voucher plans that give parents a choice where to send their children. Debate over vouchers swirls around concerns of social justice, accountability, student achievement, and value for the educational dollar. Interest groups have drawn swords to win over various constituencies. Proponents of vouchers maintain that trying to reform public schools will not work. Competition, they contend, will provide better educational opportunities for all children. Voucher plans are one way to provide choice. Opponents of vouchers contend that choice will destroy the public schools; that private schools will not admit the toughest students to educate; and that taxpayer money should not subsidize private schools, especially parochial schools. Many different voucher plans have sprouted up around the country. Among the most important are those in Milwaukee, Cleveland, Washington, D.C., and Florida. Research results on the effectiveness of vouchers are mixed. In general, parental satisfaction is shown to be higher in voucher programs, though there seem to be no significant differences in student achievement. Political interest groups will continue to play a major role in determining how the voucher controversy plays out. There is little doubt that this controversy will continue as long as dissatisfaction with the public schools, especially in poor urban areas, remains.

Discussion Questions

1. Is parental choice and competition among schools likely to improve public school education as voucher proponents contend?
2. Is government control over education a main cause of poorly performing public schools, especially in urban areas?
3. Which voucher programs, if any, do you support: district-wide schools only; district-wide and inter-district schools; public schools only; public schools and private schools, not including parochial schools; public and private schools, including parochial schools?
4. Will voucher plans lead to increased racial segregation in the schools?
5. Should voucher plans be open to all students, regardless of family income?

Class Activities

1. Divide the class into political interest groups that support and oppose vouchers. Debate the issue.

2. Assume you are a representative of your district in your state legislature. Before you propose or vote on legislation involving vouchers, devise a questionnaire to learn what the people in your district know and think about vouchers.
3. Hold a public forum at your school on vouchers. Invite interest groups to participate.

Suggestions for Further Reading

Blum, Justin. "D.C. School Vouchers Outnumber Applicants." *Washington Post*, June 11, 2004, A01.

Bolick, Clint. *Voucher Wars: Waging the Legal Battle over School Choice*. Washington, DC: Cato Institute, 2003.

Carnoy, Martin. *School Vouchers: Examining the Evidence*. Washington, DC: Economic Policy Institute, 2001.

Chan, Sewell, and Valerie Strauss. "For Voucher Program, the Lessons Begin." *Washington Post*, September 5, 2004, C01.

Harmer, David. *School Choice: Why You Need It—How You Get It*. Washington, DC: Cato Institute, 1994.

Jacoby, Jeff. "Vouchers and Equal Education." *Boston Globe*, May 30, 2004, D11.

Kafer, Krista. "Progress in School Choice in the States." Backgrounder no. 1639. Washington, DC: Heritage Foundation, July 10, 2003.

Liu, Goodwin, and William I. Taylor. "School Choice to Achieve Desegregation." *Fordham Law Review* 74, no. 2 (November 2005): 791–824.

Moe, Terry M., and John E. Chubb. *Politics, Markets, and America's Schools*. Washington, DC: Brookings, 1990.

Molnar, Alex. "Educational Vouchers: A Review of the Research." Tempe, AZ: Education Policy Research Unit, October 1999.

Nichols, Kit J. "Framing the Debate: The Case for Studying School Vouchers." Boston: Pioneer Institute for Public Policy Research. January 2006.

Paulson, Amanda. "Milwaukee's Lessons on School Vouchers." *Christian Science Monitor*, May 23, 2006, 01.

People for the American Way. *Special Report: Flaws and Failings: A Preliminary Look at the Problems Already Encountered in the Implementation of the District of Columbia's New Federally Funded Mandated School Voucher Program*. Washington, DC: People for the American Way, February 2006.

Rowan, Carl. "School-Voucher Plan Is a Cruel Sham." *The Buffalo News*, May 2, 1998, C3.

Schemo, Diana Jean. "Federal Program on Vouchers Draws Strong Minority Support." *New York Times*, April 6, 2006, A1, A16.

Tierney, John. "City Schools That Work." *New York Times*, March 7, 2006, A25.

U.S. Department of Education. "Evaluation of the D.C. Opportunity Scholarship Program: First Year Report on Participation." Washington, DC: U.S. Department of Education, April 2005.

Will, George. "A Tide for School Choice." *Washington Post*, February 1, 2007, A15.

Witte, John. "The Milwaukee Voucher Experiment: The Good, the Bad, and the Ugly." *Phi Delta Kappan* 81, no. 2 (September 1999): 59–64.

Helpful Websites

www.allianceforschoolchoice.org. The Alliance for School Choice is a leading national advocacy organization for school choice, based in Phoenix, Arizona.

www.choiceineducation.org. Website for Parents for Choice in Education.

www.friedmanfoundation.org/schoolchoice. This organization, founded by leading free enterprise economists Milton and Rose D. Friedman, is a valuable source of information for advocates of school choice.

www.pewforum.org/events. Website for the Pew Forum on Religion and Public Life. See, for example, "Judgment Day for School Vouchers: A Discussion of the Constitutionality of the Cleveland School Voucher Plan," November 28, 2001.

www.schoolchoiceinfo.org. Website for School Choice Wisconsin.

8

Political Parties and Campaigns

Case 8

Is Campaign Finance Reform Needed?

Case Snapshot

CAMPAIGN FINANCE AND LOBBYING REFORMS are polarizing issues in American politics. These issues become salient when a large scandal fuels public outrage. Voters react negatively to the excessive displays of influence by wealthy corporations and interest groups during elections. The general public views the large campaign donations, which seem to buy access to the government, as tantamount to bribery. This view is reinforced because the legislators who profit from this system also set the rules that govern it. Change from the status quo only occurs when events—such as the 1970s Watergate scandal, the 1996 presidential election, or the 2006 trial of the high-profile lobbyist Jack Abramoff for defrauding clients—serve as a catalyst. Even when spurred into action, Congress frequently finds it difficult to pass reform legislation because the process becomes mired in partisan squabbling that often ends in gridlock. Is campaign finance reform needed? You decide!

Major Case Controversies

1. *Campaign finance reform stems from a pattern of media-revealed scandals, followed by public demands for action, with a weak legislative response.*
2. *Large corporations, wealthy individuals, and big-money campaign contributors corrupt the political process by using patronage, kickbacks, bribery, and other backhanded methods to gain influence and access.*
3. *Advances in technology have made campaigns more costly and more visible to the public.* Congress developed a system that offered incentives to candidates who choose public financing of campaigns, but this has proven to be an unpopular option.

4. *The Watergate scandal precipitated the adoption of the Federal Election Campaign Act (FECA); however, it had many loopholes allowing for excessive campaign fundraising.*
5. *A Supreme Court decision in 1976, Buckley v. Valeo, ruled that several of the limits developed under FECA were unconstitutional, rendering some of the act unworkable.* It remained this way until the late 1980s and early 1990s when again the public began to address the issue of reform.
6. *There were several campaign finance abuses in the 1996 presidential election that were catalysts for modern campaign laws.* The Senate's McCain-Feingold bill and the House's Shays-Meehan bill were initially defeated, but their basis evolved into the Bipartisan Campaign Reform Act of 2002.
7. *The debate on campaign finance reform combined with the Jack Abramoff scandal forced the issue of much needed lobbying reform.*
8. *Congress needs to have money available for election campaigns, including the financial help of strong interest group lobbies, which leaves it bitterly divided on how to address the public's concerns.*

Background of the Case

A History of Attempted Reform

Money and power go together in American politics. One of the biggest areas of controversy is campaign finance reform. Polls show that public confidence in the existing political system is eroded because of the influence of money. Money does play a key role in politics, with the 2004 presidential and congressional elections having a price tag of nearly $4 billion. However, the excessive use of money and calls for reform are part of a developed cycle in American history.

Most often calls for reform are preceded by a scandal or high-profile story. An early example of this would be the series of "kickbacks" that were exposed by journalists during the 1871 reign of Boss Tweed in New York City. The reporters revealed excessive sweetheart deals in which candidates promised lucrative government deals in exchange for fees paid to elected officials. The Tweed gang was removed from office once the system of kickbacks for public works projects was revealed. In more recent times, Vice President Spiro Agnew was forced to resign in 1973 after pleading nolo contendere when it was discovered that he received 5 percent kickbacks from engineering contractors for work completed when he was the Baltimore County executive in Maryland, plus bribes while governor. The powerful chair of the House Ways and Means Committee, Representative Dan Rostenkowski, was indicted, pled guilty, and was sentenced to seventeen months in prison and given a $100,000 fine in 1996 because he accepted kickbacks from office employees. (However, he received credit for $82,095 that he returned to the Treasury Department in 1994.)

Patronage garnered attention in the latter part of the nineteenth century because of increased immigration to the United States. Major urban political machines capitalized on the new population and provided city jobs, private sector opportunities, and other benefits in exchange for their votes. The jobs ensured loyalty to the party and this tradition continued for decades. Problems arise when political appointees were expected to pay for their own jobs while continuing to contribute to the party and campaigns. The 1883 Pendleton Act was a direct consequence of the assassination of President James Garfield by a disappointed office seeker. The act established a merit system for some federal jobs rather than having them be political appointments. Subsequent presidents expanded the number of officeholders covered under the act. President Franklin D. Roosevelt continued the push for reform with the 1939 Hatch Act, which prohibits executive branch government employees from accepting campaign contributions. This protects the employees from unnecessary political pressure and prevents most civil service employees from participating in party-organized activities. However, it excludes non–civil service appointments. An example would be the eight ambassadors who contributed more than $700,000 to President Richard M. Nixon's 1972 reelection and cultivated more than $2 million in other campaign funds.

The Teapot Dome scandal of the 1920s occurred when bribes were paid to Interior Secretary Albert B. Fall by large campaign contributors in exchange for oil leases on federal land during the Harding administration. The scandal resulted in the ineffectual 1925 Federal Corrupt Practices Act, which required periodic financial reports from federal candidates. The act was not enforced and most financial records were destroyed after a short period of time. One last form of corporate influence is the "quid pro quo" system that implies "something for something." Big financial contributors expect that their donations will provide them special access to government services. The 1907 Tillman Act attempted to curb these actions by prohibiting corporate and bank contributions to federal office candidates. There were many loopholes that allowed for business executives to funnel money to political parties or donate large sums as private citizens. Senate Majority Leader Lyndon B. Johnson's former aide Bobby Baker was caught in the 1960s in a scandal that involved theft, fraud, and tax evasion. He used his influence with senators to get government contracts for campaign contributors and his own business. All these events contributed to the public's skepticism of campaign financing.

Preliminary Legislation

Two pieces of antilabor legislation from the 1940s are relevant to the development of campaign financing. The 1943 Smith-Connally Act's main purpose was to prohibit labor strikes during World War II; however, it also banned labor union campaign contributions. A loophole was created in 1943 with the formation of the Congress of Industrial Organization Political Action Committee (CIO-PAC). This was an organization that developed from a union but was not technically categorized as such, and was therefore able to donate large amounts of money to particular candidates. The 1947 Taft-Hartley Act banned campaign contributions and lobby expenditures from both labor unions and corporations.

A period of longer than two decades ensued before further major legislation concerning campaign reform again passed. Organized labor pushed for the Federal Election Campaign Act (FECA), which was passed by Congress and signed by President Nixon in 1971. However, Nixon continually evaded the fundraising limits set by FECA. The corrupt activities included such acts as extortion of illegal campaign funds from large corporations, money laundering through foreign banks, secret cash funds, and bribes paid to the Watergate burglars. In 1973 the burglars were arrested at the Watergate apartment complex in the Democratic National Committee Headquarters, where they were paid to install and remove listening devices in the chairman's telephone. Although Nixon was never directly tied to approving the break-in, he was intimately involved with the cover-up operations. The events were revealed in a sensational series of articles printed in the *Washington Post* by Carl Bernstein and Bob Woodward. The scandal forced Congress to address the dismal situation of campaign fundraising abuses.

The amended FECA law was signed in 1974 by President Gerald R. Ford. The law features limits on individual campaign contributions and party and nonparty group contributions, and reporting of requirements for all contributions. The main goal was to reduce the inequalities between the incumbent candidates and the challengers while providing more regulations for campaign financing. After some debate, the Supreme Court decision of *Buckley v. Valeo* in 1976 ruled that Congress may limit contributions to congressional candidates, but may not limit expenditures by the candidates themselves, their campaign committees, or individuals or organizations independent of the candidates. The Court did uphold individual and committee contribution limits for candidates by accepting the government's contention that the limits would help prevent corruption and keep politics above suspicion. It did uphold public funding of presidential campaigns, requiring detailed reports of campaign spending. It was ruled that limits on candidates' spending of their own money, independent expenditures, and limits on total campaign spending were prohibited by the free speech protection of the First Amendment. Congress immediately passed a revised act, but ultimately the law proved unworkable. There were no established enforceable restrictions. Politicians and interest groups were free to find ways to maximize their leverage. Although the Federal Election Commission was developed to oversee the law, the way in which its members were appointed was struck down by the Court. Two were to be chosen by the president, two by the Speaker of the House, and two by the president pro tempore of the Senate, with all six confirmed by a majority vote of the two houses of Congress. The Court felt that under our system of separation of powers, the Constitution put the appointing power in the hands of the president. Since the Commission was to conduct civil litigation in the courts to see that the law is enforced, it is acting pursuant to the president's duty in Article II, Section 3 of the Constitution to "take Care that the Laws be faithfully executed." Therefore the Commission had to be reconstituted by Congress so as to conform to the dictates of the Constitution; namely, presidential appointment and Senate confirmation. Nevertheless, despite the good intentions behind the law, campaign spending skyrocketed. In 1996 the winning candidates in the Senate spent a total of $128 million, while the winning candidates in the House spent $297 million. In the 2004 election, a combined $2.7 billion was spent on congressional campaigns.

Loopholes

When looking at the issues surrounding campaign finance reform, it is important to remember that change is resisted by those who thrive under the existing rules. Political candidates and officeholders recognize the ties between money and power and are hesitant to build too many barriers. Yet a movement in the 1980s began to try to tighten the regulations of the 1974 FECA. The attempts lasted through four presidencies, until the big business scandals of the 1990s gave enough leverage to push reforms through.

The development of Political Action Committees (PACs) became one of the largest loopholes of FECA. PACs are nonparty campaign fund organizations that are established by presidential candidates, big business, or trade unions. The biggest regulation was that PACs could not coordinate their expenditures with the candidate's campaign. PACs have become extremely powerful in politics, with expenditures in the 1974 elections at $12.5 million and jumping to over $200 million in 1996 and $250 million in 2004. PACs are also permitted to run negative ads and release campaign materials against candidates who do not support their interests. There were two large campaign finance reform bills that have dominated the last two decades of attempted reform.

The McCain-Feingold Bill

In 1995, House Speaker Newt Gingrich (R-GA) and President Bill Clinton shook hands to show support for campaign finance reform, yet after the 1996 presidential and congressional elections the media revealed the worst fundraising abuses since Watergate. A lengthy investigation into the abuses by the Senate Governmental Affairs Committee revealed that:

- President Clinton had invited contributors of $100,000 or more to the Democratic Party to spend the night in the White House's Lincoln Bedroom. He also hosted 103 coffee parties at the White House in 1995–1996 that raised more than $26 million for his reelection campaign.
- Vice President Al Gore admitted to using his White House office to solicit funds from outside contributors and argued that it was permissible under the 1883 Pendleton Act. Additionally, Gore was criticized for accepting $150,000 from a Buddhist temple in Los Angeles.
- John Huang, a former Democratic National Committee fundraiser, raised more than $3 million at a fundraising dinner for Asian Americans. It should also be noted that more than thirty members of Congress were investigated by the FBI for accepting illegal Chinese campaign donations.

At the time that these incidents were being revealed, Senator John McCain (R-AZ) and Senator Russell D. Feingold (D-WI) introduced a bill that addressed the issue of campaign finance reform. The bill sought to eliminate soft money donations by corporations and labor unions to political party organizers. "Soft" money is a form of campaign contribution not covered by FECA regulations. Wealthy individuals, corporations, and unions were permitted to make donations to political parties for expenses, party activities, and voter registration. Soft money makes a huge impact by allowing parties to channel funds into negative, issue-advocacy ads without outrightly using words like "vote for" or "vote against." The opposite of "soft money" is "hard money," and that is a donation made directly to a candidate. In addition to eliminating soft money, the McCain-Feingold bill prohibited PAC contributions and allowed for candidates that accepted public funding to receive reduced-rate broadcast time.

A version of the bill, introduced in 1997–1998, would have banned the use of soft-money contributions to political parties and eliminated the use of issue ads by outside interest groups. It was suggested that the ads could not use a candidate's name or image within sixty days of an election. The bill also included better financial record disclosure and went so far as to ban all foreign contributions. The issue was polarized in the Senate with bitter disputes over the merits of the bill. Advocates for the bill sought to eliminate the soft-money loopholes, reduce the soaring cost of elections, increase the accountability of candidates for their fundraising and spending, and level the field for incumbents and challengers. Opponents argued that voluntary spending limits unfairly penalize candidates, banning soft money limits the influence of political parties in mobilizing voters, and limiting individual expenditures might encourage more issue advocacy spending.

Senate Majority Leader Trent Lott (D-MS) developed two strategies to defeat the bill. The first was a filibuster, but the second was a "poison pill" option. He introduced the Paycheck Protection Act as a rider to the McCain-Feingold bill without any committee hearings or bipartisan consideration. It attempted to protect union members by allowing them to oppose having their dues used for political campaigns, and was aimed at punishing the pro-Democratic AFL-CIO for spending more than $35 million in issue advocacy aimed against the Republican Party in the 1996 campaign. The McCain-Feingold bill was defeated 54–46. Final Senate votes revealed that fifty-one senators supported the bill, but this was nine short of the sixty that were needed to stop Lott's filibuster. With less than the sixty votes needed, Lott declared the bill dead and ended debate.

The Shays-Meehan Bill

Following the defeat of the Senate bill, Christopher Shays (R-CT) and Martin T. Meehan (D-MA) introduced a companion measure for campaign finance reform in the House. The main points of the bill were to ban soft money donations to political parties and to require full financial disclosure by interest groups that publish advocacy ads in support or opposition of candidates sixty days before the election. Speaker Gingrich and other Republican leaders attempted to block the bill, but were unsuccessful after a discharge position forced a floor vote. Gingrich scheduled the bill for a vote but added twelve alternatives and many killer amendments. Shays-Meehan survived debate and on August 7, 1998, a bipartisan coalition approved the strong reform bill with a vote of 252–179. Majority Leader Lott declared that campaign finance reform would not be discussed in the Senate in 1998 and buried the bill when there were not enough votes to override a veto.

Bipartisan Campaign Reform Act

After the big business scandals in the late 1990s and early 2000s, the call for campaign finance reform was renewed. In 2001 the Senate passed a version of the McCain-Feingold bill that banned soft money contributions and put strict restrictions on the amount of hard money contributions to national political parties. However, the bill did allow small amounts to be donated to local and state parties and raised the individual contribution amount while limiting issue advertising by interest groups until sixty days before the election with full disclosure of sponsorship of the ads. The Senate and House agreed to a modified version and the Bipartisan Campaign Reform Act (H.R. 2356) was passed in 2002. The House passed it with a margin of 240–189 and the Senate had a final vote of 60–40. Senator Mitch McConnell (R-KY) was a loud opponent of earlier bills and filed suit against the bill, arguing that by limiting contributions the law violates the free speech protection of the First Amendment.

On December 10, 2003, the Supreme Court decided *McConnell v. Federal Election Commission* with a vote of 5–4 (for most of the provisions) in favor of upholding the key points of the bill. Title I was upheld and it prohibits the national political parties and their committees from accepting or spending soft money. Another part of it bans the solicitation of soft money by candidates themselves, and that was upheld 7–2. Title II was also upheld. It established a new category of electioneering communications television advertisements that refer to specific candidates for federal office and that are broadcast in the relevant market within thirty days before a primary and sixty days before the general election. The law says that corporations and labor unions may not pay for such advertisements from their general treasuries, but must use money from their political action committees, which are subject to contribution limits. A major theme running through the Court's opinion was that existing corporation limits had been widely circumvented with corrosive effects, such as perceptions that big money has stained the political system. The problem with big, unregulated contributions was preferential access and the influence that comes with it. The Court also upheld the record-keeping provisions imposed on broadcasters by the law, and unanimously struck down the law's prohibitions on contributions by children under the age of eighteen, finding that it swept too broadly. The dissenters in the major parts of the decision argued that corruption meant trading votes for dollars, or something very close to that, and evidence at the time of such behavior was insufficient to justify the new regulations.

The bill attempted to close the access and influence of soft money but the 2004 election showed that when one door closes, another door opens. Working in cooperation with PACs are groups called 527s. These are named after the section of the tax code that list them as tax exempt organizations designed to influence the nominations, election, appointment, or defeat of a candidate for public office. 527s are not regulated by the Federal Election Commission, nor are they subject to the same contribution limits that regulate PACs. There is a fine line here between candidate advocacy and issue advocacy. The money from 527s is not made to directly advocate for the election or defeat of an individual candidate; instead their money is spent on issue advocacy and voter mobilization. There is great debate on how 527s should be regulated and the rhetoric is often tied to debates on lobbying reform, since most are run by special interests and used to raise unlimited amounts for advocacy efforts. In 2004, 527s raised and spent over $523 million, mostly on issue ads. The elimination of soft money donations and the rise of 527s and PAC groups is also tied to the notion of lobbying reform, which in past decades has been addressed with the need for campaign finance reform.

The Supreme Court and Campaign Finance

Besides *Buckley* and *McConnell,* the Supreme Court has rendered several other decisions in the realm of campaign finance. For example, in 1978 in *First National Bank of Boston v. Bellotti,* it struck down a Massachusetts law that had banned banks and businesses from trying to influence the outcomes of political referenda. The decision said that the state, although attempting to stop big business from using its wealth to determine the outcome of political issues, was guilty of curtailing freedom of expression. Then in 1985 in *Federal Election Commission v. National Conservative Political Action Committee,* it struck down a portion of FECA under which PACS were allowed to spend only $1,000 on presidential candidates receiving public financing. The decision said that the provision favored the wealthy donors who could purchase expensive media ads with their own money, whereas in these PACS many donors of modest means are able to pool their resources for a candidate. Thus it was a denial of free expression. Again in 1986 in *Federal Election Commission v. Massachusetts Citizens for Life, Inc.,* the Court ruled that FECA did not apply to a nonprofit, non–stock corporation which had been formed solely to advocate a particular idea. All its money was obtained through donations; therefore for the government to try to limit such groups would be to take away their First Amendment right of free speech.

After these decisions against campaign finance regulation, the Court in the 1990 case of *Austin v. Michigan Chamber of Commerce* upheld a state law that forbade corporations from using general treasury funds for state elections. It concluded that there was a compelling state interest to see that huge corporate treasuries would not be used to unfairly influence election outcomes. The law was narrowly tailored so that segregated funds specifically raised for political purposes could be used. The fact that unincorporated associations are not regulated by the law and media corporations are exempt from it does not violate the Equal Protection Clause of the Fourteenth Amendment. However, in the 1996 case of *Colorado Republican Federal*

Campaign Committee v. Federal Election Commission, the Court ruled that the federal government may not limit how much political parties spend to help their candidates unless it specifically proves that party and candidates are working together. In this particular case the expenditure for radio advertisements was made independently, without coordination with any candidate. The Court then went the other way in the 2000 case of *Nixon v. Shrink Missouri Government PAC* and upheld the state's $1,000 limit on campaign contributions to candidates in statewide elections, saying it did not violate free speech rights. Similarly, in the 2001 case of *Federal Election Commission v. Colorado Republican Federal Campaign Committee,* the Court upheld the FECA limits on how much political parties can spend in coordination with candidates for public office, because without them rich donors could circumvent limits on contributions to individual candidates. The limits vary with the size of the congressional districts or the state, and the money is often used to televise commercials, underwrite mass mailings, or pay for polls. The Court felt that the limits had not harmed the political parties.

The Court again agreed with campaign finance limits in the 2003 case of *Federal Election Commission v. Beaumont,* upholding the 1971 FECA ban on direct corporate contributions to candidates or political parties in federal elections, and refusing to make an exception for corporations organized for the purpose of ideological advocacy (in this case a nonprofit antiabortion group). It stressed the need for deference to legislative choice in campaign finance, saying that there had been a century of congressional efforts to limit the corrosive effects of corporate money in politics. However, in its latest ruling, in the 2006 case of *Randall v. Sorrell,* the Court struck down Vermont's limits on campaign contributions and on campaign spending by candidates. The spending-limits part of the decision was consistent with previous cases (they ranged from $300,000 over a two-year election cycle for governors' races to $2,000 for state representative), but the contributions-limits part of the decision was inconsistent. The Court's rationale was that the limits, such as neither an individual nor a political party could contribute more than $400 to a candidate for statewide office over a two-year election cycle, including primaries, was too low (the lowest in the country) and a limit that is too low can prevent challengers from mounting effective campaigns against well-known incumbents.

Lobbying Reform

Lobbying refers to the practice of influencing a governing body by promoting a particular point of view. In the United States, the number of interest groups is growing rapidly, and as a result, so is the number of lobbyists and the money devoted to lobbying activities. The controversy arises from a lack of transparency in the system. It is often very difficult to trace the trail of money from an interest to a lobbyist to the government representative whom they are attempting to persuade. Lobbying gets its name from the story of President Ulysses Grant, who was forbidden from smoking in the White House by his wife, and instead was often found smoking a cigar in the lobby of the nearby Willard Hotel. Politicians and business representatives began to meet him there to discuss political favors. However, this has expanded to a highly funded and complex system of quid pro quo.

The 1946 Federal Regulation of Lobbying Act attempted to disclose lobbying activities to the public by requiring lobbyists to register and file a report quarterly. The 1954 Supreme Court case of *United States v. Harriss* upheld the constitutionality of the law, but significantly weakened it. The law was changed so that the only people who needed to register were paid lobbyists, those whose "principal" purpose was to influence, and lobbyists who contact members of the government directly. It became apparent that reforming lobbying activities would be difficult because there is a fine line between regulating and infringing on a citizen's right to contact an elected official. For years, lobbying was not really addressed until the Lobby Disclosure Act of 1995. This act laid out the following:

- Lobbyists are those who spend 20 percent of their time doing paid lobby work.
- Lobbying activities include preparation and research intended to influence policy, as well as direct contact with policy makers.
- Lobbyists must register with Congress and disclose the names of clients, their issue topics, and the amount they are compensated.
- Lobbyists must file disclosure reports every six months (with a fine of up to $50,000 if not completed).
- Nonprofit organizations that lobby under the IRS code 501c cannot receive direct federal grants.
- Former United States trade representatives and deputies are banned for life from lobbying for foreign interests.

After the new law came into effect, 14,912 lobbyists registered. In 2005 the number of registered lobbyists was 34,785. The 1995 law was better but was minimally enforced. Congressional probes into alleged misconduct by high-profile lobbyists triggered proposals for reform in 2005–2006. It is the scandal surrounding lobbyist Jack Abramoff that led to the Legislative Transparency and Accountability Act of 2006.

The Abramoff Affair

Jack Abramoff was a high-profile lobbyist who had ties to top lobby firms, and used his connections to influence legislation by providing lawmakers with golf trips, sporting events (he maintained four skyboxes at stadiums for over $1 million a year), or elegant meals at his swanky Washington, D.C., restaurant. In 2006, he pled guilty to fraud, public corruption, and tax evasion in his dealings with his clients, including defrauding Native American tribes. This sparked public outrage and a call for stricter restrictions on lobby activities, so Congress passed the new lobbying law in 2006. The act bars lobbyists themselves from buying gifts or meals for legislators, dictates that lawmakers get permission for privately funded trips from an ethics committee, and requires lobbyists to file more frequent and detailed reports on their activities. The bill still has many loopholes and critics in both the House and the Senate say that it will not have a major impact on changing behavior. Jack Abramoff had far-reaching ties in the Republican Party, and yet as soon as the "Abramoff scandal" receded from the front pages of newspapers, the impetus for major congressional lobbying reform quickly abated.

Policy Options

1. *Enforce existing laws.* In order for the existing legislation to be effective, there needs to be explicit criminal prosecution of illegal fundraising or lobbying activities. The problem comes in deciding who should be the enforcer. In the 1996 investigation, Republicans urged Attorney General Janet Reno to appoint an independent counsel to oversee abuses in campaign fundraising. She resisted the pressure and deemed that matter within the realm of the Justice Department. Attorney General Reno eventually decided against

further investigation into the Clinton and Gore campaigns because there was "no clear and convincing evidence" of illegal or unethical behavior. In order for the laws to be obeyed, there must be a clear consequence for when they are not followed.

2. *Create public financing options.* If the concern is truly about leveling the playing field, then there needs to be attractive public financing options that will help both incumbents and challengers win a fair fight. Public financing should come with strict rules about spending of the funds, elimination of soft money, and controlled interest group/PAC donations. Furthermore, congressional races should also have the option of accepting public financing, as a way to curb the exorbitant spending practices.

3. *Free TV time.* One of the most costly expenditures is television advertisements. By working with the Federal Election Commission and developing a system of vouchers, candidates could have an even opportunity to reach their audiences. This would also eliminate the need for amassing such budgets to cover the advertising. Also, the Internet could be used more effectively and efficiently to cut down on the need for TV spots. Development of websites, e-mails, and banner ads has allowed candidates to reach their audience quickly and easily, and without the high cost of television ads.

4. *Reform at the state level.* Because of the partisan gridlock experienced at the national level, starting reform at the state level is a viable alternative. States can administer public funds, monitor campaign spending, limit campaign contributions, and force financial disclosures. Because of the much larger size of the federal government, reform at the state level is easier to control. However, it would be imperative that states develop a level of minimum enforcement so that elections to national positions are all on an even playing field.

5. *Do nothing.* Most incumbents would argue that putting limits on anything would violate free speech rights under the First Amendment. Those that support the status quo argue that it takes large amounts of money to win elections for both incumbents and challengers, and even though incumbents usually win, the money they raise and spend might make the difference in the election. There is also the argument that those in Congress who are required to change the law are also those who are benefiting the most from the weak laws, so it is easier to do just nothing.

Conclusion

Campaign finance reform and lobbying reform are salient issues with the public but are polarizing issues that are not easily resolved in Congress. Since campaign finance is tied to money and money is tied to power, the problem will remain. With the history of reform starting in the nineteenth century and continuing today with bitter debates over proposed restrictions, it seems that an easy solution is nowhere to be found. The same can be said for lobbying reform. The efforts to promote transparency have been the source of ongoing arguments in both houses of Congress and legislation is developed without a system of regulation. However, these issues are being debated and the demands of the public to address them have been heard. As long as scandals erupt there will be discussion and proposed reforms, but how effective will they be?

Discussion Questions

1. Which has a better chance of succeeding, campaign finance reform or lobby reform?
2. What activities of the nineteenth century influenced early legislation?

3. How were the goals of early legislation different from goals of modern legislation?
4. How did FECA attempt to respond to the Watergate scandal?
5. How did the Supreme Court decision of *Buckley v. Valeo* influence the success of FECA?
6. What FECA loopholes were used in the 1996 presidential campaign?
7. How did opponents defeat the Senate's McCain-Feingold bill?
8. Should the Supreme Court play a pivotal role in campaign finance reform?
9. How has lobbying evolved with the involvement of big business and special interests?
10. How did the Lobby Disclosure Act of 1995 differ from the 1946 Regulation of Lobbying Act?
11. Do lobbying restrictions infringe on a citizen's right to contact members of government?
12. Do campaign contribution limits infringe on the freedom of speech in the First Amendment?

Class Activities

1. Debate the pros and cons of the most recent campaign finance reform and lobbying reform legislation.
2. Pick a specific piece of legislation and divide into supporting and opposing groups to debate the individual aspects.
3. Try to develop a campaign finance reform or lobbying reform proposal that is sympathetic to bipartisan support and then make plans to share the ideas with your elected representatives.

Suggestions for Further Reading

Baker, Ross. "How Lobbying Gained Its Clout." *USA Today*, January 1, 2006, 11A.

Berry, Jeffrey M. *The Interest Group Society*. New York: Longman, 1997.

Biersack, Robert, Paul S. Hernnson, and Clyde Wilcox. *After the Revolution: PACs, Lobbies, and the Republican Congress*. Boston: Allyn and Bacon, 1999.

Davidson, Roger H., and Walter J. Oleszek. *Congress and Its Members*. 10th ed. Washington, DC: Congressional Quarterly, 2006.

Loomis, Burdett A., and Wendy J. Schiller. *The Contemporary Congress*. 5th ed. Belmont, CA: Wadsworth, 2006.

Malbin, Michael J. *Life after Reform: When the Bipartisan Reform Act Meets Politics*. Lanham, MD: Rowman & Littlefield, 2004.

Morone, James A. *The Democratic Wish: Popular Participation and the Limits of American Government*. New Haven, CT: Yale University Press, 1998.

Nownes, Anthony. *Total Lobbying: What Lobbyists Want (And How They Try to Get It)*. New York: Cambridge University Press, 2006.

Oleszek, Walter J. *Congressional Procedures and the Policy Process*. 6th ed. Washington, DC: Congressional Quarterly, 2004.

Palazzolo, Daniel J. *Election Reform: Politics and Policy*. Lanham, MD: Rowman & Littlefield, 2004.

Wright, John. "Interest Groups, Congressional Reform, and Party Government in the United States." *Legislative Studies Quarterly* 25 (May 2000): 217–33.

Helpful Websites

www.brookings.edu/gs/sourcebk/default.htm. This website for the Brookings Institution contains articles discussing campaign finance reform.

www.opensecrets.org/news/campaignfinance/index.asp. This website for the Center for Responsive Politics outlines the issues of campaign finance reform.

9

Voting

Case Snapshot

VOTING IS A WAY FOR ORDINARY CITIZENS to exercise effective political power in government and be represented in government. With such value and importance attached to it, voting has come to be recognized as a fundamental right, one which is inherent to a democratic system and with which the state must not interfere without an extraordinary reason and with no lesser alternative available. Therefore, in order to most fairly ensure this right to political influence and representation, each citizen's vote should be equal to that of any other. This accepted standard expresses an ideal of equality aptly captured by the principle of "one person, one vote." Throughout history, pursuit of this equality in voting at last in 1971 extended the right to vote to all U.S. citizens above the age of eighteen by virtue of the Twenty-sixth Amendment. However, the American political system still faces challenges to truly living up to this principle of equality and fairness in voting, particularly in the decennial procedure of "redistricting." Redistricting is the process of legislative apportionment that is done by dividing and redividing states according to population counts into districts that will elect members to the U.S. House of Representatives and the states' legislatures. Traditional districting principles, such as population equality among districts, have arisen to serve as guidelines in determining boundaries, but where and how district lines are placed still has the potential to enhance or dilute the weight of a person's vote. Since the way in which congressional and legislative districts are drawn can have significant consequences on the equality of an individual's vote, redistricting can severely threaten the fair and effective representation of all citizens. Indeed, redistricting has long been used as a political tool to manipulate the influence of a voting bloc in order to benefit a certain demographic or political group in the practice of "gerrymandering." After the Voting Rights Act of 1965, racial gerrymandering went from having the objective of diluting minority voting power to enhancing it, although the Supreme Court will not allow race to be the predominant factor used in deciding district boundaries. In 2006 in *League of United Latin American Citizens v. Perry* the Supreme Court did conclude that a Texas district was an unconstitutional racial gerrymander. The Supreme Court in the 1986 case of *Davis v. Bandemer* has also declared political gerrymandering unconstitutional based on the Fourteenth Amendment's Equal Protection Clause, but the Court has yet to discern an appropriate judicial standard by which the courts could judge and prove this discriminatory gerrymandering. As this unfair practice has been allowed to continue in politics, a dissatisfied public is demanding more stringent and more neutral districting principles. Therefore, clearly and conclusively determining the fairest method of redistricting that most closely lives up to the principle of "one person, one vote" is vital to the health of American democracy. What is the fairest method of redistricting? You decide!

Major Case Controversies

1. *While the U.S. Constitution mandates that members of the U.S. House of Representatives be apportioned according to population, it does not specify how this is to be done.* Determining how electoral districts will be created has been left up to the states. Various Supreme Court decisions and congressional legislation have provided more specific guidelines, but many details of the process are still vague or even controversial.

2. *States have generally placed the responsibility of redistricting in the hands of state legislators.* Since these politicians can benefit from how districts are drawn, they have often been able to use this political power as a tool to enhance one party's power at the expense of another by determining boundary lines to maximize the seats it could gain for the U.S. House of Representatives.

3. *In many areas of the South after the Civil War, racially discriminatory redistricting was often used as a way to dilute minority voting strength and limit blacks' political representation.* However, after the Voting Rights Act of 1965 began enforcing adherence to the Fourteenth and Fifteenth Amendments, these "racial gerrymanders" have had the objective of concentrating minority strength in "majority-minority" districts (those in which a racial minority actually has a majority of the population) in order to elect candidates supported by a minority group.

4. *Politically motivated redistricting has resulted in massive gains for the political party in power in the state since it has the strongest influence over the redistricting map.* Through this partisan gerrymandering, politicians have been able to create "safe" districts by encircling large numbers of party supporters with the objective of creating a formidable supermajority that can easily elect a candidate from their party.

5. *The Supreme Court initially refused to consider cases of reapportionment, claiming redistricting was a political issue over which the courts had no jurisdiction.* Since the 1960s though, the Supreme Court has recognized apportionment as a justifiable issue, believing it could have constitutional implications. While the Supreme Court has been able to apply Article I, Section 2, of the Constitution to mandate population equality among districts and the Voting Rights Act to protect racial minorities, it still struggles to find judicial standards by which the intent and effect of partisan gerrymandering can be proven.

6. *In the 2004 U.S. Supreme Court case Vieth v. Jubelirer the Democrats of Pennsylvania alleged that the state's congressional districts were an unconstitutional political gerrymander, arguing that the Republican-controlled state legislature passed a plan after the 2000 census that*

unfairly benefited Republican candidates at the expense of Democrats. As the justices were divided in their opinions regarding the possibility of finding judicial standards to apply to a political gerrymander claim, the 5–4 decision effectively allowed partisan gerrymandering to persist.

7. *With the Texas State Legislature deadlocked in the redistricting process after the 2000 census, a state court stepped in to implement a reapportionment plan, but the Republicans did a second redistricting when they got control of the state government in 2003.* The new lines they drew broke up safe Democratic seats, which led to the Republicans picking up eight congressional seats in the 2004 elections. Bringing several cases to the Supreme Court in March of 2006, the plaintiffs alleged that the new Texas district map was unconstitutional for redistricting mid-decade, for discriminating on the basis of race, and for being a partisan gerrymander. The Court in June 2006, in *League of United Latin American Citizens v. Perry*, upheld most of the Texas plan and even said it was valid to redraw congressional districts any time there is a change in political control rather than only after the census. However, it did strike down as a violation of the Voting Rights Act a district where 100,000 Mexican Americans had been removed and an Anglo population added, even though a new district had been created with a Latino majority. The new district was not sufficiently compact and combined persons with disparate interests whose only common index was race.

8. *Many blame unfair redistricting on leaving this responsibility in the hands of state legislators, who could benefit from the results of this process.* As a response, many states have switched to giving independent commissions this task of redistricting, and some U.S. senators and representatives have proposed a constitutional amendment that would make that standard practice in the country.

Background of the Case

Redistricting and the U.S. Constitution

Article I, Section 2, of the U.S. Constitution requires that members of the U.S. House of Representatives be apportioned among the several states according to their respective populations. In leaving the specific method of legislative apportionment in the hands of the states, the Constitution merely mandates that the enumeration of representatives be delegated "within every subsequent Term of ten Years, in such Manner as [the states] shall by Law direct." In order to be in compliance with this requirement of the Constitution, a national census was instituted in 1790 to count the country's population and to note population shifts. This nationwide census has taken place every ten years since its year of inception. Although the census certainly cannot give a perfect count of the entire nation's population, and even though it is a mere snapshot into a constantly changing population, the census is still the vital primary tool that determines the national population counts that will be used in the reapportionment of seats for the U.S. House of Representatives, as well as the state legislatures.

While each state is guaranteed at least one seat in the U.S. House of Representatives, the remaining seats to be apportioned are designated for each state based on the population results as expressed in the national census. If a state has a large enough population, it is entitled to more than one representative and it must be divided up according to how many it receives. This procedure effectively creates "districts." The reapportionment, or "redistricting," that takes place after the census every ten years is the process of adjusting district boundaries according to changes in the number of seats delegated and according to shifts in population that unbalanced the population distribution among the old districts. In addition to these congressional districts, a state must also create legislative districts for the election of members to the various state legislatures; the legislative and congressional districts' boundaries often differ. Despite this common presence of districts within all states across the country, the U.S. Constitution does not mention districts specifically, nor does it explain exactly how they should be drawn. Nevertheless, since the early beginnings of the United States, this responsibility of redistricting for congressional and state legislative seats has generally been given to the elected state legislatures and, in the case of deadlock, to the courts.

Malapportionment and the Principle of "One Person, One Vote"

From the mid-nineteenth century to the early twentieth century, Congress had required that districts have equal population and that they be made up of contiguous territory, but a law that mandated these standards expired in 1911. Soon after this termination, drastic population shifts were occurring in the United States. In particular, people were moving from rural to urban areas, thereby causing the rural populations to dramatically diminish and the urban populations to swell. These shifts in population significantly altered the distribution of representatives and legislators among a given state's population. Even though this inequity effectively enhanced the influence of the voters in the sparsely populated areas relative to those in the more dense parts, many state legislatures shirked their constitutional duty to redraw district boundaries to remedy this unfairness. (Representatives from the rural areas would not want to redistrict themselves out of a seat!) But the resulting egregious malapportionment created the problem of unequal representation for citizens.

Even though the malapportionment issue that affected citizens' representation may appear to violate the fair apportionment of representatives according to population that the U.S. Constitution calls for, the U.S. Supreme Court did not assert itself in forcing state legislatures to redraw their districts' boundaries. The Supreme Court's hands-off approach was clearly articulated in its decision in the 1946 case *Colegrove v. Green*. Kenneth W. Colegrove brought a case against the state of Illinois, claiming that the state's congressional districts were unconstitutional because they "lacked compactness of territory and approximate equality of population." To the chagrin of the plaintiff, the Court decided that Illinois's districts were, in fact, constitutional because there was nothing in existing laws that specifically mandated districts to be compact, contiguous, and equal in population. Moreover, Justice Felix Frankfurter refused to further involve the court system in reapportionment cases, explaining that redistricting was nonjusticiable (i.e., not proper for the court to comment on) because it was a political issue. Therefore, rather than entering the Supreme Court into the "political thicket" of redistricting, the Court indicated that the political branches would be the most appropriate sources for resolving claims of unfair redistricting.

This distant stance of the Supreme Court changed significantly in the 1960s. In the early part of the decade, the Supreme Court intervened in redistricting claims to address the issue of malapportionment and unequal representation concerning both the state legislatures and the U.S. House of Representatives. In a decision very different from that made nearly two decades earlier, the Supreme Court ruled in *Baker v. Carr* in 1962 that federal courts did have jurisdiction to hear cases brought against legislative reapportionment issues because of the Fourteenth Amendment's Equal Protection Clause that guarantees the opportunity for equal participation and consideration to achieve fair and effective representation for all citizens. The Supreme Court used this argument for the basis of its decision in the 1964 case *Reynolds v. Sims*, which mandated that districts for state legislatures be of equal population. In the 1964 case *Wesberry v. Sanders*, the Supreme Court demanded that congressional districts also be equal in population, though its decision this time was based on a strict interpretation of Article I, Section 2, of the Constitution. Justice William O. Douglas, who wrote the decision in the 1963 case *Gray v. Sanders*, clearly articulated this principle of voting equality for which the American republic has striven: "The conception of political equality from the Declaration of Independence, to Lincoln's Gettysburg Address, to the Fifteenth, Seventeenth, and Nineteenth Amendments can mean only one thing—one person, one vote."

All these judicial decisions were intended to make a fairer redistricting process, the Court believing that by requiring population equality among districts that the vote of one citizen would be ensured equal weight with the vote of any another. "One person, one vote" then became the guiding principle for drawing district boundaries, in order to assure that each person would be guaranteed fair, equal, and effective representation in state and national government. Living up to this principle was initially understood strictly in mathematical terms; ideally, a state's districts' populations would equal the total state population divided by the total number of districts. At the same time, the Supreme Court did not require the same degree of mathematical equality for both congressional and state legislative districts. While the Court granted some leeway to state legislative districts, which were allowed a variance in populations of up to 10 percent without automatic justification, the Court's strict interpretation of Article I, Section 2, of the Constitution mandated congressional districts be mathematically equal.

The Court added some practical flexibility to this standard when it admitted in several subsequent cases that attaining this mathematical "ideal population" across all districts would not be reasonably feasible in all circumstances. This practical rationalization meant that slight population inequity among districts could be allowed, but if a challenger can show that the inequality could have been avoided or that there is something suspect about a district's boundaries, the state would then have to justify the deviation to prove that it was for a legitimate state policy. Moreover, any variance at all can be vulnerable to close scrutiny under the Constitution—no matter how small the difference may be. Such a challenge to strict population equality was upheld in the 1980 case *Karcher v. Daggett*, when the Supreme Court decided that a New Jersey redistricting plan in which the districts differed by less than 1 percent violated Article I, Section 2, of the Constitution because it believed there was not a "good faith attempt" to make them equal. Therefore, despite some reasonable flexibility, the Supreme Court generally demanded strict and loyal adherence to the requirement of population equality in order to make redistricting fairer.

Racial and Political Gerrymandering in Redistricting

The accepted method of making redistricting fairer focused on this mathematical equality of population counts based on the principle of "one person, one vote." However, despite the resolution of malapportionment through mathematical standards, a long history of manipulative use of the redistricting process was still able to persist. Redistricting is merely the process of drawing congressional and legislative district lines to distribute as equally as possible the states' changing population. On the other hand, even while still adhering to the standard of mathematical equality, legislators have demonstrated the ability to deliberately draw district boundaries with the purpose of benefiting a certain demographic or political group, effectively creating another violation of fair and effective representation. Known as "gerrymandering," this form of redistricting got its name in 1811 when Governor Elbridge Gerry of Massachusetts redrew the lines of one of his state's districts in order to bolster his party's strength within it. His politically motivated redrawing of the boundaries resulted in a district so oddly shaped that it closely resembled a salamander—thus giving us the term "gerrymander."

Gerrymandering has had a long history in the United States and it has manifested itself in the political system through various forms. For example, in many areas of the South after the Civil War, redistricting was used unfairly in order to limit the representation of African Americans in Congress. This racial gerrymandering, which arbitrarily distorted district boundaries with the intent of diluting minority-voting power, persisted even throughout the century that followed the Civil War. However, these redistricting practices that decreased the equality of black citizens' votes and representation would not remain insulated from challenge forever. The Voting Rights Act of 1965 and many Supreme Court decisions made during this same decade protected the right to vote guaranteed by the Fourteenth and Fifteenth Amendments by prohibiting the creation of any election law that could encroach upon minority voting power. These developments, which served to protect minorities from discriminatory racial gerrymanders that were intended to dilute their voting power, simultaneously encouraged the enhancement of minority voting power through concentrating a minority population in a given district to become a "majority-minority" district. The provisions in Section 2 and Section 5 of the Voting Rights Act led many states to feel obligated to create majority-minority districts, especially if the minority group is large, compact, and politically cohesive enough to make up a majority in a single-member district.

This complete reversal of the purpose for racial gerrymandering was evident following the 1990 census, when racial gerrymandering was used with the objective of getting candidates elected who were supported by a minority group in order to increase the representation of minority interests. The creation of majority-minority districts does not seemingly violate the judicial standard of "one person, one vote" because it does not affect equality in population across districts; it just alters the demographic proportions within a district's population. But the 1993 case *Shaw v. Reno* called into question the constitutionality of this form of gerrymandering. The district brought to challenge was a thin and oddly shaped North Carolina district that contained a black majority. This district was known as the "I-85 district" because some parts of it were no wider than this highway along which it stretched. The Supreme Court ruled that this district likely did represent an unconstitutional racial gerrymander because the shape of this district was so irrational that it had to be with the purpose of racially segregating voters. The decision in this case opened up oddly shaped districts for challenge as racial gerrymanders. Two years later, the Supreme Court reaffirmed this position when it ruled in *Miller v. Johnson* that while it is constitutional for race to be one of the many factors taken into account when redistricting, it could not be the predominant factor in the process. Accordingly it struck down two Georgia districts, and in 2001 in *Easley v. Cromartie* it finally did strike down the North Carolina I-85 district. However, in 2003 in *Georgia v. Ashcroft* the Court upheld the use of a variety of factors to help minorities by allowing "influence districts" rather than "packed" ones.

While standards of mathematical equality for population and protection for minority rights were resolving issues of unfairness in redistricting, the traditional form of gerrymandering, partisan (or political) gerrymandering, was more illusive to reform. This practice attempts to maximize gains in legislative seats by consciously drawing district lines to favor one political party over another. District boundaries are drawn by the political party in power to create "safe seats" for that party's candidates, or by forcing incumbents of the opposition party to run against each other. The techniques for creating noncompetitive races to protect the political party in power are "cracking" (which diminishes the power of the opposition's voting bloc) and "packing" (which enhances the power of the controlling party's voting bloc). Cracking occurs when the party in power splits an area of partisan support for the opposition among two or more districts to limit the ability for voters of this party to coalesce into an effective challenge. Packing occurs when the party in power draws district lines around as many supporters as possible to create a supermajority. Finally, in "incumbent" gerrymandering, two incumbents face each other by drawing a new district line around both their districts, forcing the opposition party to lose one seat.

Despite the threat political gerrymandering was posing to the principle of "one person, one vote," the Supreme Court continued to circumvent this issue of redistricting. Its avoidance was possible because clear standards for how a fair district should look had yet to be developed. Moreover, partisan gerrymandering was much vaguer than racial gerrymandering because, while the latter is based on a cohesive, immutable characteristic, the former involves political groups, which are less durable and much more malleable. Nevertheless, cases of alleged partisan gerrymandering made it to the Supreme Court. For example, Democrats in Indiana brought a case to the Supreme Court charging that the state's redistricting in 1981 violated their rights under the Equal Protection Clause in the Constitution because the apportionment diluted their votes in several districts. In *Davis v. Bandemer* (1986) the Court disagreed with the Democrats by arguing that the effects of the redistricting were not "sufficiently adverse" to constitute unconstitutional discrimination. This decision brought the Court to admit that partisan gerrymanders are justiciable issues under the Equal Protection Clause, but that clear judicial standards to apply to these cases had yet to be discerned. The basis for assessing cases of alleged partisan gerrymanders that was established from this decision would require proof of discrimination in both intent and effect. This rigorous standard would make partisan gerrymanders very hard to prove, and thus easier to get away with.

Current Efforts at Fairer Redistricting

Congressional legislation and Supreme Court decisions during the last half-century have been intended to make redistricting fairer by protecting the equality of citizens' votes. From these developments, a set of "traditional districting principles" that limit the freedom of elected officials to draw district lines has arisen. These seven principles encompass objective geographical and natural goals, such as a more homogeneous population, as well as more subjective political and legal goals, and are listed as follows:

1. Compactness.
2. Contiguity.
3. Preservation of counties and other political subdivisions.
4. Preservation of communities of interest.
5. Preservation of cores of prior districts.
6. Protection of incumbents.
7. Compliance with Section 2 of the Voting Rights Act.

Regardless of the established principles, many still believe that the unfairness of redistricting comes directly from the source of redistricting—the state legislators.

Criticisms for leaving redistricting up to state legislators include, among others, the following:

- Politicians draw boundaries with partisan motivations, resulting in bizarrely shaped districts that carve up communities, cities, and counties.
- Politicians redraw district boundaries to benefit themselves through noncompetitive elections that are less accessible to challengers and contribute to entrenched incumbency.
- Irrelevant elections lead to voter apathy and cynicism while the politically homogeneous districts lead parties to cater to their bases for constituent mobilization, creating greater polarization of politics.

In response, many states have moved to take the responsibility of redistricting out of the hands of the people who could potentially benefit from its results and have given this responsibility to independent commissions of a variety of appointed members. They believe that independent commissions will take partisan politics out of redistricting and use politically neutral standards to create fairer congressional and state legislative districts. In contrast to the consequences for redistricting that state legislators bring about, proponents of independent commissions believe they can attain the following:

- An independent commission would be objective in drawing boundaries, resulting in compact districts that keep communities, cities, and counties together.
- An independent commission would draw district boundaries to benefit the voter by making competitive districts, which are more open to opposition candidates and more likely to experience greater government responsiveness and incumbent turnover.
- Competitive and unpredictable elections would increase turnout by giving voters more confidence that their vote matters and would force candidates to reach out to a broader constituency.

Currently, twelve states have switched to giving first and final authority on redistricting plans to independent commissions. Action in the national legislative branch is also occurring. Some legislators have proposed a constitutional amendment that will make this system of redistricting the standard for the entire country. Also, the Fairness and Independence in Redistricting Act of 2006 has been introduced in the Senate. This bill, if enacted, would, prohibit a state from being redistricted a second time before the results of the next decennial census, and it would require redistricting to be determined through an independent commission. However, it is still inconclusive if the current system of redistricting is the sole—or even major—factor in the ills in the electoral system for which it has been blamed, and if independent commissions are able to deliver on the promises they are perceived to offer.

Policy Options

1. *The responsibility for redistricting should remain in the hands of state legislators.* Changing the system of reapportionment by taking it out of the hands of state legislators and giving it to an independent board will not ease the difficulty that the mapmakers faced when trying to reach agreement on new boundary lines. Instead, it will only prolong disputes

and heighten dissatisfaction. These delays will very likely end up leaving these decisions to be decided in the court system.

2. *The responsibility for redistricting should be given to independent commissions.* The fairness of redistricting is threatened when state legislators who can manipulate the process for partisan political gains are in control of this process. In addition, the purpose of the entire legislative branch is threatened when this process consumes the energy of state legislators while they should, in fact, be focusing on bigger problems. Iowa has instituted such a commission with the result that in 2002 four out of five congressional districts were competitive. However, voters have rejected such propositions in Ohio and California in the 2004 election.

3. *Districts should be compact and should keep already established communities, cities, and counties together.* Redistricting is fairest if it keeps together the already established community lines and keeps the territory a manageable size. Elections then are more meaningful when directed toward a more cohesive group of people and a candidate can more effectively develop his or her platform based on clearly defined groups of people.

4. *Districts should be politically heterogeneous to make elections as competitive as possible.* Fair redistricting necessitates competitiveness, and competitiveness would be better achieved without such strict adherence to maintaining city and county boundaries and with more attention to encircling a diverse group of people. Keeping cities and counties together may very likely not enhance the competitiveness of elections and may contribute to safer seats and less competitive elections, since people tend to group by similar people.

5. *Redistricting should be abandoned and a system of "at-large" candidates should replace it.* There is no need for dividing states into electoral districts. Instead, a variety of candidates can run and the state's citizens can vote for any candidate and for as many candidates that are necessary to fill the seats available. The winners of the election are the top vote-getters to fill the set of apportioned seats.

Conclusion

An intense debate regarding redistricting has gradually emerged in the country over recent years. The significant implications that district boundaries can have on equal and effective representation has lent great importance to determining the fairest method of redistricting. While the Constitution provides no explicit set of guidelines for this procedure of reapportionment, the various states have instituted on their own a system in which redistricting is a responsibility of a state legislature, an independent commission, or sometimes a mix of the two. Misuse of this power by whomever holds it, though, has led to racial and political discrimination. While advances in technology have made it easier to conduct more accurate population counts and to divide states more precisely in drawing districts for reapportionment, these same technological advancements can also be used in redistricting to advance objectives that are more partisan in nature than the fairness of equal voting and of representation. Some also argue the procedure of redistricting has contributed to an erosion of the American electoral system, as seen in low voter turnout, noncompetitive elections, entrenched incumbency, and low government responsiveness. After decades of aloofness, the Supreme Court eventually intervened in the controversial issue of reapportionment to provide some more explicit standards to follow in redistricting. While mathematical equality has held strong, other principles pose problems of vagueness, effectiveness, and practicality. Moreover, are there any wholly objective principles for redistricting? It is still unclear as to what constitutes unfair redistricting, how fairer redistricting could be accomplished, and if there truly is a fair way of redistricting.

Because the 2006 Texas decision in *League of United Latin American Citizens v. Perry* is the Court's latest pronouncement on this matter, an in-depth look at it is enlightening. In one part of the decision, Justice Anthony Kennedy upheld most of the congressional redistricting done by the Republican-dominated legislature in 2003 against Democratic and other plaintiffs' claims of a statewide gerrymander. He said the case did not present a workable test for deciding how much partisan dominance is too much, which means that a partisan gerrymander might some day be found unconstitutional. To underscore the fragmentation of the Court on this issue, two other justices (Souter and Ginsburg) thought there was nothing to be gained by expressing a view on how to assess a redistricting plan for impermissible partisanship due to the Court being deadlocked on that point; two others (Roberts and Alito) took no position on whether such claims would ever be brought; and another two (Scalia and Thomas) held to their position that claims of partisan gerrymandering were categorically invalid and could never be considered by a federal court. Only Justices Stevens and Breyer dissented, voting to strike down the Texas plan as an invalid gerrymander. However, in striking down the one district where most Mexican Americans had been removed, the Court vote was 5–4, with Scalia and Thomas again opposing all federal court intervention, and Roberts and Alito saying that the creation of the new Latino majority district meant that the Latino vote was not impermissibly diluted under this plan. Nevertheless, Kennedy's majority decision prevailed and the state legislature must redistrict so as to guarantee the Latinos in that district equal participation in the political process.

Discussion Questions

1. How did the requirements of the U.S. Constitution for the apportionment of representatives lead to the important role of state districts?
2. What role does the nationwide census play in the process of redistricting?
3. Why is redistricting such a controversial process?
4. What was the Supreme Court's position on redistricting before the 1960s?
5. How did the Supreme Court's position on redistricting change during the 1960s?
6. What condition did the principle "one person, one vote" require for congressional and state legislative districts?
7. What is a majority-minority district and how is it created?
8. What are three ways in which partisan gerrymandering could occur?
9. What parts of the Constitution do racial and political gerrymanders violate?
10. What conditions are necessary to prove an unconstitutional racial gerrymander?
11. What conditions are necessary to prove an unconstitutional political gerrymander?
12. Why has it been easier to develop standards to judge racial gerrymanders than political gerrymanders?
13. What are the "traditional districting principles"?
14. How do proponents of giving redistricting responsibilities to independent commissions believe redistricting will become fairer?
15. What implications can the Supreme Court's decision in *Vieth v. Jubelirer* have on redistricting?

Class Activities

1. Have students choose which of the seven "traditional districting principles" they believe is the most important in assuring fairness in the redistricting process. Have them form groups according to the principle chosen and give a presentation defending their chosen principle.
2. Discuss the difficulty in creating a district that is both competitive and compact. Have the students form a group according to which condition they believe is more important in making a fair district. Hold a classroom debate between the two positions.
3. The Supreme Court still has not found an appropriate standard by which a partisan gerrymander can be judged and proven. Through class discussion and student ideas, try to formulate such a standard that the class thinks can fulfill this role.
4. The principle of "one person, one vote" has not met much criticism. Stage a debate on the fairness and practicality of this principle. Is population equality truly necessary across districts to attain greater fairness?
5. Present to the class a Supreme Court case involving a racial gerrymander. Have the class judge the case based on the evidence presented and write a decision citing provisions in the Constitution or in the Voting Rights Act. See if the class's decision matches that of the Supreme Court.

Suggestions for Further Reading

Backstrom, Charles, Samuel Krislov, and Leonard Robins. "Desperately Seeking Standards: The Court's Frustrating Attempts to Limit Political Gerrymandering." *Political Science & Politics* 39, no. 3 (2006): 409–15.

Forgette, Richard, and Glenn Platt. "Redistricting Principles and Incumbency Protection in the U.S. Congress." *Political Geography* 24, no. 8 (2005): 934–51.

Galderisi, Peter F., ed. *Redistricting in the New Millennium*. Lanham, MD: Lexington, 2005.

Marquart, Deanna, and Winston Harrington. "Reapportionment Reconsidered." *Journal of Policy Analysis and Management* 9, no. 4 (1990): 555–60.

Mignot, Jean-François. "Racial Redistricting in the United States: An Introduction to Supreme Court Case Law." *International Social Science Journal (NWISSJ)* 183 (2005): 143–51.

Rush, Mark E. "Gerrymandering: Out of the Political Thicket and into the Quagmire (Election Systems and Representative Democracy)." *Political Science & Politics* 27, no. 4 (1994): 682–86.

Helpful Websites

www.ncsl.org/programs/legman/elect/redist.htm. A comprehensive report compiled by the National Conference for State Legislatures Redistricting Task Force that details the provisions of redistricting law and its implementation throughout the 1990s. Up-to-date information on redistricting laws, developments, and news.

www.oyez.org. Overviews on redistricting cases brought before the Supreme Court.

www.senate.leg.state.mn.us/departments/scr/redist/red2000/red-tc.htm. Gives the contents of "Redistricting Law 2000," a project of the Redistricting Task Force of the National Conference for State Legislatures.

10

Elections

Case 10
Is the Electoral College the Best Way to Elect U.S. Presidents?

Case Snapshot

SINCE THE BIRTH OF THE REPUBLIC, the Electoral College has been the mechanism through which the United States has elected its presidents. In this system citizens do not directly elect the president; rather they employ electors to the College to determine the election. The original objective of this system was to protect smaller states from being misrepresented in a presidential election. Luther Martin, a small-state advocate who was also Maryland's attorney general, was the person who devised the Electoral College, and his plan carried the day because of the general distrust of democracy by the Framers. For the most part they represented the elite of the colonies and just did not think the masses were capable of complete self-governance. Direct election to the House of Representatives was as far as they were willing to take that idea. Therefore, they did not approve of direct election of the president as proposed by James Wilson from Pennsylvania. Under the Electoral College system each state is entitled to as many electors as it has representing it in the two houses of Congress. The District of Columbia also is given three electors due to the Twenty-third Amendment in 1961. The current number of electors is therefore 538, making 270 the magic number to win the presidency.

The political parties generally choose the slate of electors, who often are state and local politicians. Each state legislature determines which slate wins the election. Currently electors are popularly elected on a statewide, winner-take-all system (except for Nebraska and Maine, where they are elected by districts). Thus, when a presidential candidate carries the state's popular vote, all the electors for that candidate are victorious. There is no provision in the Constitution or federal law which requires electors to vote in accordance with the popular vote, but either by state law or by tradition there is seldom any deviation.

Despite its intent, the Electoral College has drawn controversy as at times it has produced election outcomes where a presidential candidate loses the popular vote but wins the electoral vote and thus the presidency. Should the Electoral College be reformed or perhaps even abolished? This question is highly debatable with many possible solutions. The options range from various formulas to protect the original intent of the Electoral College to the direct election of presidential candidates. Electoral reform is not completely new to the United States. The concept of direct election by popular vote found favor in the debate over the election of senators at the turn of the twentieth century, producing the Seventeenth Amendment to the Constitution in 1913.

It may be time now to take a hard look at the Electoral College system, especially after the election of 2000, where Vice President Al Gore won the popular vote but narrowly lost the state of Florida—and consequently the Electoral College vote—to George W. Bush. The winner of this bitterly contested election ultimately had to be determined by a politically divided Supreme Court. Is the Electoral College the best way to elect U.S. presidents? You decide!

Major Case Controversies

1. *In United States presidential elections, four candidates have won the office by winning the electoral vote while losing the popular vote:* John Quincy Adams in 1824, Rutherford Hayes in 1876, Benjamin Harrison in 1888, and George W. Bush in 2000. These represent some of the most controversial elections in the history of the United States. Despite losing the popular vote these candidates garnered a majority of the electoral vote.

2. *If no candidate wins the electoral vote (receiving at least 270 of 538 total votes at present), the election is thrown into the House of Representatives, where each state delegation casts one vote.* This practice has also not been without controversy. For example, in the 1824 election the House of Representatives chose the president because Article II of the Constitution as modified by the Twelfth Amendment gives it that power. That amendment was added because the 1800 election produced a tie for the presidency between Thomas Jefferson and Aaron Burr due to the original Constitution not mandating that there be separate ballots for president and vice president. The decision of the House was controversial because it did not award the presidency to the person who had garnered the most popular votes.

3. *In the 1876 election an Electoral Commission was created in order to decide how twenty disputed electoral votes would be counted.* It was controversial because the vote taken on each of the disputed votes was on a straight partisan basis. A "deal" seems to have been made wherein the Republican candidate (Rutherford Hayes) would be elected, with the understanding that he would withdraw the last of the U.S. military that was stationed in the South to enforce Reconstruction. This indeed did occur.

4. *The 2000 election was decided when the Supreme Court ordered an end to the recount of votes in some of the counties of one of our states (Florida).* It was controversial because the Court split along liberal-conservative lines.

5. *Third parties do not fare well in the Electoral College system.* For example, Ross Perot in 1992 won 19 percent of the popular vote but got no electoral votes due to the winner-take-all system whereby the winner of the popular vote in a state receives (with two exceptions) all that state's electoral votes.

6. *Under the "winner-take-all" system, many people in the country have their votes essentially nullified.* As an example, if one candidate receives 51 percent of the popular vote in a state, that person receives all the state's electoral votes, meaning that 49 percent of the popular vote translates into zero electoral votes. It effectively makes the 49 percent meaningless.

7. *Because the outcome of many elections hinges upon which candidate carries certain crucial states, there is disproportionate campaigning done in those states.* Candidates visit them time and time again, while they pay very few visits to the other states. It sends a message to the voters in those neglected states that they are not all that important, and it tells the voters in the crucial states that they are the key to the election.

Background of the Case

Over the years the Electoral College system often worked well, as intended. However, it has also revealed a number of serious flaws. Several elections are illustrative.

Presidential Election of 1824

After years of one-party rule in the United States under the Democratic-Republicans, the party fractured, producing four major candidates in the election: John Quincy Adams, Andrew Jackson, William Crawford, and Henry Clay. Despite Jackson's clearly gaining a plurality in both the popular and electoral vote, no one candidate gained a majority of either. The vote was thrown to the House of Representatives and, as per the Twelfth Amendment, only the top three candidates were eligible. This left out House Speaker Clay, who threw his support to Adams. In the first ballot in the House, Adams won with thirteen votes while Jackson received seven and Crawford received four. Adams became the sixth president of the United States. Allegations of a "corrupt bargain" were heard when he then appointed Clay secretary of state, the traditional stepping stone to the presidency. That same amendment provides for the Senate's choosing the vice president from the top two vote getters if there is no electoral vote majority. It only occurred in 1837 when Richard Johnson was chosen to be President Martin Van Buren's vice president.

Presidential Election of 1876

In this election Democrat Samuel Tilden defeated Republican Rutherford Hayes in the popular vote by nearly 250,000 votes and appeared to have carried the Electoral College. However, some Republicans noticed the closeness of the results in key states and decided to contest twenty electoral votes. One elector from Oregon was declared illegal and thrown out, while four votes in Florida, eight in Louisiana, and seven in South Carolina were disputed due to voter fraud. Facing a crisis, on January 29, 1877, an Electoral Commission was created through the Electoral Commission Act to settle the dispute. The fifteen-member commission included five Supreme Court justices and members from each of the parties in both houses (three Democrats and two Republicans from the House; three Republicans and two Democrats from the Senate). The commission, by an 8–7 vote, ultimately awarded all twenty disputed electoral votes to Hayes, swinging the election in his favor 185–184. This election was the second closest in U.S. history, with a margin of victory of only 889 popular votes in South Carolina. The election had significant policy consequences, because the Republicans agreed to curtail many Reconstruction efforts in the South in order to placate the Democrats for "losing" the presidency.

Presidential Election of 1888

This election pitted Democrat Grover Cleveland against Republican Benjamin Harrison. It must not be overlooked that the Prohibition Party fielded Clinton Bowen Fisk as its candidate and garnered nearly a quarter million popular votes. This strong third-party showing allowed Cleveland to win a plurality of the popular vote by almost 100,000 ballots. Despite this, the southern states that Cleveland carried did not yield a sufficient number of electoral votes. Harrison received 233 electoral votes from all the northern and western states, defeating Cleveland's 168. Regardless of the popular vote, Harrison won the election. For the third time in U.S. history a candidate who lost the popular vote ascended to its highest office.

Presidential Election of 2000

This election was controversial for many reasons. By a razor-thin margin of 539,897, Democrat Al Gore won the popular vote over Republican George W. Bush. On the evening of the election, some media outlets declared the wrong winner. The effect this had on voter turnout is not necessarily known, but problems with "butterfly" ballots in Palm Beach County, Florida (two leaves in book form, with chads to be punched out from the center), and with some African Americans who claimed they were turned away at the polls after being told they were not on voter registration lists, plus the closeness of the vote in that state led to a month of recounts and bitterness. In response to litigation in the Florida Supreme Court (*Palm Beach Canvassing Board v. Katherine Harris*), the Bush campaign filed suit at the federal level not to allow the extension of deadlines for the manual recount being conducted in Florida. In the Supreme Court case *Bush v. Gore*, the justices were concerned with the irregularity of standards in the county-by-county recounts, and the lack of a single judicial officer's oversight. All the voters in the state were not being treated the same way. In a 5–4 decision, the justices held that these incidents constituted a violation of the Equal Protection Clause of the Fourteenth Amendment to the Constitution, ending the recounts with Bush leading. George W. Bush was sworn in as the president despite losing the popular election by nearly one million votes. This election ended up being the closest in U.S. history with a margin of victory of only 537 votes in Florida.

Seven of the nine justices actually agreed with the equal protection argument, but only Chief Justice William Rehnquist and Justices Sandra Day O'Connor, Antonin Scalia, Anthony Kennedy, and Clarence Thomas voted to end the recounts. Rehnquist, Scalia, and Thomas wrote a joint concurring opinion stressing that the intent of the Florida legislature must prevail, and it had charged the Florida secretary of state, who had imposed a deadline for the ballots to be counted, with that responsibility. They also made the point that the Florida Supreme Court had ordered the recount to proceed, but the votes could not be counted in the four days following the decision to meet the safe harbor date necessary to meet various deadlines.

The dissenting justices were John Paul Stevens and Ruth Bader Ginsburg, who disagreed with the entire decision, and David Souter and Stephen Breyer, who agreed with the equal protection argument but disagreed with ending the recount. The dissenters said the decision disfranchised an unknown number of voters and was a federal assault on the Florida election procedures. They would have remanded the case to the Florida courts with instructions to establish uniform standards for the recounts. They also stressed the importance of dual sovereignty, which would result in deferring to the Florida Supreme Court. Also, the majority had said that an adequate recount was impractical, but the dissenters said that judgment could not be tested, due to ending the recount. Finally, they said that the Framers of the Constitution and Congress had sought to minimize the Court's role in resolving close presidential elections. Nevertheless, the decision was accepted by both sides and the election was over.

Electoral College Debate

The original purpose of the Electoral College was protecting the interests of smaller states. However, the debate over the Electoral College soon focused on the very foundation of the Constitution and the United States, because the concept of majority rule was undermined in those instances where a person won the popular vote but lost the electoral vote, and the votes of many people were negated due to the winner-take-all system. To understand the various policy proposals for possible change of the Electoral College system, it is useful to review basic arguments for and against this institution.

Points Critical of the Electoral College

Voter Inequality

Detractors of the Electoral College criticize the fact that within the system not all votes are equally weighted. Voters in smaller states may have a greater say in a presidential election because they have electoral votes disproportionate to their population. For example, according to 2000 census data, the combined voting-age population of the four least populous states (Alaska, North Dakota, Vermont, and Wyoming) plus the District of Columbia was nearly three million. Within the Electoral College, this "bloc of states" receives fifteen electoral votes. Yet New Jersey, with a population of nearly nine million, receives the same number of electoral votes, fifteen. As a result, this "bloc of states" receives 5 electoral votes for every million voters; New Jersey receives only 1.6 electoral votes for the same number of voters. Ultimately, a voter in New Jersey has less weight in a presidential election than a voter from Wyoming.

An argument can also be made that large states may wield a disproportionate influence on the Electoral College. The electoral votes of a large state, such as California, become very important, especially if the election is closely contested in that state. This gives the voters in that state an undue influence on the outcome of the election, since California has approximately one-fifth of the total electoral votes needed to capture the presidency. While the Electoral College clearly distorts votes being counted equally, it is arguable whether small states or large states benefit more from the system.

Under the current presidential campaign process, candidates tour the country attempting to appeal to the nation's voters. Despite the attempts of the Electoral College to protect smaller states from larger ones, campaigns do not focus on winning in less populated states. The bulk of the campaign usually focuses on "battleground" states that are closely contested by both parties. These are the states with large numbers of electoral votes where the outcome of the election is in doubt. This leads to an inequality of focus during the presidential campaign among the states. Because there are more small states than large ones, the variety of political views of the numerous small states make it difficult for them to combine their interests to enable them to overtake the larger states. The unequal value of a voter during the campaign and all the way to the ballot box is a clear disadvantage of the Electoral College system.

Popular and Electoral Vote Discrepancies

As we have seen, in four U.S. presidential elections the winner did not win the majority of the popular vote. The fact that a candidate can be elected president without winning the popular vote strikes some as a major flaw in the system. However, many proponents of the Electoral College believe the current system protects us from this very problem because it forces a candidate to garner votes from around the country. Yet it did occur in the presidential elections of 1824, 1876, 1888, and 2000. To detractors of the Electoral College this is one of the major concerns. The majority will of the people, therefore, can be ignored. In truth, there is *no* national popular vote in the U.S. It is very misleading to assume that by combining the state popular votes there will be an actual national popular vote. Therefore, truly quantifying the effect of a popular vote and its relation to the electoral vote is impossible, with far too many interfering variables.

The Problem with Swing States

Almost all states use the winner-take-all method when awarding electoral votes in a presidential election. Maine and Nebraska are the exceptions because these states split themselves into districts to determine its electors. Even with this alternative method, with few exceptions, seldom has a state split its electors. Because of the winner-take-all system, candidates campaign mainly in larger states where there is a tight race. They are considered as "swing states" because they can determine (swing) the outcome of the election. Despite the large populations in California and Texas, these states are usually predictable for one party or another, causing candidates at times to overlook extensive campaigning there. This, in turn, might affect voter participation when a person does not vote because their state is "safe" for a candidate. In addition there are some smaller states, such as Nevada, which may be winnable by both parties, yet yield few electoral votes, causing them at times to be ignored in campaigns. Large states, such as Florida, Ohio, and Pennsylvania, are winnable for both parties and have many electoral votes. These swing states are important to win in a presidential election, as seen in 2000 and 2004. Because of this, campaigns focus on these states and their voters, rarely paying heed to voters in smaller or "safe" states. Disproportionate campaigning may lead to a false popular mandate for a candidate.

Hindrance to Third Parties

Critics of the Electoral College contend that the winner-take-all method of allotting electors favors a two-party system. By awarding all electors to the plurality or majority winner, third parties may garner some popular support without receiving a single elector. For instance, Ross Perot, a candidate in the 1992 presidential election with no majority party affiliation, won almost 19 percent of the popular vote but received not a single electoral vote by not winning a plurality in any state. Because of the winner-take-all system a third-party candidate simply does not have a realistic chance at winning the presidency.

There have been exceptions. For example, in 1968, former governor of Alabama George Wallace carried five southern states as the American Independent Party candidate by running an anti–federal government campaign on the issue of federal intervention over civil rights policies. On the whole, however, third parties do not fare well in our Electoral College system.

Elections Decided by the House of Representatives

One of the possible outcomes of the Electoral College vote is that there is no winner. Currently, a candidate needs at least 270 electoral votes, and it is possible for no candidate to receive that amount. In this case, according to the Twelfth Amendment, the election is given to the House of Representatives where each state delegation has one vote to cast, regardless of the population of the state. In the event of the election being decided by the House, smaller states gain a greater advantage over the normal Electoral College system. This occurred in the 1824 presidential election, with the House of Representatives electing John Quincy Adams over the popular vote receiver, Andrew Jackson. If there is no president or vice president by the time of inauguration, the Speaker of the House of Representatives becomes acting president until Congress can select a proper candidate. With elections thrown into Congress the voter is completely disenfranchised and divorced from the selection of the president. Critics of the Electoral College contend that this possibility flies in the face of the idea of self-determination. When a voter has no say in the selection of the president, as happens in the case that no candidate wins a majority of the electoral vote, then that election is neither free nor fair and completely undemocratic.

Points in Support for the Electoral College

Allocation of a National Endorsement

Supporters of the Electoral College maintain that the original intent of the Electoral College helped solve the problem of a large nation with a scattered population electing a candidate for president. The Electoral College allows smaller states to be represented fairly. A system in which smaller states carry the same weight as larger states ultimately protects voters. In the Electoral College system a candidate must sustain popular support over a large part of the country. It is difficult to win a presidential election by focusing solely on large states and cities and this counters totally majoritarian rule. Through the Electoral College, every voter has the ability to vote for president with confidence that a true national mandate must be attained to win the election.

Protecting Federalism

The United States is a layered republic consisting of overlapping governing bodies. This union consists of states and a central government. By maintaining the Electoral College, the federalist aspect of the republic is preserved. With each state casting its electoral vote according to who carried that state, the will of the people coexists with the federal character enshrined in the Constitution. If the Electoral College were to be thrown out, then there is a danger that the United States will become a single immense, central government because the role of the states in determining the election would be negated. Under direct elections the importance of states is diminished, allowing candidates to pursue popularity only, instead of building a league of supporting states. The Electoral College is necessary to maintain the federal character of the United States.

Protecting Minority Groups

Minority groups must be protected in a presidential election in accordance with the Constitution. The Electoral College provides this protection by allowing minority groups to make a difference in an election. Almost all the states utilize a winner-take-all system of electors.

Minority groups, therefore, can provide a critical margin for a single candidate. The winner-take-all system, where the favored candidate receives all that state's electors, forces candidates to garner the support of certain interests and minority groups. If ignored, a minority group or special interest could destabilize a candidate's campaign. Without the Electoral College, candidates seeking pure majoritarian support would easily overlook minority groups.

Voter Turnout Discrepancies

The Electoral College system addresses various concerns with voter turnout. Many variables affect the turnout of voters in presidential elections. A large storm in any area of the country can push down the voter turnout of an affected state. States with senatorial or gubernatorial elections seem to push up voter turnout. In these cases the Electoral College mitigates the various turnouts in different states. Without the Electoral College the strength of a state's weight in the national vote would be in jeopardy due to uncontrolled variables such as weather conditions. The Electoral College protects states that may have a low voter turnout. Despite the lack of turnout, a state maintains a consistent number of electoral votes, preserving the state's representation in the national outcome. The Electoral College maintains consistency despite voter turnout irregularities among states.

Protection from Deceased or Inappropriate Candidates

The Electoral College is made up of electors, each having been chosen via the popular vote in their state. If a candidate dies or is otherwise found unsuitable before the Electoral College meets, the electors pick a new candidate, usually from the same party. This allows the nation to continue operating despite a volatile disruption in the election process. This worst-case scenario actually occurred in the presidential election of 1872. The election pitted the Republican incumbent Ulysses Grant against the Democratic candidate Horace Greeley. Unfortunately, Greeley died before the Electoral College could convene. The Democratic electors were thrown into turmoil, resulting in the electors splitting their votes among four different Democratic candidates. Despite the scramble, incumbent Grant won the election. Without the Electoral College, a death of a candidate or unsuitability of a candidate would throw the nation into chaotic disarray. The Electoral College provides a system that can account for these unlikely scenarios.

Policy Options

Possible reforms attempt to address many of the perceived problems associated with the Electoral College system. One of the problems to address is the possibility of a candidate winning a presidential election despite not attaining a popular majority. The winner-take-all system exacerbates this problem while leading to voter apathy when one party dominates a state. Another problem to address is the two-party system that the Electoral College seems to favor, hence hindering third parties. Many argue that the mere fact that the Electoral College is undemocratic warrants reform. From winning candidates who did not carry the popular vote to faithless electors, there have been many calls for possible reform of the Electoral College System.

1. *Direct elections.* Within this system, each voter casts his or her vote for one candidate. The candidate who gains the majority of votes wins the election. This upholds the democratic

spirit of all voters having equal say. One of the disadvantages of this system is that it would require an amendment to the Constitution. In the event that no candidate receives a majority, the election would be thrown to the House of Representatives, where partisan representatives would decide the election. Another form of direct election could use plurality rather than a majority to determine a winner in the election. This does not solve the major problem of a winning candidate not gaining a popular mandate. Other modifications of this plan include a runoff election after the popular election. This runoff would be between the two highest-vote-receiving candidates. This presidential election system is used, for example, in France. While a runoff election has its benefits there are some drawbacks. A disadvantage of this model is the voter turnout discrepancy between the original vote and the runoff. The runoff election could have less voter turnout than the original election, producing a winning candidate with a false mandate. For any of these modifications to be implemented a constitutional amendment would be needed, requiring two-thirds approval in each house of Congress and ratification in three-fourths of the states.

2. *Preferential voting.* Preferential voting is a system in which a voter ranks the candidates on a ballot from most favorable to least favorable. Preferential voting in a popular election could alleviate some of the problems associated with the current Electoral College system without requiring a constitutional amendment. Instead of a person only voting for one candidate, a voter has the opportunity to choose from a list of candidates they approve. Many call this an instant runoff system. The way the ballot would work is that voters would rank their top three candidates, or more. If their first choice does not win, their vote is transferred to their second most favorable candidate. The candidate with the fewest first choice votes is eliminated, creating the so-called instant runoff. This instant runoff would continue until a candidate gains a majority. The ballot could consist of a voter's top three choices, or may be more complicated in asking for four or five candidates. This system is already in use in Australia, New Zealand, and Ireland with some variation.

3. *The Borda system.* Another form of this instant runoff system in a popular election is the Borda system. In this variant candidates are given preferential rankings with point values. For instance, if there are three preferential rankings, voters will rank their favorite candidate first with three points, their next favorite second with two points, and their least favorite with one point. The candidate who gains the most points wins the election. Whether with the Borda system, or plain ranking, the drawback of preferential popular voting is the fact that constituents can manipulate the vote by disproportionately ranking fringe candidates above their rival party in a two-party system. This could produce fringe candidates winning elections in partisan battles, leaving a winner without a real popular mandate. In tough partisan contests a third party could take the election without true popular support. Yet another disadvantage to preferential voting is the complicating of the ballot. The voting process would be more involved, let alone the vote-counting system needed to tabulate results. With current problems with electronic voting and its accuracy and reliability, a technological advancement would be needed to effectively implement this system. Since the Constitution delegates to the states the power to decide voting systems, preferential popular vote would not require a constitutional amendment.

4. *Approval-based voting.* This system is similar to the preferential voting system, but simpler. A voter does not rank candidates, but merely votes "yes" if they could tolerate that candidate, and "no" if not. Instead of being locked into ranking candidates, constituents can vote for as many or as few candidates as they wish. The candidate who gains the most

"yes" votes would win the popular election. The advantages of this system are similar to preferential voting in that it could eliminate the bias against third parties in the Electoral College system. However, the winner-take-all aspect of states in the Electoral College, approval-based voting, and preferential voting for that matter, may not solve any problems. A clear disadvantage of the approval-based voting system is the problem with mediocre candidates. Bland candidates that seem neither to be exceptional or repulsive may win an election because many voters voted "yes" on their tolerability. This could also produce a false mandate, and allow a truly unpopular candidate to ascend to the presidency.

5. *National bonus plan.* Noted historian Arthur Schlesinger Jr. originally introduced the national bonus plan that attempts to solve the problem of a candidate winning the popular election but losing the electoral vote as happened in the 2000 presidential election. Schlesinger's plan maintains the legitimacy of the Electoral College but awards a bonus of electoral votes to the popular vote winner. For the winner of the popular election, a national bonus of 102 electoral votes is awarded, consisting of two electoral votes from each state and two electoral votes from the District of Columbia. In this way it is nearly impossible for the winner of the popular vote to lose the electoral vote. This plan does not desert the Electoral College system but compensates for the uneven distribution of weight within the College. This plan does not seem to assist third parties in gaining strength, but leaves their role as spoilers intact. Yet, it does alleviate voter apathy in uncontested states by giving a voter the initiative to vote in the popular election to affect the national bonus award of 102 electors. For instance, this gives Republicans in California and Democrats in Texas incentive to vote, despite the probability of their state's being "locked up" by the opposing party.

6. *Proportional electoral vote.* This system has been in practice in Maine and Nebraska for some time, and recently has been brought to the forefront in Colorado. The proportional electoral vote system eliminates the entrenched winner-take-all system of distributing electors in a state. If a candidate were to lose a state while gaining 30 percent of the popular vote there, that candidate would be awarded 30 percent of the electors, rather than no electors under the winner-take-all system. This plan would encourage voter turnout and change the presidential campaigning dynamic. With all states splitting their electors, all constituents would live in battleground states. One of the drawbacks of this system is apportioning partial electors. If the apportionment is done by percentage vote, rounding off electors will lead to inaccuracies. Another problem may be encountered if not all states adopt proportional vote. For example, imagine if Texas adopted proportional vote and California maintained winner-take-all. Undoubtedly, problems would ensue.

7. *National popular vote.* The most current idea is one that would involve interstate compacts, that is, states making agreements with each other. The agreement would be that whoever wins the national vote will receive all the electoral votes of each state in the compact, even if that person did not win that state. The good point is that it could be done without amending the Constitution. In fact the California legislature passed such a bill in 2006, but Governor Arnold Schwarzenegger vetoed it. It would have taken effect only if states with a combined total of 270 electoral votes (the number required to win the presidency) agreed to the same process. However, it is doubtful that many states will want to award their electoral votes to someone who did not win their popular vote, and therefore it is unlikely that this proposal will ever come to fruition.

Conclusion

Enshrined in the Constitution, the Electoral College is an institution that draws critical debate among scholars today. For many reasons, critics of the Electoral College have suggested policies of reform that adjust the system, or even call for its complete elimination. The way in which a nation chooses its leaders is of the utmost importance.

Because of the Electoral College, four presidential races in the history of the United States have elected a candidate who did not win a majority of the popular votes. These elections seem to point to the shortcomings of the Electoral College. Supporters of the College contend that these elections are insignificant compared to the benefits of the status quo and the many successful elections the College has produced. Detractors suggest that the College is antiquated, undemocratic, and in need of reform, to guarantee that every citizen's vote carries the same weight.

Should the Electoral College be reformed? Should it be preserved? Or, should the Electoral College be eliminated altogether? These questions require more than a one-word answer. Reform could maintain the original intent of the Electoral College as set forth in the Constitution. Regardless, if the Electoral College is to be reformed, it may require a combination of policy reforms. Some policy reform options may require a Constitutional amendment, while others may be implemented at the state level. Whether the Electoral College is to be reformed or not, the costs and benefits need to be crucially examined, as elections—and especially those for president—are the core of the American Republic.

Discussion Questions

1. If the two-party system were done away with, how would this affect the Electoral College? Would this make the system more fair and balanced?
2. What is the intent of the Electoral College in presidential elections?
3. How does the Electoral College affect the presidential election campaign process?
4. How would a critic of the Electoral College respond to the argument that the College makes certain that a candidate attains a true national endorsement to win the presidency?
5. How would a proponent of the Electoral College respond to the argument that the College hinders third-party development?
6. What are the disadvantages of the policy option of direct elections for president?
7. How would preferential voting help third-party candidates?
8. In what way could approval-based voting and preferential voting produce fringe or mediocre candidates?
9. How could the national bonus plan policy option change voter turnout in the United States?
10. What are the disadvantages of the winner-take-all system, and would proportional electoral voting alleviate those problems?

Class Activities

1. Split the class into five groups with each group responsible for a different policy option. After giving the groups time to prepare, begin to discuss the costs and benefits of each

system. Be sure to consider opposing points of view when presenting your reform option. Also, provide feedback through debate of each policy option.

2. Divide students among the two opposing views concerning whether or not the Electoral College should be reformed. Regardless of personal viewpoints, be prepared to defend the viewpoint you have been assigned. Through a process of debate, present arguments defending your viewpoint.

Suggestions for Further Reading

Bennett, Robert W. *Taming the Electoral College.* Palo Alto, CA: Stanford University Press, 2006.

Berthoud, John E. "The Electoral Lock Thesis: The Weighting Bias Component." *Political Science & Politics* 30, no. 2 (June 1997): 189–93.

Edwards, George C. III. *Why the Electoral College is Bad for America.* New Haven, CT: Yale University Press, 2004.

Gregg, Gary L. II, et al. *Securing Democracy: Why We Have an Electoral College.* Brentwood, TN: ISI, 2001.

Hardaway, Robert M. *The Electoral College and the Constitution: The Case for Preserving Federalism.* Westport, CT: Praeger, 1994.

Parris, Judith H., and Wallace S. Sayre. *Voting for President: The Electoral College and the American Political System.* Washington, DC: Brookings, 1970.

Polsby, Nelson, and Aaron Wildavsky. *Presidential Elections: Strategies and Structures of American Politics.* 11th ed. Lanham, MD: Rowman & Littlefield, 2004.

Ross, Tara. *Enlightened Democracy: The Case for the Electoral College.* Torrance, CA: World Ahead, 2004.

Helpful Websites

www.archives.gov. Website for the National Archives.

www.fairvote.org. Website for the Center for Voting and Democracy.

www.fec.gov. Website for the Federal Election Commission.

www.library.louisville.edu/government/subjects/elections/electoral.html. This website of Louisville University contains a section on the Electoral College.

www.midwestdemocracy.org. Website for the Midwest Democracy Center.

www.votepair.org. Website for Pair the Vote.

11

Congress

Case 11
Should the Senate Continue the Practice of the Filibuster?

Case Snapshot

UNDER THE U.S. CONSTITUTION THE SENATE has the authority to confirm presidential nominations. Specifically, Article II of the Constitution gives the president the authority to nominate ambassadors, other public ministers and consuls, judges of the Supreme Court, and all other officers of the United States with the advice and consent of the Senate. In today's politically divided environment, the filibuster is used as a means to level the playing field and give the minority a means of power.

The filibuster is one of the Senate's unique features. Throughout Senate history, the filibuster has been a source of controversy. In recent years, the future of the filibuster has become uncertain. The use of the filibuster has increased immensely in the last several decades. It is used to delay, modify, or prevent legislation (e.g., the southern senators used it extensively in opposition to civil rights bills) and it is used to try to prevent presidential nominations, especially federal judges, from being confirmed. For this latter reason, during the 108th (2003–2005) and 109th (2005–2007) Congresses, the battle between the Republican majority and the Democratic minority was heated as the Democrats continuously threatened to block President George W. Bush's judicial nominations. In response, Senate Majority Leader Bill Frist (R-TN) began a campaign for the "nuclear option," in which a simple majority vote rather than sixty votes could stop this type of filibuster, starting the latest controversy over the future of the filibuster. Should the Senate continue the practice of the filibuster? You decide!

Major Case Controversies

1. *The filibuster is not found directly in the U.S. Constitution.* However, the practice derives from the fact that the Consitution allows each House to set its own rules. From the beginning of Congress in 1789, both the Senate and the House of Representatives had the option of the filibuster. As the House grew in size, rules limited debate. However, in the much smaller Senate, the filibuster remained. The Founding Fathers envisioned the Senate as a more deliberative body than the House because, since it was chosen by state legislatures rather than by popular vote, it would serve to curb the excesses of popular government.

2. *In 1841, a Democratic minority attempted to block a bill initiated by Senator Henry Clay (Whig-KY).* In response, Senator Clay threatened to change Senate rules to allow the majority party to close debate. Senator Clay's threatened rules change was thrown out as an attempt to limit the Senate's right to debate.

3. *In 1872, Vice President Schuyler Colfax ruled that "under the practice of the Senate the presiding officer could not restrain a Senator in remarks which the Senator considers pertinent to the pending issue."*

4. *The attempt to end filibuster debate continued into the 1900s. In 1917, Senate Rule XXII was established.* Rule XXII, known as the cloture rule, allowed senators to end debate with a two-thirds majority vote. However, even with the new cloture rule, obtaining a two-thirds vote to overcome a filibuster was extremely problematic.

5. *Throughout the middle of the twentieth century, the filibuster was used by southern senators to consistently block civil rights legislation.* In response, in 1975, the Senate changed its rules on cloture, requiring only three-fifths of the Senate (sixty members) to limit debate.

6. *In recent years, the Republican majority in the Senate has threatened to destroy the filibuster.* The "nuclear option" would change the current Senate rules to allow for straight majority voting on judicial nominations. The debate over the change of Senate rules caused concern in both the Senate and throughout the country.

7. *The underlying theme is the relationship of the filibuster to democracy: the issue of minority rights or impact.* Should the minority have the right to paralyze the Senate? Is that how democracy should work? Is the filibuster important so that the minority can add input to a bill? Does the filibuster waste the limited time of the Senate? You decide!

Background of the Case

Early Debates over the Filibuster

The term "filibuster" has been traced to several variations of the term for pirates; for example, it comes from a Dutch word meaning "pirate," and from the Spanish word "*filibustero*," which was a mercenary who tried to destabilize the government. In fact, the latter has been used by Senator Orrin Hatch (R-UT) as a point in the argument for making it easier to end filibusters of judicial nominees, as he and others feel the tactic hampers rather than protects the democratic process. The filibuster was first used in the U.S. Senate in the early nineteenth century in order to prevent votes from reaching the Senate floor. Filibuster is defined as the use of extreme dilatory tactics in an attempt to delay or prevent action in a legislative assembly. It is a time-delaying tactic associated with the Senate and used by a minority in an effort to prevent a vote on bill or an amendment that probably would pass if voted on directly. The most common method is to take advantage of the Senate's rules permitting unlimited debate, but other forms of parliamentary maneuvering may be used. The filibuster was not a major issue until World War I but it has been contentious since then. The stricter rules of the House of Representatives make filibusters more difficult, but delaying tactics are employed occasionally through other procedural devices. The word "filibuster" was first used to describe efforts to hold the Senate floor in order to prevent action on a bill.

The House of Representatives used to have its own version of filibustering, or using dilatory tactics, through the disappearing quorum in the nineteenth century (members would simply not answer to their names during roll call). Those tactics were abolished by Speaker Thomas "Czar" Reed (R-ME) in the late nineteenth century (he would count them toward the quorum even if they did not answer to their names). When the Democrats took control of the House they at first reintroduced dilatory tactics, but found them so frustrating they adopted Reed's rules also. Ever since the House has had few means of extending debate.

Throughout much of the nineteenth century, the filibuster was not a main concern in the Senate. At the time, the smaller Senate did not have a heavy workload and the filibuster was not seen as a means to stop legislation. With a smaller number of senators, it was easier to compromise. For example, in 1841, a Democratic minority attempted to filibuster a bank bill initiated by Senator Henry Clay. Senator Clay was angered by the threat of the filibuster and in turn attempted to change Senate rules, allowing the majority party to limit debate. At the time, the Senate saw it as a way to limit debate, a key aspect of the structure of the Senate.

The use of the filibuster without restrictions remained intact until 1917. Then, at the request of President Woodrow Wilson, the Senate established Rule XXII, also known as cloture. This rule allowed senators to end debate with a two-thirds majority. The cloture rule gave senators a formal procedure to end filibusters. A motion of cloture can be applied to any measure before the Senate, including proposals to change Senate rules. Once cloture is approved, debate in the Senate is limited, granting each senator one hour, but no more than a total of thirty hours.

The Senate had been prompted by Wilson to pass a rule limiting debate after a filibuster killed a bill that would have allowed arms on U.S. merchant ships to deter attacks by German submarines during World War I. The new cloture rule was first put to the test just two years later, when the Senate invoked cloture to end a filibuster against the Treaty of Versailles.

Over the next several decades, the Senate attempted to invoke cloture on a number of occasions. However, even with the cloture rule, it remained extremely difficult to end a filibuster. Obtaining a two-thirds vote in the Senate basically meant that two-thirds of the Senate would need to be in favor of the bill. In the decades following the creation of Rule XXII, cloture was invoked an average of two to four times per Congress.

During the 1930s, Senator Huey Long (D-LA) used the filibuster against several bills he thought worked against the common man (shades of actor Jimmy Stewart in the 1939 movie *Mr. Smith Goes to Washington*). Senator Long would filibuster by reciting Shakespeare and reading recipes. Throughout the history of the filibuster, senators have been known to exercise their right to filibuster on the Senate floor.

During the 1950s and 1960s, civil rights legislation was on the congressional agenda. In 1957, Senator Strom Thurmond, then a Democrat from South Carolina, set the filibuster record. Senator Thurmond spent twenty-four hours and eighteen minutes speaking against the 1957 Civil Rights Bill. Yet another filibuster against civil rights became one of the most famous filibusters in history. A debate over the Civil Rights Act of 1964 lasted fifty-seven days before cloture was invoked.

Once civil rights legislation cleared Congress, the use of the filibuster began to increase. According to Walter J. Oleszek, a congressional scholar, the increase in the filibuster has been attributed to several factors. First, most "freshman" or new senators prefer to pursue their own agendas regardless of the problems this may cause in the Senate. Another reason for increased filibustering is that filibusters have enhanced potency in an organization that is workload-packed and deadline-driven. Time is a very precious commodity in the Senate and any threat or use of a filibuster gives senators leverage. In addition, Oleszek attributes the lack of internal incentives that at one time fostered deference to seniority and party leaders to the increased use of the filibuster. Finally, partisanship has contributed to the gridlock and stalemate in the Senate.

In 1975, senators sought to change the Senate rules. Senators wanted to make it easier to invoke cloture, but were also worried that lowering the required number of votes would make it easier to change the Senate rules. As a compromise, the Senate changed Rule XXII to allow a three-fifths majority to invoke cloture on all matters except future rules changes, including changes in the cloture rule, which require a two-thirds vote. Following the new rule, only sixty votes were necessary to overrule a filibuster. However, although easier than sixty-seven votes, cloture has remained difficult to invoke.

The Increasing Use of the Filibuster and the Senate's Efforts to Change the Rule

In the last decade, the use of the filibuster has increased substantially. For example, during the 1960s, there were on average only 5.2 cloture votes per Congress. In just the 108th Congress, there were fifty cloture votes. Senators have begun to use the filibuster as a tactical device to achieve goals more frequently during the last several years. An interesting event in recent Congresses is the increase in the number of cloture petitions filed on the majority leader's motion to bring legislation to the floor, thereby enabling the majority to act on its agenda. In a politically divided country, senators see the filibuster as a tool for compromise. Obtaining the necessary sixty votes for cloture in a politically divided Senate can be very difficult and even the threat of a filibuster can mean the demise of a bill.

Another reason why filibustering has become more prevalent is that ever since the Republicans took control of Congress after the 1994 elections, they have often used the Conference Committee (members of each house meet to work out a compromise if each house has passed a different version of the same bill) as a partisan device to essentially devise new legislation. The Democrats, most notably during the debate over the Medicare Prescription Drug Benefit bill in 2003, have been ignored or actually excluded from the Conference Committee's deliberations, therefore letting them have no impact in shaping the final bill. Thus in the Senate the only way for them to make their voice heard is through the use of the filibuster.

After the election of President George W. Bush, a political divide in the country created serious gridlock in the Senate between the Republicans and the Democrats. After the Democrats had successfully filibustered a number of the president's judicial nominees, frustration among Senate Republicans increased. President Bush had a confirmation rate of 67 percent, the lowest in modern times. This frustration led to a Republican desire to change the filibuster in the judicial nomination process. It should be noted that partisan ideologues often make strong demands on the president to appoint persons who hold their beliefs to the judiciary. While Democratic President Bill Clinton consulted Republicans when he appointed Justices Ruth Bader Ginsburg and Stephen Breyer to the Supreme Court, Republican President George W. Bush felt he had to listen to his conservative base more than to Democrats when he made his appointments. Hence, among the reasons for President Bush's withdrawal of the nomination of Harriet Miers was pressure from conservatives who believed that she was not conservative enough.

The Senate Republicans decided to initiate hearings on the constitutionality of the filibuster for judicial nominees. Ironically, it was this group along with some southern Democrats who successfully used the filibuster in 1968 to prevent President Lyndon B. Johnson from elevating Supreme Court Associate Justice Abe Fortas to the position of Chief Justice, and that ushered in the modern era of fighting about judicial candidates. In 2003, Senate Republicans spent thirty hours in an around-the-clock debate on the nominations process. During these hearings, Senate Majority Leader Bill Frist sponsored a resolution to bypass Rule XXII to change Senate rules for judicial nominees. The resolution would have changed the rule to sixty votes required on the first vote, fifty-seven votes on the second, fifty-four on the third vote, and a simple fifty-one votes on the last one. Senator Frist's plan would have given the majority party power over judicial nominees. Nothing changed as a result of the hearings.

In 2004, President George W. Bush was reelected and resubmitted several of his judicial nominees that were filibustered during his first term, reigniting the issue with the filibuster as the Senate Democrats threatened once again to filibuster the nominations. In response, President Bush granted a nominee that had previously been subject to a filibuster, a recess nomination. The recess nomination allowed the president to put his judicial nominee in office, at least until the end of the next Senate session. However, the nomination created a stir among Senate Democrats.

As the Democrats' threat to filibuster continued, in May 2005, Senator Frist once again began campaigning for change, arguing for the use of the "nuclear option." Called the nuclear option because it would mean danger for the Senate, it was later called the constitutional or majority rule by Republicans. Republicans argued that filibusters imposed an unconstitutional super-majority requirement on judicial confirmations. As a result of the problems the Republicans faced confirming judicial nominees, they began to argue for straight majority voting on judicial nominees.

More specifically, Senator Frist planned to ask Vice President Dick Cheney, president of the Senate, to change the rules so that there would be no filibustering of judicial nominations. His plan was to make filibustering judicial nominations out of order. The nuclear option would occur in a series of steps designed to bypass Rule XXII to change Senate rules:

1. The Senate moves to vote on a controversial nominee.
2. At least forty-one senators call for a filibuster.
3. Senate Majority Leader Bill Frist raises a point of order stating that debate has gone on long enough and that a vote must be taken within a certain time frame.
4. As presiding officer, Vice President Cheney sustains the point of order.
5. A Democratic senator appeals the decision.
6. A Republican senator moves to table the motion on the floor.
7. The vote to table the appeal is procedural and cannot be subjected to a filibuster. This vote only requires a majority vote.
8 With debate ended, the Senate would vote on the nominee requiring only a majority of those voting.

Senator Frist spent the next several weeks debating with Democratic leader Senator Harry Reid (D-NV). Senator Frist suggested limits on the amount of time spent on filibustering judicial nominees. As an example, he suggested a one-hundred-hour limit on the filibustering of judicial nominees. Senator Reid disagreed, arguing that there should be no limit on the filibuster. Any limit would invalidate the filibuster.

The debate continued, Senator Frist argued that the use of the filibuster was effective in legislative matters, but ineffective for judicial matters because legislation could be changed, but a person could not. He also argued that filibustering judicial nominees affected all three branches of government.

In response, the Democrats argued that the Constitution authorizes each chamber to "determine the rules of its proceedings." The Democrats reiterated that the current procedure establishes a sixty-vote requirement under Rule XXII. If cloture is invoked, then senators have the right to confirm judges by majority vote.

One day before a vote on the nuclear option was scheduled to take place, a group of seven Democrats and seven Republicans met to work out another solution. The Democrats agreed not to filibuster the remaining three nominees, and the Republicans agreed not to support the vote on the nuclear option the next day. This bipartisan agreement, in effect, killed the bill.

As an example of how partisan our country has become, those fourteen moderate senators took some criticism from extremists from their own parties because of their compromise agreement.

The idea or even thought of the demise or change of the filibuster for judicial nominations created a firestorm in the country. The media produced stories on the filibuster with everyone having an opinion on whether or not the filibuster should remain in the Senate. Once the media were deeply involved, the Senate began to feel pressured by their constituents to act in a series of ways.

The Debate over the Filibuster

The Argument against Changing the Current Senate Rules

Blocking judicial nominees has been a part of the U.S. Senate since the very beginning. In fact, George Washington's nomination of John Rutledge to be Chief Justice of the United States was rejected by the Senate. This example shows that from the very beginning the U.S. Senate did not want to be seen as a rubber stamp for the president. The Senate sent a message to future presidents that it has an equal responsibility in the nomination process and that it intended to exercise that responsibility. By simply requiring a majority, the Senate would be almost left out of the nomination process, particularly the minority. One of the biggest arguments for keeping Senate rules intact is that the Constitution grants the entire Senate the right to confirm nominations—not just the majority party.

More specifically, at the Constitutional Convention, a compromise had been reached to give both the president and the Senate a hand in the nomination process. Those who defend the filibuster point out that one of the dominant themes during the Constitutional Convention was protecting the rights of the minority. Thus the filibuster is a tactic that protects the minority.

Scholars also argue that preserving the filibuster in judicial nominations is important in protecting against ideology as the prime factor in selecting the nominee. The filibuster prevents the president from nominating a friend of the party when both the president and the majority party are the same. It is argued that the independence of the judicial branch from the other two branches is necessary to the success of the government. The filibuster serves as an effective means of ensuring that party is not the only credential for confirming appointments.

In addition, there is no term limit on judicial appointments; they are made for life. The average tenure of a federal judge is twenty-four years. It can then be argued that because the appointment is for life, all confirmation options should be left available to the Senate. By discontinuing the filibuster, the majority party is left to decide the fate of judicial nominees, which can be problematic for the minority if as mentioned both the president and the majority are from the same party.

Yet another argument for the filibuster is that it serves as a means for the minority to be heard. Without the filibuster, the minority would have no way to have its voice heard. The argument is that the filibuster protects minority rights. Regardless of party, the minority should be given a means of power.

There are numerous arguments for keeping the filibuster. A major one is that it protects the minority party in the Senate. Specifically, the filibuster has been used effectively on numerous occasions to block both legislation and nominations that could have been detrimental to the future of the United States.

The Argument for Changing the Current Senate Rules

There are also several arguments for changing the current filibuster rules. One of the biggest is that a filibuster—or even the mere threat of a filibuster—can kill a nomination. Senators are concerned about time, which is very valuable. Time is the reason that even the threat of a filibuster can cause the defeat of a nomination. The committee process of drafting bills is tedious and takes time. For this reason, any time wasted on judicial nomination filibusters is time that could be used for making America a better place. Allowing a majority vote on judicial nominations would save time.

Scholars who are in favor of getting rid of the filibuster also cite major principles of the Founding Fathers. A common criticism of the filibuster is that it goes against the democratic foundation of the country. However, other scholars also point out that the Framers did not agree on granting the Senate the power to advise and consent to nominations.

Filibusters also create and maintain gridlock in the Senate. Gridlock occurs as a result of partisanship. It can be alleviated by an election that changes the voting pattern in Congress, or by more bipartisan compromise. Gridlock prevents the Senate from moving forward.

Policy Options

1. *Do nothing.* The Senate could elect to keep its current rules intact. A change would require either unleashing the nuclear option, creating havoc in the Senate, or obtaining a two-thirds majority, highly unlikely in a politically separated nation. By doing nothing, the filibuster will continue to give the minority the ability to have some power in the Senate.
2. *Vote to change Senate Rule XXII.* Although difficult to achieve, the Senate has the option to change the rules. By obtaining a two-thirds majority, the Senate would be able to change the cloture rule and only require a majority vote to overcome filibusters. This option would be very difficult to achieve because, as noted previously, it would require sixty-seven votes. The minority party is unlikely to vote with the majority to vote for a change that takes away one of its only methods of influence.
3. *The nuclear option.* Senator Frist laid out the framework for the nuclear option, also known as the constitutional or majority rule. The nuclear option would make filibustering judicial nominations out of order by having the president of the Senate change the rules so that there would be no filibustering of judicial nominations. The nuclear option would

allow the Senate to change the current rule without obtaining the two-thirds majority. The problem with this option is the possible chaos that it would create in Congress. The minority party could argue that the change violates the spirit of the Constitution by stopping debate.

Conclusion

The filibuster is an intriguing tool used in the Senate that has arguably served an extremely useful purpose on many occasions. Throughout its history, debate rules of the Senate have changed, adding in particular the cloture rule to allow for a means of stopping a filibuster. They may change many more times in the future.

The filibuster has been used most frequently in the past several decades and most recently to block President George W. Bush's judicial nominations. In response, Senate Majority Leader Bill Frist attempted to unleash the nuclear option, causing a stir among the Senate and the nation out of fear of what might result from such a dramatic change to Senate rules. There are a number of arguments for changing Senate rules to either keep the current rule intact or make filibustering judicial nominees out of order.

The future of the filibuster is uncertain, especially in an era of partisanship. Both parties have used the filibuster to block judicial nominees and neither party wants to see a chaotic disruption in the Senate over the filibuster as a result of the nuclear option. It is questionable if the nuclear option is in the future of the Senate, but in the foreseeable future the filibuster remains controversial.

Discussion Questions

1. How was the filibuster used by senators in the nineteenth century and why was Rule XXII not passed until 1900?
2. How has the cloture rule changed throughout the history of the filibuster in the Senate?
3. What are some arguments for the increased use of the filibuster in the last several decades?
4. How was the filibuster issue decided in the debates over President George W. Bush's judicial nominations?
5. How would the use of the nuclear option affect the future of the Senate?
6. Should the filibuster still be allowed to be used for the purpose of delaying, modifying, or preventing legislation?
7. Can you provide another argument against the filibuster?
8. Is the filibuster a wise procedure for our democracy?

Class Activities

1. Have a class debate over the pro and con arguments of using the nuclear option to change the Senate rules.
2. Have a class discussion on how the Senate may be able to change Rule XXII to remove the option of the filibuster for judicial nominations. The discussion should include how various obstacles need to be overcome to achieve a two-thirds majority.

Suggestions for Further Reading

Alter, Alison B., and Leslie Moscow McGranahan. "Reexamining the Filibuster and Proposal Powers in the Senate." *Legislative Studies Quarterly* 25, no. 2 (May 2000) 259–84.

Beth, Richard S., and Stanley Bach. "Filibusters and Cloture in the Senate." 28 March 2003, at www.senate .gov/reference/resources/pdf/RL30360.pdf .

Binder, Sarah A. *Minority Rights, Majority Rules.* New York: Cambridge University Press, 1997.

Davidson, Roger H., and Walter J. Oleszek. *Congress and Its Members.* 10th ed. Washington, DC: Congressional Quarterly, 2006.

Fisk, Catherine, and Erwin Chemerinsky. "The Filibuster." *Stanford Law Review* 49, no. 2 (1997): 181–254.

Gill, Kathy. "U.S. Senate: Filibuster." At http://uspolitics.about.com/od/usgovernment/i/filibuster.htm.

May, Robert E. *Manifest Destiny's Underworld: Filibustering in Antebellum America.* Chapel Hill: University of North Carolina Press, 2002.

Oleszek, Walter J. *Congressional Procedures and the Policy Process.* 6th ed. Washington, DC: Congressional Quarterly, 2004.

United States Senate. "Filibuster and Cloture." At www.senate.gov/artandhistory/history/common/briefing/ Filibuster_Cloture.htm.

Wawro, Gregory, and Eric Schickler. *Filibuster: Obstruction and Lawmaking in the U.S. Senate.* Princeton, NJ: Princeton University Press, 2006.

Helpful Website

www.senate.gov/artandhistory/history/common/briefing/Filibuster_Cloture.htm. This website gives a good synopsis of the history and use of the filibuster and cloture.

12

The Presidency

Case 12

How Limited Should Presidential Power Be in Wartime?

Case Snapshot

ALTHOUGH THE CONSTITUTION GIVES CONGRESS the power to declare war, it has not done so since World War II in 1941. In fact, Congress has declared war only four other times: the War of 1812 against England; the Mexican War in 1846; the Spanish-American War in 1898; and World War I in 1917. The Constitution gives the president the power to fight, utilizing any and all resources that Congress authorizes. The president is expected to use this power to protect the nation and its people. However, in the past, presidents such as Woodrow Wilson, Franklin D. Roosevelt, Lyndon B. Johnson, and Richard M. Nixon expanded this power, which ultimately divided the opinion of the country and put the United States at more risk for future extension of presidential power during wartime. One reason presidents have been able to do this is because the president is, according to the Constitution, commander in chief of the armed forces, meaning the military is under his authority. The United States has continuously been preoccupied with the problem of defining and confining executive power. Particularly in wartime, the government needs to be decisive about the authority that the president holds. The foremost danger of this would be arbitrary power.

Many believe that President George W. Bush is misusing this power after declaring the Global War on Terror. On the evening of September 11, 2001, the White House proposed that Congress sanction the use of military force to "deter and pre-empt any future acts of terrorism or aggression against the United States." Although Congress believed this language was too broad, it nevertheless authorized, on September 14, 2001, "all necessary and appropriate force against those nations, organizations or persons the president determines planned, authorized, committed or aided the attacks of September 11, 2001." With this resolution, called the Authorization for Use of Military Force (AUMF), Congress denied the president the more extensive power he sought and asserted that his authority would be used only against Osama bin Laden and al Qaeda. However, following the 9/11 attacks on the United States and the subsequent strikes on London, Madrid, Bali, and Baghdad, President Bush contended that the War on Terror provided him with enough reason to establish a domestic surveillance program within the United States, along with the formation of new rules and regulations surrounding the enemy combatant detainees within the United States and abroad, including the constitutional-legal question whether the U.S. Naval Base at Guantanamo Bay, Cuba, is under U.S. constitutional jurisdiction. Has President Bush abused his wartime presidential power? You decide!

Major Case Controversies

1. *The United States Constitution gives the president the power to engage in armed conflict and to fight with any and all resources Congress authorizes.*
2. *The War Powers Act of 1973 limits the power of the president of the United States to engage in or wage armed conflict for longer than sixty days without the approval of Congress. The 1973 War Powers Act gives Congress some power over the deployment of troops in military situations.*
3. *President Richard Nixon abused his wartime power in the 1970s by authorizing warrantless wiretap surveillance on domestic groups opposed to the Vietnam War.*
4. *The 1978 Foreign Intelligence Surveillance Act (FISA) created the Foreign Intelligence Surveillance Court for the purpose of approving or disapproving requests for surveillance and physical searches aimed at foreign powers and their agents, plus an appeals panel to hear appeals from denials of the applications.*
5. *The USA Patriot Act, enacted in response to the September 11, 2001, attacks, expanded the power of the executive branch and also the Foreign Intelligence Surveillance Court in order to better fight against terrorist acts within the United States and abroad.*
6. *President George W. Bush, Vice President Dick Cheney, and Attorney General Alberto Gonzales defend and justify the use of domestic surveillance.* The American public provides mixed reviews on warrantless wiretapping in the twenty-first century. In August 2006 a federal district court judge ruled the program unconstitutional as an infringement of free speech and privacy and ordered an immediate halt to it.
7. *The U.S. Supreme Court held that Yaser Esam Hamdi, an American citizen captured in Afghanistan and then detained without trial in the United States, was denied due process of law.*
8. *The Supreme Court has questioned the procedures set for enemy combatant detainees outside the United States.*
9. *The practice of extraditing some enemy combatant detainees back to their home countries or sending them to Eastern Europe or elsewhere where the United States knows they may be tortured (called "extraordinary rendition") is troublesome for many people.*
10. *There is a controversy over the expansion of presidential power during the War on Terror and the accompanying contraction of civil liberties (e.g., section 215 of Patriot Act). There is also a split within the Supreme Court over the possible utilization of international law and treaties in presidential decision making.*
11. *There is a controversy over the use of presidential signing statements—when bills are signed with accompanying statements by presidents that they can disregard certain provisions in the bill or interpret them in an arbitrary way.*

Background of the Case

Origins of Presidential Power during Wartime

Under Article II, Section 2, of the United States Constitution, the president is given the power to fight with any resources made available by Congress. In particular, in the Constitution the Founding Fathers divided war powers: Congress was allotted the authority to declare war and the president was granted the power to wage and engage in war. Therefore, under the specific article, the president cannot legally wage war until given the consent by Congress to do so; any other decision would be deemed illegal and unconstitutional. In addition, under the United States system of government, although the president might believe that waging war on a particular country or nonstate actor such as al Qaeda is morally just, he is forbidden by law to engage in that war unless given congressional permission through a declaration of war or congressional resolution, such as the 1964 Gulf of Tonkin Resolution that gave President Johnson authority to expand United States operations in Vietnam.

In current society and with each newly elected president, the Constitution must evolve into something fundamentally different in order to endure the new challenges and conditions surrounding the administration. The continual and most recent difficulty, in particular within the George W. Bush administration, concerns presidential power over national security, which has been something that many U.S. presidents have attempted to strengthen while in office. For example, Thomas Jefferson increased presidential authority during the 1803 Louisiana Purchase when he did not wait for congressional approval and did not seek a constitutional amendment for the purchase of the land. This resulted in the doubling of the land mass within the United States and, although some thought it unconstitutional because acquiring territory is not mentioned specifically in the Constitution, confirmed that the office of the presidency would act on its own interests for the good of the country and not wait for overall congressional support. Andrew Jackson, approximately thirty years later, also extended presidential authority when, due to events such as Indian wars, he defied the Supreme Court by expelling the Indian tribes from lands to which they held title by treaties with the government. Abraham Lincoln followed Jackson's lead when he suspended the writ of habeas corpus during the Civil War, an action not supported or approved by Congress. Franklin Delano Roosevelt made use of executive agreements, which have the binding force of treaties but are not subject to congressional approval, to conduct foreign affairs, such as his letting England have naval destroyers in exchange for allowing U.S. military bases on English soil. More recently, Bill Clinton was able to bomb Serbian forces in Kosovo without the approval of Congress, which otherwise would have violated the War Powers Act of 1973.

Following the attacks of 9/11, the Bush administration received complete support from the Republican Congress for a more concentrated presidential power regarding national security. Problems began to develop, however, because the president is legally protected under the Constitution to fight wars as he sees fit, which may not be what Congress believes to be the solution to the problem. Regarding the War on Terror, Congress has argued that Bush has violated Congress's antitorture law concerning the detainees at the Guantanamo Bay Naval Base prison in Cuba, and also international treaties around the world, in order to fight the war his way. The administration views Congress's statute against the use of torture to be applicable only within the United States, therefore making its actions at the U.S. Naval Base in Guantanamo Bay, Cuba, legal. Also, some enemy combatant detainees are returned to their home countries although some of those countries condone the use of torture. Presumably, the most aggressive use of presidential power is the administration's ability to arrest American citizens and others anywhere in the world and detain them without a trial as enemy combatants. This, private surveillance programs, and other presidential encroachments on civil liberties, has affected the opinions of both the legislative branch and the American people regarding presidential power. Presidential power was created to protect the United States and its citizens; however, it is now argued that President Bush and many past presidents have overstepped the boundaries of their constitutional rights and gone too far. The irony is that President Bush frequently complains about "activist" judges who do not adhere to the Founding Fathers' intentions and legislate from the bench, yet when it comes to presidential war powers he, like all other recent presidents, has no wish to be bound by what many consider to be the intentions of the Framers.

The War Powers Act of 1973

The War Powers Act of 1973 was established after the House of Representatives and the Senate achieved the two-thirds majority required to guarantee that Congress and the president would share decision-making capabilities in situations that might put the United States in hostile or adverse situations. The approval occurred after President Nixon's veto in early November 1973, at a time when Nixon was severely weakened by the Watergate scandal. There has been constant tension over it between the two branches ever since, because historically presidential power increases during wartime. One section of the act requires that the president make an official written request to Congress before conducting military operations, and also that he continue to consult with Congress until all hostilities have ceased. Congress also has the ability, under the act, to remove any U.S. armed forces from hostilities if it has not prepared a declaration of war or passed resolutions sanctioning the use of force within sixty days. The sixty days can then be extended for another thirty days after the president makes an official request and affirms that there will be a safe withdrawal of troops once the hostilities have come to an end.

The War Powers Act was fairly successful shortly after being passed, with presidents submitting the required reports to Congress. However, all presidents since the act was passed have declared that it violated their presidential powers and have deemed it unconstitutional. The courts have not yet directly addressed this question.

There are two main arguments for the unconstitutionality of the War Powers Act. The first concerns Congress's control over the U.S. armed forces through appropriations while the president leads, which indicates that the ability to declare war does not mean congressional dominance. The second constitutionality dispute involves the separation-of-powers doctrine, with the legislature attempting to carry out the president's duties. However, this could be seen as unconstitutional through Article II, Section 1, of the U.S. Constitution, which includes the oath that the president "will faithfully execute the Office of President of the United States, and will to the best of my Ability, preserve, protect and defend the Constitution of the United States."

Since the act was passed in 1973, Congress's role in war declarations has been minimal, especially with the presidency becoming a more powerful institution than it ever has been before; no president has accepted or followed the act's constitutionality, which is one reason why Clinton was able to bomb Kosovo and George W. Bush was able to commit troops to Iraq without waiting for the United Nations to act.

Warrantless Wiretaps during the Nixon Administration

During the early 1970s, President Nixon was accused of misusing the office of the president, the Federal Bureau of Investigation (FBI), the Secret Service, and other executive branch entities; and of breaching the constitutional rights of U.S. citizens by conducting and authorizing electronic surveillance investigations. Although he claimed that the purpose of the surveillance was to keep track of certain domestic groups associated with and opposed to the Vietnam War, he did not use the surveillance just for this justification but also for his own political agenda. These "certain groups" that Nixon targeted included five members from his national security staff, a member of the Department of Defense, and two newsmen, all of whom had contested the Vietnam War and helped get stories published in such newspapers as the *New York Times.* Nixon believed that he had a reasonable national security justification for the wiretaps; however, as indicated above, he did not use the surveillance solely for this justification, but also for his own political agenda. Not only did Nixon permit the use of warrantless wiretaps, he also attempted to cover up the surveillance and his utilization of the FBI. This, among many other things, contributed to his impeachment and trial.

Following Nixon's resignation, a committee chaired by Senator Frank Church (D-ID) was organized to investigate the uses and abuses of warrantless wiretaps. It was at this time that Congress passed the 1978 Foreign Intelligence Surveillance Act (FISA), which set limits on electronic surveillance and created a court that would have the ability to allow law enforcement applications for the future use of electronic surveillance and physical searches of foreign powers and their agents. The court consists of eleven federal district judges appointed by the Chief Justice of the United States, with no more than three of them living within a twenty-mile radius of the District of Columbia. Its records are not made public. If it turns down a government request, an appeals panel consisting of three district or courts of appeals judges appointed by the Chief Justice will look at the request.

The USA Patriot Act of 2001

The USA Patriot Act, officially the Uniting and Strengthening America by Providing Appropriate Tools Required to Intercept and Obstruct Terrorism Act of 2001, was passed shortly after the 9/11 attacks on the United States. It was enacted to radically increase the authority of U.S. law enforcement to better fight terrorist acts both within the United States and abroad. Section 215 allows searches to be conducted if the records involved are relevant to an ongoing counterterrorism or counterinsurgency investigation, which is a lower standard than the probable cause for suspected criminal activity. The act has also been utilized to identify and prosecute other crimes concerning terrorism. The reauthorization of most of the provisions in the USA Patriot Act was signed into law on March 9, 2006, by President George W. Bush.

With regard to terrorism, the Patriot Act defines terrorism within the United States as "domestic terrorism," which is expounded upon in the U.S. criminal code at *18 U.S.C. § 2331.* Domestic terrorism from Section 2331 represents the following:

1. Any activities that involve acts dangerous to human life that are a violation of the criminal laws of the United States or of any state.
2. Any activities that appear to be intended:
   a. To intimidate or coerce a civilian population.
   b. To influence the policy of a government by intimidation or coercion.
   c. To affect the conduct of a government by mass destruction, assassination, or kidnapping.
3. Activities that occur primarily within the territorial jurisdiction of the United States.

This particular section also includes crimes concerning international terrorism, which is similar to domestic terrorism, except that it occurs beyond our national borders.

Along with complying with the U.S. criminal code, the USA Patriot Act also amends other acts relating to foreign intelligence investigations, including FISA and the Financial Anti-Terrorism Act. With regard to FISA, section 218 allows for searches and surveillance to be authorized if intelligence gathering were a significant purpose rather than the primary purpose. As for financial terrorism, under the Patriot Act the government has the authority to block assets pending investigation and the justification for so doing is examined in secrecy in federal court. The controversy surrounding the USA Patriot Act, similar to FISA, involves the power that the president believes he has over the law and without working with the legislative branch in order to protect the country as he sees fit. Technically, perhaps, George W. Bush has violated sections of both the Patriot Act and FISA in his attempts to protect the nation and its citizens against terrorism.

Twenty-first-Century Presidential Wartime Power vs. Congress and the U.S. Supreme Court

President George W. Bush has consistently given a very expansive interpretation of presidential wartime power, whether concerning the Global War on Terror, the Guantanamo Bay detainee trials, or the surveillance program; he has incessantly provided constitutional justifications for his actions. Given this situation, what, if anything, can the U.S. Supreme Court or Congress do in order to limit wartime power within this administration and presidencies to come?

As for the Supreme Court, it responded first by ruling 6–3 in the 2004 case of *Rasul v. Bush* that federal judges have jurisdiction to consider petitions for habeas corpus from the hundreds of noncitizens confined at the United States Naval Base at Guantanamo Bay, Cuba, who argued they were being unlawfully held. Justice John Paul Stevens in his majority opinion stressed the nature of Guantanamo Bay, calling it a territory over which the United States exercises exclusive jurisdiction and control under its 1903 lease. Justices Antonin Scalia, William Rehnquist, and Clarence Thomas dissented, saying the Court was extending "the scope of the habeas statute to the four corners of the earth." As Scalia put it, "war is war, and it has never been the case that when you captured a combatant you had to give them a jury trial in your civil courts." The Supreme Court subsequently handed down decisions in the *Hamdi* and *Hamdan* cases, which will be discussed in full later. The issue of surveillance has not come before the Supreme Court yet, but that does not mean that it never will. Since Chief Justice John Roberts has replaced Chief Justice Rehnquist and Justice Samuel Alito has replaced Justice Sandra Day O'Connor as an associate justice, the Supreme Court may considerably lessen Congress's chances in limiting presidential wartime power, as both Roberts and Alito have been part of the conservative movement that has presented the Bush administration with many of its legal justifications regarding the detainee trials, the War on Terror, and also the private surveillance program.

With regard to enemy combatant detainee trials, the Bush administration has stated that it will attempt to work with Congress to have military hearings for the detainees, which it feels would also comply with the Court's objections. This, however, is about the most that the Court is able to do to reinstate congressional authority. In the past, if Congress attempted to engage in oversight, the president could refuse to turn over information by citing "executive privilege," which is not mentioned in the Constitution. The only options that Congress has are either to cease its cooperation with the presidential agenda or to suspend financing for pertinent programs. If Congress were to hold hearings on the issues concerning the administration's secrecy, it would make the public more aware of the situation; however, hearings are very difficult to hold as they require extensive documentation. The ultimate penalty put forth by Congress would be the beginning of impeachment proceedings. All of these options would be viable for Congress, even in the case of the Bush administration. However, each of these methods requires extensive funding, which would most likely draw a lot of contention with the public. Instead, Congress usually waits for public interest groups to ask the Court to enforce a subpoena, which ultimately eliminates most of the costs. Therefore, some other approaches that Congress could take to redeem its authority within the legislative branch might include:

1. Clarifying that it did not give the president a "blank check" to defy existing laws without notifying Congress about the violations.
2. Passing new laws stating, without equivocation, that Congress proposes to bind the president and his administration and staff on issues relating to the conduct and declaration of war.
3. Creating more oversight programs to guarantee that the president will abide by the laws as stated by Congress and the U.S. Constitution.
4. Establishing new ways to sanction the president if he violates laws.

President George W. Bush has taken one of the most historically aggressive positions regarding presidential wartime powers and now it is up to both Congress and the Supreme Court to either limit or expand presidential power.

White House Justifications and American Opinions of Domestic Surveillance

There are many instances of domestic surveillance and eavesdropping that take place every day within the United States. The difference between President Bush's program and past eavesdropping programs is the fact that Bush's surveillance was not authorized by Congress. The case for domestic surveillance in this situation is being argued by the president, Vice President Richard Cheney, and Attorney General Alberto Gonzales, among others, through the avenue of the AUMF, which stated that "the President is authorized to use all necessary and appropriate force against those nations, organizations or persons he determines planned, authorized, committed or aided the terrorist attacks that occurred on 9/11 or harbored such organizations or persons, in order to prevent any future acts of international terrorism against the United States by such nations, organizations or persons." They feel this gives the president the right to protect the nation to the best of his ability and with as much force as he and his administration deem realistic.

President George W. Bush's Justification and Defense of Surveillance. President Bush has defended the legality and necessity of the domestic eavesdropping program, which was created with help from the National Security Agency (NSA) in 2002. After the *New York Times* leaked the surveillance program to the public, Bush produced this statement in January 2006: "I think most Americans understand the need to find out what the enemy is thinking, and that is what we are doing. They attacked us before, they will attack us again if they can and we are going to do everything we can to stop them." Although increasingly controversial, Bush continues to defend his position by declaring that he is conducting the surveillance under the Constitution and the power given to him by Congress on September 14, 2001 (the AUMF), which included any and all decisions that would result in the protection and ultimate security of the United States and its citizens. He continues on to state that "the NSA program is a necessary program. I was elected to protect the American people from harm. And on September 11, 2001, our nation was attacked. And after that day, I vowed to use all the resources at my disposal, within the law, to protect the American person, which is what I have been doing and will continue to do so." He produced this statement in January 2006 and still defended it in May 2006 when he referred to electronic surveillance as a program that was and continues to be a program designed to pursue terrorists and not intrude on the private telephone calls and e-mail messages of Americans. Bush added: "We are not mining or trolling through the personal lives of millions of innocent Americans. Our efforts are focused on links to al-Qaeda and their known affiliates. So far, we have been very successful in preventing another attack on our soil. The intelligence activities I authorized are lawful and have been briefed to appropriate members of Congress, both Republican and Democrat." According to President Bush, he and his administration were acting in the best interest of the citizens of the United States.

Vice President Richard Cheney's Justification and Defense of Surveillance. Vice President Cheney, whose defense of the administration's surveillance program has been unremitting, justifies the president's actions by stating that had the NSA not been authorized to run wiretaps, more attacks like that on 9/11 might have occurred. "No one can guarantee that we will not be hit again," Cheney said, "but neither should anyone say that the relative safety of the last four years came as an accident. America has been protected not by luck but by sensible policy decisions." Cheney goes on to declare that, in current times, the United States needs a leader who is fierce and not afraid to anger the legislative branch: "I believe in a strong, robust executive authority and I think that the world we live in demands it." Although receiving numerous opposing arguments surrounding the surveillance legality, Cheney has not faltered in the media when discussing the issue. As of late June 2006, Cheney, along with President Bush and several Republican congressional leaders, suggested that the *New York Times* could face criminal charges for exposing its report on the U.S. government surveillance program, specifically concerning the eavesdropping on international financial transactions. Cheney went as far as to single out the publication during a speech at a Republican fundraiser in Nebraska, where he stated that "some of the press, in particular the *New York Times*, have made the job of defending against further terrorist attacks more difficult by insisting on publishing detailed information about vital national security programs." The statements made by Cheney and various White House officials were spoken to discourage the media from printing untrue or secret information that could result in a security breach for the United States. While no prosecution was called for or has been called for to date by Bush or Cheney, Congressman Peter King (R-NY), chairman of the House Homeland Security Committee, joined the president and vice president in criticizing the *New York Times*, including its publisher, editor, and staff writers who helped publicize the story.

Attorney General Alberto Gonzales's Justification and Defense of Surveillance. Attorney General Gonzales maintained that the White House was justified in authorizing the NSA to conduct wiretaps on any persons in connection with or in suspicion of terrorist activities. To facilitate his defense of the program, Gonzales stated that "the domestic eavesdropping operation derived its legality from the congressional resolution permitting the use of force to fight terrorism as well as from the 'inherent powers' of the president as commander-in-chief." He continued by declaring that, while the surveillance program would regularly be illegal under the rules and regulations established by FISA, it was not in this situation because FISA does, in fact, make an exception for eavesdropping when "otherwise authorized," in this case by the AUMF. Gonzales insisted that the president was justified in the eavesdropping and, along with General Michael V. Hayden, the former director of the NSA, went on to state that, in the case of violating FISA, the president does not abuse the rules and regulations set forth by the intelligence agency. He argued that FISA "forbids warrantless domestic wiretapping that is not authorized by statute, but in authorizing the use of military force against al Qaeda, Congress implicitly authorized the monitoring of overseas calls of those linked to the group. The president has the inherent constitutional authority to conduct such surveillance, whatever the statutes may say. And he is using it only where we have a reasonable basis to conclude that one of the parties of the communication is either a member of al Qaeda or affiliated with al Qaeda."

Justice Department Defense of Surveillance. The Justice Department has taken a defensive stance against the domestic surveillance program. In a December 2005 letter to Congress, the department stated that the president possessed full authority to conduct the wiretaps without warrants under the regulations provided by the AUMF. Assistant Attorney General William Moschella went as far as to proclaim that the "intercepting [of] communications into and out of the United States of persons linked to al Qaeda in order to detect and prevent a catastrophic attack is clearly reasonable." The Justice Department continues to see the warrantless surveillance as "an early warning system" following the 9/11 attacks.

The American Public's Mixed Reviews of Surveillance. There have been numerous reviews by the American public surrounding Bush's domestic surveillance program, with some supporting it and others opposing it.

Proponents of the surveillance program have stated the following arguments:

1. They endorse the White House's assertion that Bush's authority as commander in chief allowed him to dismiss the warrant law and conduct eavesdropping programs on the American public.
2. Because of the enormity of the September 11, 2001, attacks on U.S. soil, which transformed America into a "battlefield," Congress should not be able to restrict a president's constitutional authority to carry out war as he sees fit.
3. The president should be able to abide by what he swore to during his inauguration, which is to "preserve, protect and defend" the Constitution. Bottom line—it is not an outrage for the president to run the government and his administration according to his own personal understanding of the Constitution.

Opponents of the surveillance program have stated the following objections:

1. The rationale used by the Bush administration could equally justify "mail openings, burglary, torture, or internment camps, all in the name of gathering foreign intelligence. Unless rebuked, it will lie around like a loaded weapon ready to be used by any incumbent who claims an urgent need," stated Bruce Fein, a former lawyer in the Reagan administration.
2. Bush's theories are immoral and reckless, such as his argument that his wartime powers allow him to bypass the courts and use warrantless surveillance on Americans' e-mails and international calls.
3. By ignoring the oversight of the courts and avoiding the language set forth by Congress, Bush has defiantly been turning away from the Constitution and the rules and regulations stipulated by Congress. Therefore, he has not, as the commander in chief, upheld his obligation to protect the nation and abide by the Constitution.

The opponents won the first round in court. The American Civil Liberties Union filed a lawsuit on behalf of journalists, scholars, and lawyers who say the program has made it difficult for them to do their jobs. They believe many of their overseas contacts are likely targets. In August 2006 a federal district court judge in Detroit agreed, calling the program an unconstitutional infringement of free speech and privacy and ordered an immediate halt to it.

Yaser Esam Hamdi and the U.S. Supreme Court

Yaser Esam Hamdi, an American citizen born in Louisiana, was imprisoned by the United States government after being found an "enemy combatant" for purportedly taking up arms with the Taliban before and during the 9/11 attacks. He was captured in Afghanistan and detained until the Supreme Court ruled in the 2004 case of *Hamdi v. United States* that the U.S. government could not legally keep him in custody any longer since there was no evidence that he had actually worked against the United States.

Eight of the nine justices (all but Justice Thomas) thought Hamdi's detention was wrong. Justices O'Connor, Anthony Kennedy, and Stephen Breyer, along with former Chief Justice Rehnquist, concluded (with O'Connor writing the opinion) that the detention was permissible if his designation as an enemy combatant proved to be correct, but his inability to appear before a judge, challenge the government's evidence, and tell his side of the story, had denied him of his constitutional right to due process.

O'Connor stated that a citizen held as an enemy combatant was entitled to know why and should be offered the chance to challenge it before someone neutral. These are "essential constitutional promises" and the administration was wrong to try to limit the role of the courts, as it condenses "power into a single branch of government." One cannot be held indefinitely for the purpose of interrogation, since that can lead to "oppression and abuse of others." The lower courts would have to weigh Hamdi's liberty against the government's interest in now allowing those who have fought against us to return to do battle. In balancing these interests, one must consider our values and "the privilege that is American citizenship." Hamdi had on his side "the most elemental of liberty interests—the interest in being free from physical detention by one's own government." She concluded that the government's contention that it just needed "some evidence" if it had to give Hamdi a hearing was not enough to evaluate the basis of detaining a citizen. "Plainly, the 'process' Hamdi has received is not that to which he is entitled under the Due Process Clause."

Justices David Souter and Ruth Bader Ginsburg said that Hamdi's detention lacked a legal basis as a matter of statutory authority, so there was no need to delve into constitutional issues. Justices Scalia and Stevens said that Hamdi was entitled to a habeas corpus petition ordering his release unless the government prosecuted him for treason or Congress exercised its constitutional authority to suspend habeas corpus. They thought O'Connor's opinion had not gone far enough to protect Hamdi's civil liberties. Scalia said that "if civil liberties are to be curtailed during wartime, it must be done openly and democratically, as the Constitution requires, rather than by silent erosion through an opinion of this court."

Although Justice Thomas thought the detention did fall within the federal government's war powers, he did join O'Connor and her three allies in providing the fifth vote for her finding statutory justification for detaining Hamdi in the AUMF, which authorized "all necessary and appropriate force" to pursue and prevent international terrorism. Souter and Ginsburg, on the other hand, said the use-of-force resolution said nothing about detaining citizens.

The legal significance of the *Hamdi* case defended an unprecedented separation of powers between the judiciary and the executive branch. The Bush administration claimed that the Constitution does not relate to "illegal enemy combatants" and that the administration will decide which U.S. citizens are considered enemy combatants, whose rights are not protected by the U.S. Constitution. Although this issue continues today and keeps challenging the Supreme Court, Justice O'Connor, in a closing statement, reaffirmed that "we have long since made clear that a state of war is not a blank check for the president when it comes to the rights of the nation's citizens." On October 9, 2004, Yaser Esam Hamdi was released from a Virginia prison and deported to Saudi Arabia (his ancestral home) after relinquishing his U.S. citizenship and agreeing to comply with the travel restrictions to never again visit Afghanistan, Israel, Iraq, Pakistan, the West Bank, Gaza, or Syria. He also had to promise that he would not sue the United States government over his incarceration.

The U.S. Supreme Court Questions Laws on Detainee Trials

President Bush made a signing statement at the beginning of 2006 after signing the Detainee Treatment Act that outlawed the torture of detainees; he reserved the right to bypass the law under his power as commander in chief. There has been growing controversy over Bush's use of signing statements. In fact, in 2006 a panel of the American Bar Association said that the president was flouting the Constitution and undermining the rule of law by claiming the power to disregard selected provisions of bills that he signed. After approving the antitorture bill, Bush stated that "the executive branch shall construe the law in a manner consistent with the constitutional authority of the President . . . as Commander in Chief" and further added that "this approach will assist in achieving the shared objective of the Congress and the President . . . of protecting the American people from further terrorist attacks." Some government officials argued that the statement simply alleged that Bush would conform to the law when he wants to, and if something were to happen concerning terrorism, then he would have the ability under his power as the president to do what would be best to protect the nation. Since the 9/11 attacks, the administration has also asserted that it will bypass both domestic and international laws in deciding how to deal with enemy combatants and detainees in the War on Terror. In response to this declaration, Senator John McCain (R-AZ) filed an amendment to a Defense Department bill that clearly stated that the cruel and inhumane punishment and treatment of detainees in U.S. custody is illegal in spite of where they are held. The primary reason for McCain's amendment was to close every loophole; however, the president has reopened the loophole by avowing the constitutional power to act in violation of the statute where it would aid the War on Terror.

In March 2006, the Supreme Court received a new case, one concerning Osama bin Laden's former chauffeur and bodyguard, Salim Ahmed Hamdan, whose lawyer asked the justices to declare the U.S. military charge that he conspired with his former boss to perform terrorist attacks against the United States unconstitutional. Hamdan, a Yemeni citizen, was captured in Afghanistan in 2001, taken to Guantanamo the next year, and formally charged with conspiracy in 2004. Historically, the courts have been reluctant to take on cases concerning the president during wartime. However, this case is different. In his client's defense, Hamdan's attorney stated that "neither the broadly worded September 14, 2001 House-Senate resolution that endorsed the use of force against al Qaeda [AUMF] nor older statutes gives Bush the clear legislative approval he needs to set up the commissions." He continued on to contend that the commissions violate the Geneva Conventions, which are enforceable by U.S. courts and give Hamdan the right to the same type of trial that a U.S. soldier would receive in a court-martial. After the Supreme Court agreed to hear Hamdan's case, the administration asked that the Supreme Court dismiss the case on the basis that the Detainee Treatment Act, which provided that "no court, justice, or judge" had jurisdiction to hear habeas corpus petitions filed by detainees at Guantanamo Bay, reinforced the president's power under the AUMF. The administration also argued that the proper time for Hamdan's constitutional challenge would be after his trial.

On June 29, 2006, the U.S. Supreme Court ruled in *Hamdan v. Rumsfeld* that President Bush did not have the authority to arrange military commissions at Guantanamo Bay, Cuba. It violated the Uniform Code of Military Justice and also the Geneva Convention. Justice Stevens authored the 5–3 decision. He was joined by Justices Kennedy, Souter, Ginsburg, and Breyer. (Chief Justice Roberts did not take part due to his involvement with the United States Court of Appeals for the District of Columbia, which endorsed the government's initial position regarding the *Hamdan* case before Roberts was confirmed to the Supreme Court.)

Stevens held that the president had established the commissions without congressional authorization (the AUMF cannot be interpreted to legitimize military commissions). He also said that a provision of the Geneva Convention known as Common Article 3 applies to Guantanamo detainees and is enforceable in federal court for their protection (the administration had contended that the article does not cover followers of al Qaeda). The provision requires humane treatment of captured combatants and prohibits trials except by "a regularly constituted court affording all the judicial guarantees which are recognized as indispensable by civilized people." It requires observance of protections for defendants that are missing from the rules the administration has issued for military tribunals; for example, the failure to guarantee the defendant the right to attend the trial, and the prosecution's ability under the rules to introduce hearsay evidence, unsworn testimony, and evidence obtained through coercion are all prohibited. Stevens went on to say that the historical origin of military commissions was in their use as a "tribunal of necessity" under wartime conditions. According to Stevens, "Exigency lent the commissions its legitimacy but did not further justify the wholesale jettisoning of procedural protections." As Justice Breyer said in his concurrence: "The court's conclusion ultimately rests upon a single ground: Congress has not issued the executive branch a blank check." Stevens further said that because the charge against Hamdan, conspiracy, was not a violation of the law of war, it could not be the basis for a trial before a military panel.

Justices Scalia, Thomas, and Alito dissented, with Scalia arguing that the 2005 Detainee Treatment Act had stripped the Court of jurisdiction to proceed with this case (the majority said it did not apply to cases pending at the time it was enacted), while Thomas called the decision "untenable" and "dangerous" and disregarded "the commander in chief's wartime decisions."

The Supreme Court's June 2006 decision in *Hamdan* has not affected the Justice Department's view on the legality of the NSA's antiterrorism surveillance program in conjunction with the enemy combatant detainees. According to Senator Charles Schumer (D-NY), Assistant Attorney General Moschella stated that the Supreme Court decision on detainee trials "does not affect our analysis of the Terrorist Surveillance Program for several reasons, although the Department of Justice is carefully considering the ramifications of the decision."

Policy Options

Since nothing, to date, has been accomplished in lessening the power of the president during wartime, there are a few policy options that might aid in the ability to limit and control White House authority.

1. Congress could amend the AUMF in order to exemplify to the president that it does not accept violations of domestic espionage laws. Therefore, if the White House identifies problems that would obstruct the rules and regulations found within FISA, Congress would then consider the claims made by the administration and determine whether or not civil liberties have been violated.

2. The administration might consider asking Congress to give it more authority and flexibility in rapidly planting wiretaps on international calls and e-mails. Although the Bush White House decided to avoid another argument with Congress, which would draw more unwanted attention to the domestic surveillance program, it still has the ability to do so when the opportunity presents itself. Attorney General Gonzales strongly supported this idea.

3. Congress could clarify that its new military-commission statute supersedes Common Article 3, which is applicable to al Qaeda detainees and requires that they must be treated humanely by the U.S. government. It would also explain the standards for managing unlawful enemy combatants.

4. Congress could become more assertive in invoking the War Powers Act and trying to hold the president more accountable to its provisions.

5. Congress or some other plaintiff might bring a lawsuit challenging the constitutionality of presidential signing statements.

6. Lawsuits have already been started concerning some of the president's domestic surveillance tactics, done under the aegis of national security, as an infringement upon civil liberties.

7. An attempt might be made, especially in Congress, to try to curb the use of international law and treaties in judicial decision making. The Supreme Court is divided on this issue, with Justices Kennedy and Ginsburg favoring their use and Justice Scalia opposing.

8. Due to the Supreme Court, the administration must make a distinction in its treatment of U.S. citizens and noncitizens.

9. Due once again to the Supreme Court, Congress might examine the administration's use of military tribunals to try enemy combatant detainees.

10. Congress and/or the courts might review the CIA policy of "extraordinary rendition" of enemy combatant detainees to countries that use torture.

11. Congress might begin an inquiry into the alleged use of torture of enemy combatant detainees at Guantanamo Bay as well as in Iraq and Afghanistan.

12. A legal challenge might be made to the changes that the Patriot Act made to the original intent of FISA.

Conclusion

It is very difficult to definitively "limit" presidential wartime powers, especially following the 9/11 attacks on the United States. Unfortunately, terrorism has interfered with many resolutions and sanctions that have previously been put into place in order to keep the U.S. and its government operating efficiently and securely. The president, as commander in chief, has taken actions he believes to be in the best interest of the United States and also its citizens. Some of these decisions, as stated above, however, may have violated statutes passed by Congress. It has been stated within the current administration that President George W. Bush has "taken matters into his own hands" when dealing with challenging issues such as domestic surveillance and detainee trials. Although he has met vast opposition to his actions, he has also maintained a great amount of support. Therefore, where is the line drawn concerning presidential wartime powers? Will too many limits be constricting, and could they inevitably cause more threats to America's citizens? Or will too few limitations create the environment for a type of "tyrannical" government?

The Founding Fathers intended that the president serve the country under the authority of Congress, but throughout the past two centuries, presidents have attempted to circumvent that relationship. Historically, Abraham Lincoln blockaded southern ports, freed the slaves, and established a draft—all without constitutional support. Ronald Reagan cited "inherent powers" to justify the illegal financing of the war in Nicaragua and the illegal sale of arms to Iran. Congress after 1982 did attach the "Boland Amendments" to various bills to forbid nonhumanitarian aid to the contra rebels in Nicaragua. Nevertheless, short of impeachment, Congress could only deny funds for this and future illegal actions. George W. Bush challenged Congress with his surveillance program and justification for detainee trials, but only after he was allotted the ability to use his authority as he saw fit based on the language in the AUMF. Although presidents such as these have defied Congress, the Constitution declares that the president shall exercise his executive authority and shall perform the duties as commander in chief of the armed forces; it does not articulate what those powers are, which is perhaps why presidents have created "inherent powers" that allow them the ability to run the country as they want. Therefore, what type of solution would be possible in this situation? One might recognize the balance of power within the government and conclude that the executive branch, Congress, and the United States Supreme Court all work together to protect the nation that the Founding Fathers created over two centuries ago. After all, America's strength lies in its confidence in the rule of law. Congress has constitutional power equal to the president's when civil liberties are concerned and is able to modify acts pertaining to surveillance and prisoner treatment if new circumstances justify a legislative solution. However, exploiting the fears of Americans to validate unconstitutional behavior may ultimately result in the sacrifice of the very freedoms that the United States is fighting to preserve.

Discussion Questions

1. How much power should be given to the president during wartime?
2. What were President George W. Bush's arguments for increased executive power during times of war?
3. Does the Constitution give the president virtually complete control during wartime?
4. What occurs if Congress does not comply with the president's requests?
5. How has Congress tried to limit presidential wartime power?
6. When does government surveillance become unconstitutional?
7. Should detainees be given the same protection as Americans in trials and should those trials be conducted by military tribunals?
8. Was the treatment of prisoners at Guantanamo Bay inhumane and against the Geneva Convention?
9. What can the U.S. Supreme Court do and what has it done in response to the detainees? Look specifically at the cases concerning Yaser Esam Hamdi and Salim Ahmed Hamdan.

10. Should both the Supreme Court and Congress have more control over the president in wartime? If yes, how would both branches achieve such an objective?

Class Activities

1. Have a class debate on the pro and con arguments concerning private surveillance programs.
2. Have a class debate on the pro and con arguments concerning treatment of war criminals and terrorists in United States naval bases and secret prisons.
3. Hold a class discussion about Article II, Section 2, of the U.S. Constitution and argue whether or not the Constitution should ever be stretched in regard to presidential power during wartime. Should Congress be given more power over final executive decisions? Why or why not?

Suggestions for Further Reading

American Journal of International Law. "Vice President Cheney Applauds Strengthened Presidential Powers." *American Journal of International Law* 99, no. 2 (April 2005): 492–93.

Byman, Daniel. "Renditions: Reject the Abuses, Retain the Tactic." *Washington Post*, April 17, 2005, B1.

Corwin, Edward S. *Presidential Power and the Constitution.* Ithaca: Cornell University Press, 1976.

Eagleton, Thomas F. *War and Presidential Power: A Chronicle of Congressional Surrender.* New York: Liveright, 1974.

Fisher, Louis. *Presidential War Power.* Lawrence: University Press of Kansas, 2004.

Fisher, Louis, and David Gray Adler. "The War Powers Resolution: Time to Say Goodbye." *Political Science Quarterly* 113, no. 1 (Spring 1988): 1–20.

Garcia, Michael John. "Renditions: Constraints Imposed by Laws on Torture." Washington, DC: Congressional Research Service, 2005.

Henkin, Louis. *Constitutionalism, Democracy, and Foreign Affairs.* New York: Columbia University Press, 1990.

Neustadt, Richard E. *Presidential Power and the Modern Presidents: The Politics of Leadership from Roosevelt to Reagan.* New York: Maxwell and Macmillan, 1990.

Paolucci, Richard C., and Richard C. Clark, eds. *Presidential Power and Crisis: Government in the Age of Terrorism.* Smyrna, DE: Griffon House Publications, 2003.

Salih, Zak M. "Use of Extraordinary Renditions Has Changed: Risk of Torture Hasn't, Panelists Say," February 21, 2006, at www.law.virginia.edu/html/news/2006_spr/rendition.htm.

Shapiro, Robert Y., Martha Joynt Kumar, and Lawrence R. Jacobs, eds. *Presidential Power: Forging the Presidency for the Twenty-first Century.* New York: Columbia University Press, 2000.

Helpful Website

www.hqda.army.mil/library/warpowers.htm. This website contains a selected bibliography on war powers.

13

The Judiciary

Case Snapshot

THE DECISION FROM THE 2005 SUPREME COURT case *Kelo v. City of New London* remains a lightning rod for controversy, even a year and a half after being handed down. The 5–4 decision held that cities may use eminent domain to take private houses and hand them over to corporations for reasons of economic development. Public reaction was as intense as it was immediate, and some thirty-four states subsequently enacted measures to limit such a practice. *Kelo* has become a battle cry for advocates of property rights nationwide. The case has been berated as judicial activism by the political left and right, and has spawned a host of legislative efforts on the state and local levels. The media and many grassroots lobbying camps have subscribed to the sentiment set forth by former Justice Sandra Day O'Connor in her vociferous dissent. With the degree of political and social fervor surrounding the decision, the case appears to be a landmark decision, in the mold of *Roe v. Wade* or *Gideon v. Wainwright*. Oddly enough, it is questionable whether the case warrants the public uproar. In fact, the political salience of the case seems to significantly outweigh the legal importance and implications. After all, even after the decision, states maintain the right and ability to restrain their own public authorities without the consultation or approval of the Supreme Court, which leaves politically elected branches of government to curb any actions deemed legal by the Court but perceived as undesirable by society en masse. So, should the Court revisit this issue, taking a more narrow approach to its interpretation of the Takings Clause of the Fifth Amendment of the U.S. Constitution? Or should society interpret the decision in light of the institutional room that has been left for legislative bodies to protect property? Is it the responsibility of American jurists to protect property rights? If so, to what extent should the Court abide by precedent that does not offer the protection sought after? You decide!

Major Case Controversies

1. *Eminent domain is the inherent power of a governmental entity to take privately owned property, especially land, and convert it to public use.* When the entity chooses to invoke this power, it is obligated to compensate the displaced property owner for his or her losses, per the Fifth Amendment of the United States Constitution. Often there are discrepancies as to what constitutes "public use." In eminent domain cases, the Court must decide whether the proposed end use of the property can be considered "public" as required by the Constitution. Oftentimes, the Court will agree that a "public purpose" will suffice, which is contentious because land can be placed into the hands of private companies.

2. *Americans throughout history have passionately defended property rights.* During the ratification stages of the Constitution, however, no state convention demanded that the federal government pay just compensation when and if it took private property for public use. In fact, the proposal was tucked away into an omnibus amendment whose other procedural provisions were widely supported. Americans commonly look to the Court to defend these property rights when other political avenues may be more appropriate.

3. *The historical use of the Takings Clause of the Fifth Amendment tends to support a broad reading.* In the late nineteenth and early twentieth centuries, it was almost customary for governments to delegate eminent domain powers to private interests for "public purposes." The Court's unwillingness to rule otherwise in the *Kelo* case was probably dictated by the legal doctrine of stare decisis, under which it is necessary to follow earlier judicial decisions when the same points arise in another case. For example, in the 1954 case of *Berman v. Parker* the Court upheld a redevelopment plan targeting a blighted area of Washington, D.C., in which most of the housing of the area's 5,000 inhabitants was beyond repair. In the 1984 case of *Hawaii Housing Authority v. Midkiff* the Court upheld a statute whereby fee title was taken from lessors and transferred to lessees (for just compensation) in order to reduce the concentration of land ownership. Also in 1984, in *Ruckelshaus v. Monsanto Co.*, the Court upheld a federal law under which the Environmental Protection Agency could consider the data (including trade secrets) submitted by a prior pesticide applicant in evaluating a subsequent application, so long as the second applicant paid just compensation for the data.

4. *The issue of public versus private takings lay dormant for some time prior to the Kelo case.* When the case was decided, the outcome seemed offensive and unattractive to many. The holding, however, may be on solid constitutional and precedential ground.

5. *One key question that arose in the Kelo case is the taking of the private homes for private gain which may ultimately benefit the public.* That is because the property in question was to be developed with office space for research and development, a conference hotel, new residences, and a pedestrian "river walk."

Background of the Case

Before we examine the question of whether or not the *Kelo* case should be revisited, it is necessary to look at the fact pattern leading up to the case. The city of New London is situated at the mouth of the Thames River in Connecticut. It is the second smallest municipality in the state, founded by settlers from the Massachusetts Colony. Although once the center of a thriving whaling industry, New London had fallen on difficult economic times in recent decades. This state of decline led a Connecticut agency to designate New London a "distressed municipality" in 1990. By 1998, the unemployment rate of New London was twice the statewide average, and at 24,000 residents, the population was at its lowest since 1920.

In, and because of, this socioeconomic context, the city of New London began to make plans for redevelopment of the waterfront area near the Fort Trumbull neighborhood. The New London Development Corporation (NLDC) is a privately held nonprofit entity that had been established years prior to aid New London in formulating an economic redevelopment plan. The NLDC was to plan and oversee the redevelopment project. In January of 1998, the state of Connecticut approved a $5.35 million bond issue to support the proposed activities. In the following month, the pharmaceutical company Pfizer Inc. announced plans to build a $300 million research facility in the immediate area of Fort Trumbull. The NLDC went through the necessary formal stages of environmental assessments and evaluations per Connecticut state law. Ultimately, the plan was to include commercial, retail, and residential properties, a conference center, museum, marina, and waterfront hotel. The NLDC expected to create between 1,736 and 3,169 new jobs and generate up to $1.25 million in tax revenue. Upon state approval, the NLDC focused the final plan on a ninety-acre area of land located in Fort Trumbull.

The Fort Trumbull area consists of 115 privately owned properties. The NLDC planned on using this land to help revitalize the city of New London by making the city more attractive and creating recreational opportunities around the waterfront. The plan was approved in January 2000 by the city council, and the NLDC (who had no independent power of eminent domain) was designated as the agent that would lead implementation. The council authorized the NLDC to either purchase the necessary property or acquire it by invoking the power of eminent domain on behalf of the city. The NLDC was able to obtain most the land necessary for the plan, but nine owners of fifteen properties refused to sell. Among them were Susette Kelo and several other petitioners of the case. These petitioners brought suit in the New London Superior Court in December 2000 claiming, among other things, that the taking of their properties violated the Public Use restriction of the Fifth Amendment. The Superior Court granted a permanent restraining order for some of the areas involved, but denied relief to other areas.

Both parties appealed to the Supreme Court of Connecticut, which held that the city's takings were valid under the plan, partially because a local municipal development statute mandated that the taking of land for an economic redevelopment project is indeed a "public use." The Supreme Court of Connecticut also looked to federal precedent in this area. The Supreme Court of the United States granted certiorari to determine whether or not the city's taking satisfied the Public Use requirement.

The Supreme Court Decision

Despite popular convention, the *Kelo* decision did not in any way alter existing eminent domain doctrine. Relying exclusively on precedent, it is actually a legally conservative decision, failing to create any new laws or expand old ones. This notwithstanding, most Americans have come to view the decision as egregious because of the taking of private residences and the turning of them into commercial development by a private entity, and it has sparked an onslaught of grassroots efforts to restrict eminent domain. We will briefly examine the highlights of the decision. As we will see, despite being politically offensive, the decision was likely correct on constitutional grounds.

The Majority

Justice John Paul Stevens wrote for the majority of the Court (joined by Justices Anthony Kennedy, David Souter, Ruth Bader Ginsburg, and Stephen Breyer), basing the decision almost entirely on other previous Supreme Court decisions. Citing some earlier cases, Stevens concluded that "[p]romoting economic development is a traditional and long accepted function of government." As such, it seemed settled that the Public Use Clause did not require that land be necessarily "put into use for the general public." This, of course, is not carte blanche for American cities. Rather, there needs to exist some identifiable public purpose or benefit from the proposed taking. Upon articulating some kind of determination that the taking will serve a public purpose (or is at least in the public interest), the city is free to exercise eminent domain. The majority of the Court refused to second-guess that determination, and as per one of its norms it would not displace the judgment of locally elected officials in favor of their own judgment.

The Court held that New London's plan for redevelopment did not benefit a particular class of individuals. While the plan may have incidentally benefited certain individuals over others, this would not invalidate the plan under the Public Use Clause. Essentially, New London had made the determination that redevelopment of the proposed area would confer a benefit on the public, and consequently the taking of the Kelo house and various other properties was necessary to accomplish this development. Also, the Court determined that the government could delegate their power of eminent domain to a private entity.

One very important aspect of the majority decision needs to be mentioned, and that is the room that Justice Stevens leaves for a political and legislative role in limiting the use of eminent domain. Leaving a conceptual template for state and local action, he wrote:

> We emphasize that nothing in our opinion precludes any State from placing further restrictions on its exercise of takings power. Indeed, many States already impose "public use" requirements that are stricter than the federal baseline. Some of these requirements have been established as a matter of constitutional law, while others are expressed in state eminent domain statutes that carefully limit the grounds upon which takings may be exercised.

The Concurrence

Justice Kennedy provided the fifth vote necessary for the majority. (Justice Kennedy, much like Justice O'Connor, would often prove to be the swing vote in a given case. In a fashion that has become recognizable to legal scholars, he wrote a concurring opinion that agreed in judgment, but softened the edges of the argument.) He explained that there seemed to be no favoritism at play in the case, which signifies that the Court might use "heightened scrutiny" if it suspects preferential treatment. Under "heightened scrutiny" the Court will not simply defer to the law in question but will look to see if it serves an important governmental objective and if the means employed are substantially related to the achievement of that objective. Also, he emphasized, in accordance with the majority, that a well-developed plan was necessary to qualify as a legitimate purpose.

The Dissents

Justice Sandra Day O'Connor penned a dissent, taking great care to distance herself (and those joining her, including the late Chief Justice William Rehnquist, and Justices Antonin Scalia and Clarence Thomas) from the majority opinion. She thought the Court had strayed from precedent by endorsing economic development as an appropriate land use. In her view, "all private property is now vulnerable to being taken and transferred to another private owner, so long as it might be upgraded—*i.e.* given to an owner who will use it in a way that the legislature deems more beneficial to the public—in the process." She feared that the majority's qualification of "public use" would effectively eviscerate "any distinction between private and public use of property." The dissent was concerned with protecting those people whose political heft may be significantly outweighed by those wealthier and more powerful, and who are subject to unfair takings. Justice O'Connor advocated an external check (in the form of judicial action) on these potentially unfair practices.

Justice Thomas authored his own originalist dissent. In his opinion, Thomas condemned the majority opinion as "simply the latest in a string of our cases construing the public use clause to be a virtual nullity." Thomas favors a more narrow reading of the Public Use Clause because this is, in his view, what is mandated by the original meaning of the Constitution (for a more detailed analysis of this jurisprudence, see chapter 1). He accuses the majority of the Court of essentially replacing the necessary "public use" with a "public purpose" test, which logically strays from the confines of the intended meaning. This shift in phraseology stands in stark contrast with Thomas's originalist principles.

The Takings Clause

The bedrock of the issue of *Kelo* involves the Fifth Amendment of the U.S. Constitution. The relevant text reads as such: " . . . nor shall private property be taken for public use, without just compensation."

A few pertinent observations must be made upon examining the text, because so much of the case rests on this clause. The text of the Fifth Amendment (despite popular opposition) does not in any way say that property may *only* be taken for public use. As some scholars have noted, the Founders could have very easily placed an overt limitation on takings but chose not to, opting instead only to require just compensation in those situations in which takings do occur. A plain reading of the clause will reveal that the Amendment attempts to differentiate when compensation is due and when it is not. As such, there seems to exist no evidence that the Takings Clause was meant to serve as a limit on the purpose of the taking.

Perhaps this is why the Supreme Court has continued to embrace a broad view of the clause throughout its history. According to this broad view, nearly anything that improves the public welfare will amount to a "public use." Property may thus be taken if the result is of some (even if only slightly) discernable public benefit. This public benefit may come in the form of an increased tax base, job creation, and/or economic renewal.

Modern U.S. Supreme Court decisions have afforded great deference to a government's determination of "public use." Add to this a simple consideration of history—a history in which the taking of land to build private roads and dams was commonplace, and during which the necessary and actual use of the taken land varied. While contingent on the ebb and flow of political factors during most of the nineteenth century, liberal use of eminent domain became firmly established in American case law in the twentieth century.

Subsequent Action

In the wake of *Kelo*, there has been plenty of action on the front of eminent domain and property rights. The decision has become collectively and universally reviled. Early polling numbers were staggering. Approximately 80 percent of people nationwide were opposed to the decision and wanted something to be done about it. At the same time, local city planners and developers, along with powerful and high-ranking politicians, seemed to be embracing the decision, creating tension in legislatures across the country.

The potential problems with eminent domain abuse are very real. Between 1998 and 2002, more than 10,000 different properties were either condemned or threatened with development via eminent domain. In the year following the *Kelo* decision, 5,700 properties were threatened or taken. In light of these figures, state legislatures around the country have sprung into action. Twenty-five states have reacted to the public chorus of disapproval, passing laws that in some way restrict the use of eminent domain. Additionally, three other states attempted to pass similar legislation, only to be met with opposition from veto-wielding governors. Six states, including Louisiana, Georgia, Florida, South Carolina, New Hampshire, and Michigan, have constitutional amendments limiting the use of eminent domain to be presented to voters. In an entertaining if not effective measure, libertarians in New Hampshire actually attempted to seize the local homes of Justices Souter and Breyer to build a hotel and park, respectively. Not surprisingly, this did not occur.

State legislatures are not alone in the fight. The U.S. Senate and House of Representatives have also proposed measures to curb potential eminent domain abuse in light of the decision. In 2005, Texas Senator John Cornyn (R) introduced a bill "[t]o protect homes, small businesses, and other private, property rights, by limiting the power of eminent domain." The language of the bill would deem eminent domain necessary only for public use, which would not include economic development. In the House, the Private Property Rights Protection Act was approved by a vast majority, and included provisions to prohibit federal economic development funds from reaching the state and local levels in cases of proposed eminent domain use for commercial development.

Additionally, the executive branch entered the dispute. On June 23, 2006, on the first anniversary of the decision, President George W. Bush issued an executive order to control eminent domain abuse. The order had the following language in addition to instructions to the attorney general as to how to carry out the policy:

> It is the policy of the United States to protect the rights of Americans to their private property, including by limiting the taking of private property by the Federal Government to situations in which the taking is for public use, with just compensation, and for the purpose of benefiting the general public and not merely for the purpose of advancing the economic interest of private parties to be given ownership or use of the property taken.

Policy Options

Eminent domain abuse can be inflicted upon nearly anyone. However, the results, while possibly unsavory, are not necessarily unlawful. Efforts to curb the abuse would likely be more effective if generated within, and carried out through, the various legislative branches. It has been noted that numerous state legislatures have enacted laws with an aim to rein in eminent domain abuse. Some will say, however, that the political backlash has fallen short in terms of results, despite the massive public outrage. Advocates of property rights and all those otherwise concerned with curbing or ending eminent domain abuse might consider these options:

1. *State legislative reform as an alternative to judicial interpretation and limitations of/on public use.* Many states nationwide are embracing this alternative, to varying degrees of success. One study shows that only five states, Indiana, Georgia, Pennsylvania, South Dakota, and Florida, actually provide strong protection for property rights. Many other states simply restate existing laws and pass laws that allege to restrain eminent domain but do no such thing in practice. Additionally, those states that have enacted meaningful legislation sometimes exclude large cities in which the problems of eminent domain abuse are most prominent. For example, the Pennsylvania law excludes Pittsburgh and Philadelphia, where most of the state's condemnations occur. States would be more successful in making similar legislation comprehensive. Furthermore, states should go to some length to educate voters on the potential dangers of eminent domain. Developers and city planners will naturally have a more sophisticated knowledge in this area, and might consequently have the upper hand in the political process.

2. *Anti-Kelo legislation passed in the U.S. Congress.* If the bills proposed by the House and Senate come to full votes and pass, they may make a difference in the national fight. However, implementation issues will undoubtedly arise on the state level, where most abuse occurs. Another potential problem with these federal bills is the wording, which often undercuts the goal of forbidding federal agencies and others from using eminent domain for economic purposes.

3. *A presidential executive order.* President Bush has made an effort to restrain the federal government from using eminent domain for certain purposes. Again, since the abuse most often occurs at the state and local level, the overall impact of such orders may be diminished. Also, similar to those proposed federal bills, the order allows property transfer to continue for economic development only if such a transfer benefits the general public. Herein lies the problem. Public officials will *always* claim that the taking is justified based on some abstract public benefit, and with no language specifying exactly what constitutes a public "use" or "benefit," the same pattern of deference to the local government is likely to continue.

4. *Banning economic development takings by means of state constitutional amendments.* In doing this, states should take great care to avoid loopholes and adequately target "economic development." By doing this, governments retain the power to exercise eminent domain and can still pursue economic development independently of this power. Government would be forced to buy desirable property on the open market, which could help eliminate some of the unfairness and inequality that undermine the process of eminent domain.

5. *The Supreme Court's reconsideration of the nature of the Public Use Clause.* This is not likely to happen anytime soon, especially since *Kelo* was just recently decided. If the Court were willing (at least to a certain extent) to break the confines of precedent to revisit the issue de novo, perhaps it might be inclined to adopt a more narrow reading of "public use."

Conclusion

Kelo v. City of New London raised important concerns over eminent domain abuse after the issue had lain legally dormant for some time. Ultimately, the majority of the Supreme Court decided that if a (thoroughly and legitimately planned) economic redevelopment project served to increase tax and other revenues and help revitalize the economy of a struggling area, that end satisfied the Public Use requirement of the U.S. Constitution. This decision provoked a political firestorm nationwide and was viewed negatively by most observers. Upon examining the case and some of the relevant legal history and texts involved, it appears as if the political backlash is at least a bit misdirected—misdirected in the sense that eminent domain abuse is indeed an egregious practice, but a practice that would be better dealt with in the political arena as opposed to the judiciary.

In fact, property rights advocates nationwide have simply blindly adopted the dissent's rhetoric instead of taking care to offer a viable solution. Such a solution might include a carefully worded amendment to restrict or ban takings for the purpose of economic development, a practice which, according to the decision, is practical and legal. Even though the decision handed down is collectively vilified, this institutional room was left for a reason. Was this, then, a successful display of judicial restraint, or a judicial failure to protect one of the most passionate held American rights? The answer will likely vary.

So, should the case of *Kelo* be revisited by virtue of a case with a similar fact pattern? Surely there are plenty of potential cases to challenge *Kelo*. Or, should a disgruntled nation turn instead to the political process, in hope that the decision may become discredited (if not overruled)? This political process would be successful if the Court has no future occasion by which to squarely reconsider the precedence at issue. Is *Kelo* a silver lining for property rights advocates, affording them a national spotlight under which scrutiny will undoubtedly underlie eminent domain pursuits? Or is the decision the deathblow to private property? Only time and the progression of political events will tell.

Discussion Questions

1. How do you think the Public Use Clause should be properly interpreted? Does "public use" necessarily mean that the land is "used" by the "public"?
2. Is the *Kelo* decision a Pyrrhic victory for developers? Will the consequent national backlash prevent developers from taking property for reasons of economic development?
3. How legitimate is a Supreme Court decision that is based on potentially flawed precedent? How willing should the Court be to disregard precedent? Or does the need for stability in law outweigh these concerns?
4. Having examined the text of the Fifth Amendment, do you think the federal judiciary is the proper means of remedying eminent domain abuse?
5. Is *Kelo* a formalistic tragedy? In other words, what kind of balance should be struck between procedural justice and substantive justice?
6. Should the Court revisit an issue because of an overwhelming national opposition or disapproval?
7. Has the distinction between public and private use been obliterated?
8. How possible is it that states will overreact to the decision, destroying a necessary although sometimes painful government power?

Class Activities

1. Debate the merits of the majority and dissenting opinions of the *Kelo* decision and discuss which side seems more favorable.

2. Divide the class into three groups. Nine class members serve as Supreme Court Justices, and the rest of the class divide equally and work together to present the case for either Susette Kelo or the city of New London. Create briefs based on the pertinent facts and act out a short session of oral argument. The nine Justices should be prepared to make a ruling.

Suggestions for Further Reading

Adler, Jonathan H. "Property Rights and Wrongs." *National Review Online*, June 29, 2005, at www.national review.com/adler/adler200506290806.asp.

Broder, John M. "States Curbing Right to Seize Private Homes." *New York Times*, February 21, 2006, A1.

Bullock, Scott. "The Specter of Condemnation." *Wall Street Journal*, June 24, 2006, A3.

Cohen, Charles E. "Eminent Domain after *Kelo v. City of New London*: An Argument for Banning Economic Development Takings." *Harvard Journal of Law & Public Policy* 29 (2006): 491–569.

Cole, Daniel H. "Why Kelo is not Good News for Local Planners and Developers." *Georgia State University Law Review* (forthcoming). Abstract available at http://ssrn.com/abstract=880149.

Sandefur, Timothy. "The 'Backlash' So Far: Will Americans Get Meaningful Eminent Domain Reform?" Program for Judicial Awareness Working Paper Series No. 05–015 (2006): 1–111. Abstract available at http://ssrn.com/abstract=868539.

Somin, Ilya. "Controlling the Grasping Hand: Economic Development Takings after Kelo." George Mason Law & Economics Research Paper No. 06–01 (2006). Abstract available at http://ssrn.com/abstract=874865.

Helpful Website

www.opinionjournal.com/weekend/hottopic/?id=110009196. This website discusses the anti-*Kelo* property rights initiatives in many states.

14

Foreign Policy

Case Snapshot

By the end of November 2006, the U.S. had fought longer in Iraq than it had in World War II. Although the U.S.-led coalition forces had rather quickly and easily defeated the Iraqi resistance, as proudly announced by President George W. Bush in his historic "mission accomplished" speech on May 1, 2003, their job was far from over. There were some early notable accomplishments, including the capture of Saddam Hussein and the formation of a democratically elected government. But there were also some serious mistakes, perhaps none bigger than carrying out a de-Ba'athification campaign that drove thousands of Ba'thists underground who might have smoothed the transition to the post-Saddam era. This campaign contributed to the fact that U.S. troops were not able to fully restore basic services, particularly electricity and water; nor could they provide stability and security for the Iraqi population or train Iraqis to do so. Instead, armed militias, death squads, and suicide bombers representing both Sunni and Shiite Muslims, as well as factions within these groups, began fighting one another and U.S. "occupation" forces simultaneously. Sectarian violence was stoked by neighboring Iran, foreign fighters, and "jihadists" from al Qaeda. By the end of 2006, sectarian violence in Iraq seemingly had spiraled out of control, leaving the country in near anarchy. President Bush thus faced a terrible dilemma. As UN Secretary-General Kofi Annan noted in a speech on November 21, 2006, the United States had become trapped in a country where its military forces could neither leave nor remain without terrible consequences; in fact, the presence in Iraq of U.S. forces arguably was a major cause of the escalating violence. At the same time, the high public support for the war that President Bush enjoyed initially had dropped significantly to a low of 31 percent. Americans had become disenchanted early on when no weapons of mass destruction (WMD) were found, and later on as casualties mounted and the war seemed to drag on with no end in sight. The November 2006 election victory by

Democrats who regained control of both houses of Congress was in effect a referendum against the war. With the U.S. increasingly isolated at home and abroad because of the Iraq War, pressure was mounting on President Bush to decide on an exit strategy. Just before Thanksgiving 2006, the Pentagon outlined three basic options: Send in more troops, reduce forces but stay longer, or leave Iraq (referred to informally as "Go Big," "Go Long" and "Go Home"). But each of these options, or their hybrids, could not be implemented easily or without dangers and risks. A couple of weeks later, the Congress-authorized bipartisan Iraq Study Group (ISG), chaired by former Secretary of State James A. Baker III and former congressman Lee H. Hamilton (D-IN), made its recommendations. The ISG, noting that it offered no "magic bullets," called for a gradual withdrawal of U.S. forces in Iraq, though with no specific timeline; more reliance on Iraqis to deal with the insurgency and sectarian violence; and a bolder diplomatic effort to involve regional players, particularly Syria and Iran, in a multilateral effort to resolve Iraq's problems. President Bush finally accepted the fact that since previous U.S. strategies in Iraq had not worked, a new course of action was needed. After studying the ISG report and consulting a number of Middle East experts both inside and outside the government, on January 10, 2007, he announced his decision. He would send an additional 21,500 American troops to "clear, hold and build" mainly in Baghdad and the heavily violence-prone Anbar Province. At the same time the U.S. would push the Iraqi government much harder to take responsibility for providing security and stability. Most Americans were highly skeptical that this strategy would work, but they were not confident anything else would. Thus the question remained as to what the U.S. "endgame" should be in Iraq. Questions were being raised more frequency and loudly: Who is the enemy in Iraq? What is the mission of U.S. troops in that country? How long should they stay there? When and under what circumstances should they leave? And the ultimate question: How should the U.S. extricate itself from this seemingly intractable dilemma? You decide!

Major Case Controversies

1. *By fall 2006, there was deepening concern over the extent to which the situation in Iraq was spinning out of control and controversy over whether the country had fallen into civil war.* UN Secretary-General Kofi Annan said that Iraq was "on the brink of civil war"; former secretary of state Colin Powell commented that the war in Iraq "could be considered a civil war"; and former President Jimmy Carter stated that what was going on in Iraq was "civil strife." Nevertheless, President Bush kept insisting that because the daily violence was being fomented by al Qaeda "jihadists" and because there was no organized fighting against the Iraqi government, the violence could not be called a civil war. Moreover, Bush realized if it were a civil war people would start asking what side the U.S. was on, or why U.S. forces were put in the middle of someone else's battles. On March 4, 2007, the Pentagon released its quarterly report (*Measuring Security and Stability in Iraq*) on the period from October through December 2006. For the first time it described some of the violence as civil war; this reflected similar language found in the National Intelligence Estimate (NIE) released a few weeks earlier. However, according to many media sources and political pundits, what had been occurring for some time was indeed civil war. Whatever the semantic differences and labels, Iraq was surely in the throes of complex ethnic, religious, tribal, and political violence. Kurds were struggling to secure their newly won autonomy; the majority Shiite Muslims (about 60 percent of the population), now in at least titular control of the government, were fighting Sunnis (about 20 percent of the popula-

tion); Sunnis, who were the dominant political group under Saddam Hussein, were bat-
tling to resist Shiite domination and feared their retribution for anti-Shiite actions they
were involved in under Saddam Hussein's rule; foreign "jihadists" (in President Bush's
words) and Iranians were stoking this sectarian violence and the insurgency while trying
to drive out the U.S.-led forces; and all these groups, including factions within each group,
were fighting one another and U.S. forces simultaneously. A mishandled U.S. exit plan
would certainly exacerbate all these growing conflicts.

2. *Americans were confused over identification of the main enemy in Iraq.* Was it armed Sunni
   unsurgents? The Mahdi Army of the rebellious Shiite cleric Moqtada al-Sadr? Foreign "jihadists" under the control of al Qaeda? Saudi Arabia (for supporting Sunni insurgents)?
   Iran (for supporting Shiite militias)? Iraq's tribal leaders who command intense loyalty?
   Bandits, thieves, and thugs who run amok? Some or all of the above? And could the main
   cause of continued violence actually be the continued presence of Coalition "occupation"forces, mainly Americans?

3. *It was unclear what the U.S. military mission was in Iraq after the defeat of Saddam Hussein's
   forces and his subsequent capture and execution.* American soldiers seemingly were asked to
   do the impossible: rebuild a war-torn nation; grow democracy; hunt down terrorists affiliated with al Qaeda; supply, support, and train Iraqi troops; and stop sectarian violence—
   all simultaneously and without adequate training. A related question, of course, was
   whether the U.S. had enough troops in Iraq to perform these multifaceted duties.

4. *After three years of fighting in Iraq, whatever dwindling hope was left for the war to end in victory or with a positive military solution seemed to have vanished.* When in November 2006 former secretary of state Henry Kissinger, an early supporter of the war, stated to a British audience that the Iraq War was unwinnable, his words quickly reverberated in the American
   political arena. Kissinger's prediction was clearly at variance with President Bush's remark just
   a few days earlier during his trip to Vietnam that "we can succeed [in Iraq] if we don't quit."

5. *President Bush was increasingly worried that as the Iraq War dragged on without a positive
   end in sight his administration was losing its credibility at home, in the Middle East, and in
   the world at large.* Moreover, the image and reputation of the U.S. abroad was being severely
   tarnished and reaching an all-time low. Bush may have lost credibility at home, as the results of the November 2006 elections suggested. Some pundits downplayed the credibility
   factor in foreign policy. For example, retired general William Odom, an outspoken critic of
   the U.S. war in Iraq, argued that "a hyperpower need not worry about credibility." However, others like Kissinger placed a high premium on credibility—reminiscent of the situation the U.S. faced during the last years of the Vietnam War. In Kissinger's view, if the U.S.
   suffered a military disaster in Iraq it would also suffer a crushing political setback in the
   oil-rich and volatile Middle East; moreover, this would weaken American influence in
   other regions around the world. According to Bob Woodward of the *Washington Post* in his
   book *State of Denial*, published in October 2006, Kissinger had made frequent visits to the
   White House to advise the president on the war when presumably he stressed the importance of victory in Iraq, which would enhance U.S. credibility. Senator Chuck Hagel (R-
   NE) gave a slightly different slant on the credibility factor. According to Hagel, as the U.S.
   continued fighting in Iraq, Americans were "perceived as a nation at war with Muslims . . .
   which will complicate America's global credibility, purpose and leadership."

6. *The economic costs of the Iraq War faced resistance by an increasingly skeptical Congress and
   American public.* In fall 2006 there were estimates that the war in Iraq was costing nearly $2
   billion a week. This was 20 percent more than the previous year and significantly more than

the funds allocated to the U.S. military effort in Afghanistan. Congressional estimates also placed the cost of both the Iraq and Afghanistan wars since the terrorist attacks on September 11, 2001, at $509 billion, with the lion's share (about $300 billion) going to Iraq. Early predictions on the future cost of the war in Iraq after the U.S. initial military success were not realized. For example, Vice President Dick Cheney said that Iraqis would greet the Americans as liberators. Moreover, no WMD were found. Finally, initial plans for paying for the Iraq War—notably Deputy Defense Secretary Paul Wolfowitz's expectation that Iraq could "really finance its own reconstruction" through oil revenues—proved unrealistic. Finally, other American politicians had grossly underestimated the costs of a protracted war.

7. *With such big spending in the face of burgeoning budget deficits and perceived failures to achieve desired goals in Iraq, public support for continued high expenditures to prosecute the war was clearly eroding.* However, there were lingering pockets of support among those who feared that a cutback of U.S. financial aid and perhaps withdrawal of some U.S. forces would leave an even weaker and more unstable Iraqi government which, if it fell, would leave an anarchic vacuum in the region.

8. *Congress was increasingly seen as abdicating its oversight role in the war.* Not only did Congress authorize the war—though with limited information, debate, and poor intelligence—according to Senator Hagel it continued "funding this war dishonestly, mainly through supplemental appropriations, which minimizes responsible congressional oversight and allows the administration to duck tough questions in defending its policies." In effect this "emergency" budgeting was cloaking the true cost of the war.

9. *Innumerable comparisons between the exit strategies the U.S. used in the Vietnam War and the ones it was considering in the Iraq War left a number of troubling questions.* For example, could "Iraqization" succeed where "Vietnamization" failed? Some argued that handing over responsibility for security to the Iraqi army and police would lead to greater stabilization of the country. But with their highly suspect loyalty and allegiance, and with poor U.S. training and deployment, how soon—if ever—could the "U.S. stand down when the Iraqis stand up"? There was related concern over at least two catch-22s in Iraq: First, the more the U.S. supported an Iraqi government controlled by Shiites, the more the Sunnis would resist this government and the more Iraq was destabilized; and second, how could the current Shiite-dominated Iraqi government work with U.S. forces to quash radical Shiite militias when it was so heavily dependent on their support for political survival? Finally, there was the concern that the Iraqi government existed mainly on paper, without any real control over what went on in the country.

10. *U.S. government officials could not agree on an appropriate timetable for withdrawal of U.S. forces, or whether a timetable should be set at all.* Should U.S. troops simply "stay the course," or when the White House dropped this phrase just before the congressional elections in November 2006, maintain essentially the same strategy but show more "flexibility"? Or should there be a "phased withdrawal" over the course of several months, years, or even decades? And if there is to be complete withdrawal, should there be a certain date? After the November 2006 elections, some Democratic leaders stepped up calls for a timetable for withdrawal. For example, Senator Carl Levin (D-MI), the new chair of the Senate Armed Services Committee, talked publicly about U.S. forces leaving in about four to six months; and Senator John Kerry (D-MA), Representative John Murtha (D-PA), and newly elected Speaker of the House Nancy Pelosi and the new Senate Majority Leader Harry Reid (D-NV) all argued that since the U.S. military strategy in Iraq already was a clear failure with no hope of success, the U.S. should withdraw its forces as soon as possible. However, crit-

ics of a set timetable (sometimes referred to as a set "surrender date"), mainly in the White House, believed this would seriously weaken chances for the U.S. to stabilize Iraq because the "enemy," however defined, would simply wait to pounce until after the U.S. withdrawal. Consequently, President Bush made it clear that he would veto any legislation that contained a timetable for withdrawal. Complicating this situation was the fact that moderate Sunnis tended to want American forces to stay in Iraq as protection against Shiite radicals who wanted U.S. forces to leave as soon as possible. Indeed, to make this point in April 2007, Moqtada al Sadr withdrew six ministers from the Iraqi cabinet.

11. *Some critics contend that the original U.S. goal of establishing a democracy in Iraq was unrealistic given Iraq's vastly different history, culture, religion, and values and the deepening violence in the country.* These critics argued that democracy is always difficult to transplant or grow in another country's soil. This is especially so where the people have been victimized by a brutal dictatorship for many years. Instead, they maintained that democracy must be home-grown, which would be very difficult in Iraq's inhospitable soil. Others, mainly neoconservatives, still held onto this idea, arguing that establishing democracy will take time but is vital to the future stability, security, and peace in the region. Still others argued that authoritarian rulers and their supporters in neighboring Arab states will learn the lesson from a failed Iraqi experience that democracy is too risky a venture, potentially causing chaos and despair; instead these rulers may decide to step up their authoritarianism. After the November 2006 elections, President Bush seemed to have realized the impracticality of achieving his original goal of making Iraq a beacon of democracy when he explained his new goal of "a government that can defend, govern and sustain itself."

12. *The Bush administration identified Iraq as the central front in the U.S.'s Global War on Terror at the time of the U.S.-led invasion in 2003.* However, it is ironic that there were many more al Qaeda forces in Iraq three years later, and there was good likelihood that continued U.S. military "occupation" of Iraq would continue to attract even more al Qaeda terrorists. In fact, al Qaeda leaders announced they wanted U.S. forces to remain in Iraq, at least for the time being, where they would continue to suffer increased casualties and political humiliation. Interestingly, the wording from the Bush administration started to change after the November 2006 elections. For example, in testimony before a congressional committee, General Michael V. Hayden, director of the Central Intelligence Agency, spoke of Iraq as an "absolutely critical battlefront" in the War on Terror, though not as the main front.

13. *Commitment of U.S. forces in Iraq may have weakened the U.S. military effort in Afghanistan, the original locus of the U.S. War on Terror, and possibly other regions around the world where U.S. forces may be needed.* The Bush administration must be careful not to spread its military too thin. Some argued that it was bad for Iraq to overshadow or even eclipse the U.S. military effort in Afghanistan, especially when U.S. forces reportedly were closing in on Osama bin Laden. Critics also pointed to a war-weary volunteer armed services and the overuse—and even misuse—of the National Guard in Iraq, where soldiers were being deployed for repeated tours of duty.

14. *In March 2007, investigative reporters revealed deplorable conditions for wounded Iraq war veterans in Walter Reed Hospital and other veterans' medical facilities.* Critics demanded immediate corrective action. Implicit in this criticism was that if the U.S. government was unprepared to handle existing war casualties, as the war dragged on how could it handle even more?

15. *There has been a call for a reinstitution of the draft.* Supporters of a draft, like Representative Charles Rangel (D-NY) proposed legislation to this effect. According to Rangel, a draft would not only increase the numbers in the military but also more equitably share the burden of war. Whatever the merits of a draft, the idea was given the cold shoulder by both Democratic and Republican leadership in both houses.

16. *The Iraq War may have significantly weakened U.S influence in the United Nations.* Many world leaders still harbor resentment against President Bush for going to war without authorization from the Security Council. The longer the war drags on, the more necessary help from the UN may be. Many assert that the U.S. must compromise to some degree in an effort to save face internationally and defer some responsibility to the organization, regardless of prior disagreements.

17. *The U.S. was increasingly fighting alone in Iraq as forces from "the Coalition of the Willing" began to depart the country.* Even the United Kingdom, America's main ally in the war, announced on February 21, 2007, that it planned a "moderate reduction" of most of its 7,100 troops in southern Iraq by late 2007. At the same time, other countries in the "Coalition of the Willing" such as Denmark announced plans to draw down their troops.

18. *President Bush was criticized for relying too heavily on the "Rumsfeld Doctrine."* Critics charged that the U.S. should not have gone to war in Iraq under the "Rumsfeld Doctrine," which depended heavily on technology, utilized realitively small numbers of troops, and had an unclear postwar plan and uncertain exit strategy. Instead, they claimed that the U.S. should have been guided by the "Powell Doctrine," which stressed going to war only with a defined mission, overwhelming military force, and a clear exit strategy—but also with flexibility to reassess when there is a change in mission. Moreover, critics argued that the U.S. was unprepared—especially as regards knowledge of Iraq's history and culture—for what happened in Iraq after Bush declared "mission accomplished." Secretary of Defense Donald Rumsfeld, the main architect of the U.S. military effort in Iraq, bore the brunt of such criticism as pressure mounted for his dismissal or resignation. Finally, he resigned the day after the November 2006 elections, taking at least a little steam out of the criticism of Bush's war policy. Rumsfeld was replaced by Robert M. Gates, former CIA director under President George H. W. Bush and former member of the ISG. It was unclear whether the Gates appointment indicated a possible shift in the administration's Iraq strategy. Before his confirmation, Gates gave some clues to his position when he stated that he opposed a swift pullout from Iraq, fearing this would leave the country "in chaos" that "would have dangerous consequences both in the region and globally for many years to come." Moreover, he favored U.S. diplomatic engagement with both Syria and Iran, though on a regional rather than unilateral basis.

19. *The Iraq war sharpened a constitutional debate over the respective powers of Congress and the president in war time.* The president as commander in chief has the power to deploy troops, whereas Congress with the power of the purse can cut off funds whenever it wants. But if Congress does this, it could be accused both of micromanaging the war and of encroaching on presidential power. Whatever the constitutional argument, most legislators understandably are very reluctant to cut funding for troops in the field.

20. *One of the ISG's recommendations was to involve countries in the region in trying to stabilize and eventually establish peace in Iraq.* Two of the countries considered for this role were Syria and Iran. But President Bush had been isolating and criticizing these countries—Syria for its meddling in Lebanon and support for terrorist groups, and Iran for training, arming, and funding sectarian violence in Iraq. Moreover, the president in his

first State of the Union address had included Iran in his "axis of evil" (along with Iraq and North Korea), had labeled it a state sponsor of terror in the Middle East, and had criticized it for developing a dangerous nuclear weapons program. However, in March 2007 President Bush reversed course. He agreed to U.S. participation in a regional meeting in Baghdad where American diplomats talked face to face with both Iran and Syria, although not on a bilateral basis. However, in May at a regional conference on the stabilization of Iraq hosted by Egypt at the resort city of Sharm el-Sheikh, Secretary of State Condoleeza Rice met privately with Syrian Foreign Minister Walid Moallem.

21. *The Iraq War was caught up in controversial euphemisms and wordings.* Here are some notable examples:

    a. In 2003, did President Bush launch a preemptive or preventive war against Iraq? The official White House designation was preemptive war, which meant that Iraq at the time of the U.S.-led invasion had both the capability and the intention for an imminent attack against its neighbors or the United States. However, critics argue that since Iraq had neither the means nor the intent for an imminent strike, the invasion should have been labeled a preventive war. This distinction is not just semantical, for a preventive war where the threat is not imminent is much harder to justify.

    b. Should the enemy in Iraq be called "Islamofascists," "jihadists," "insurgents," or "dead-enders"? Instead of "withdrawal," which became too closely associated with "cut and run," should "phased redeployment" be used? For comparison purposes, according to reminiscences by Leslie Gelb, president emeritus of the Council on Foreign Relations and a Pentagon official during the Vietnam War, at that time the U.S. began using "talks" with Hanoi rather than "negotiation," as it was believed much of the public did not want this country to negotiate with a "devil" enemy; and the U.S. was dropping "ordnance" on Vietnam rather than "bombs." Just before the November 2006 elections, the Bush administration dropped "stay the course" when the public began associating this term with a failed exit strategy from Vietnam; and it scaled down the goal of the U.S. in the Iraq War to "success" rather than "victory." The president soon made another modification when on November 28, 2006, he stated in a speech to NATO members in Latvia that U.S. troops would not leave Iraq "before the mission is complete." Shortly before this, Senator John McCain (R-AZ) had expressed the hope that the U.S. could "prevail" in Iraq.

    c. In early 2007 President Bush announced he would soon send 21,500 troops to Iraq. To the White House, "surge" probably sounded more vigorous and hopeful than either "enhancement" (too bland) or "escalation" (too reminiscent of failure in Vietnam).

22. *The Iraq War became a major issue in partisan politics.* Kissinger has argued that the kiss of death to an American military venture is when it becomes caught up in partisan politics. Some argue that the November 2006 elections that saw the Democrats regain control of both houses of Congress, in effect, was a national referendum on the Iraq War. If so, the election was a stunning defeat for President Bush's Iraq policy. The stage was set in a Democratic-led Congress for a change of course, but it remained uncertain what this course would be.

23. *As hopes for a positive outcome of the Iraq War dwindled, some people began asking "Who lost Iraq?"* This was reminiscent of earlier setbacks or defeats for the U.S., such as "Who lost Eastern Europe?" "Who lost China?" and "Who lost Vietnam?" Americans recalled President John F. Kennedy's quip that "victory has a thousand fathers but defeat is an orphan." It will be interesting to see how the "blame game" plays out. Surely whatever exit strategy the U.S. eventually adopts will impact heavily on who receives the brunt of the blame.

Background of the Case

Effects of the First Gulf War and Saddam Hussein's Violations of Postwar Agreements

Following Iraq's invasion of Kuwait on August 2, 1990, and its ensuing defeat by U.S.-led coalition forces under UN auspices, Saddam Hussein's regime was placed under strict UN sanctions until it complied with several conditions. These included recognition of Kuwait's sovereignty and the inviolability of the Iraq-Kuwait border, accountability for Kuwaiti prisoners, financial restitution for the pillaging of Kuwait, and submission to a no-fly zone. However, the largest stumbling block to removal of sanctions was Iraq's refusal to allow UN inspection of its capabilities for WMD and possible weapons sites.

After the cease-fire in February 1991, criticism began to mount that President George H.W. Bush should not have ended the first Gulf War without removing Hussein from power. The eventual difficulties with sanctions enforcement and effectiveness only heightened such criticism. Critics charged that U.S. policies toward Iraq had become too reactive and passive in the face of Hussein's continual flouting of UN-imposed restrictions. After several relatively minor skirmishes in the early and mid-1990s surrounding no-fly zone and Kuwaiti sovereignty infractions, a series of crises from winter 1997 to fall 1998 seemed to have brought matters to a head. These crises, triggered by Hussein's repeated refusal to allow the UN Special Commission (UNSCOM) complete and unfettered freedom to inspect weapons sites, resulted in several U.S. and U.K. missile strikes on Iraq.

With concerns mounting surrounding Hussein's lack of compliance with Resolution 687 calling for immediate declaration and destruction of all WMD, Secretary-General Annan tried in early 1998 to broker an agreement allowing UNSCOM inspectors more complete access within Iraq. President Bill Clinton cautiously accepted this agreement, as did all other involved parties, but U.S. distrust of Hussein continued. In summer 1998, chief UN arms inspector Richard Butler outlined a set of requirements for Iraq to end weapons inspections:

- Hand over information on long-range missiles that it had imported.
- Prove that it had scrapped all biological and chemical warheads and missile fuel.
- Provide documentation on the domestic production of long-range missiles.
- Prove that it had dismantled unaccounted-for chemical munitions.
- Fully account for what it had done in producing the deadly chemical agent VX that reportedly Hussein had used against Iraqi Kurds in Halabja near the end of the Iran-Iraq War.

Hussein claimed these requirements were politically motivated, and in August 1998 he barred UNSCOM inspectors from visiting new sites with suspected stores of biological and chemical weapons and long-range missiles. In response, Scott Ritter, the top American on UNSCOM, resigned in anger, calling the inspection a dangerous "illusion." In his resignation letter, Ritter wrote: "The issue of immediate, unrestricted access is . . . the cornerstone of any viable inspection scheme." Ritter added, "Unfortunately, others don't share this opinion, including the Secretary-General of the United Nations." Ritter was upset with Annan for not being tough enough with Iraq. He was also perturbed at what he deemed the weakness of President Clinton's use of economic sanctions rather than the threat of military action to pressure Iraq to comply with the obligations imposed after the Gulf War. Some time later, Ritter became an outspoken critic of President Bush's position that the UN inspectors had not done a thorough job in looking for WMD sites. In Ritter's view, the inspectors had done their job and he was confident Iraq did not have WMD.

On October 31, 1998, Iraq announced that it was halting all dealings with UNSCOM. After a period in which Hussein continuously vacillated between compliance and provocation, in December the U.S. and U.K. unleashed "Operation Desert Fox," a four-day missile and bomb assault on Iraqi weapons facilities. While this temporarily halted Hussein's defiance, problems continued in late 1999 with the creation of a new UN monitoring verification and inspection commission (UNMOVIC) and Iraq's consequent rejection of the resolution.

The Clinton presidency ended with some critics still contending that Hussein should have been removed from power during the first Gulf War. Hussein's continuing noncompliance with UN weapons inspectors had already caused mounting U.S. military strikes and a great deal of speculation regarding lingering WMD programs. The American public was often reminded that Hussein had used poison gas against Iraq's Kurdish population and Iran in the last days of the Iran-Iraq War. The election of George W. Bush to office in 2001, coupled with an ensuing drastic turn of events, would lead to intensification of this conflict. Soon Iraq was in the headlights of what became a new, bolder, and more assertive U.S. foreign policy.

The Impact of the 9/11 Attacks and Escalating Conflict

President Bush was elected with a campaign platform that included "full implementation" of 1998's Iraq Liberation Act (legislation passed under Clinton that called for a democratic Iraq and support to opposition leaders like Ahmed Chalabi). This stance hardened as a result of the terrorist attacks of September 11, 2001. Shortly thereafter, Bush declared there was a connection between Osama bin Laden and the Hussein regime. While the special 9/11 Commission found no such connection, terrorists attacks on the Twin Towers and the Pentagon did provide an impetus for the Bush administration to begin its War on Terror. Cracking down on state sponsors of terror later became one of Bush's motivations for removing Hussein. In his January 2002 State of the Union address, the president listed Iraq as part of an "axis of evil," along with Iran and North Korea. This classification helped set the stage for the ensuing conflict over Iraq's alleged noncompliance with UN inspections and sponsorship of terror.

Hussein continued his defiance toward UN inspectors in 2002, refusing to allow their return aside from a brief stint in September that was quickly retracted. Secretary-General Annan was unable to persuade Hussein, and with pressure from Bush and British Prime Minister Tony Blair mounting for multilateral military action, the Security Council passed Resolution 1441 on November 8, 2002, calling on Iraq to cooperate with inspection teams and declare all its WMD within one month. This resolution did not authorize the use of force to implement these terms, but the U.S. Congress had recently passed the Authorization for Use of Military Force against Iraq Resolution of 2002. That legislation permitted Bush to attack Iraq if Hussein did not give up his WMD and comply with past UN resolutions involving inspections, terrorism, and human rights. When Iraq submitted the requested documentation on December 7, the U.S. government did not accept the report, claiming it was incomplete and unconvincing regarding WMD.

The beginning of 2003 saw a growing schism in the UN between those calling for a second resolution authorizing military force (led by the U.S. and U.K.), and those who opposed the idea (led by France, Germany, and Russia). In the spring, France announced it would veto any second resolution authorizing UN force against Iraq. In the meantime, chief UN weapons inspector Hans Blix requested more time for UNMOVIC to complete its tasks. Despite facing such opposition to military action from within the UN, Bush addressed the nation on March 17, 2003, announcing he had given Hussein and his two sons forty-eight hours to surrender and leave Iraq. When this demand was rejected, Bush decided to invade Iraq without UN authorization. However, the president's goal of stabilizing and democratizing Iraq proved far more daunting than anticipated. The invasion unleashed sectarian violence between Sunnis and Shiites and provided an opportunity for al Qaeda and foreign fighters from the Muslim world to add to the chaos that soon enveloped Iraq. These developments created policy dilemmas for which there seemed no easy and quick solutions.

May 1, 2003, marked the conclusion of major military operations, but regrettably this did not lead to peace in Iraq. U.S. troops continued to clash with resistance movements concentrated largely in the "Sunni Triangle," the dense area northwest of Baghdad that contains Fallujah, Samarra, Ramadi, and Tikrit. Clashes also occurred in Baghdad itself, along with serious looting of historical treasures and antiquities from museums. These resistance movements would eventually burgeon into the larger insurgency that began to engulf Iraq, spreading to new areas and gradually including new groups of Sunnis, Shiites, Kurds, and jihadists. The insurgency was largely carried out by three distinct groups: disgruntled Sunnis and former Ba'ath Party loyalists, local Shiites such as Moqtada al Sadr and his Mahdi Army, and foreign fighters using Iraq as a breeding and training ground for terrorists like those led by Abu Musab al-Zarqawi. Zarqawi was a Jordanian who, once imprisoned by Jordan's King Hussein for extremist political opposition, after the U.S. invasion traveled to Iraq where he assumed leadership of al Qaeda forces. Although U.S. forces killed him in 2005, he was replaced immediately and terrorist activities soon even increased.

After a brief period of relative optimism after an initial military victory over Hussein's forces, the president found himself increasingly subjected to public criticism regarding the war, which dragged on after his "mission accomplished" speech. The main criticism involved reliance on faulty prewar intelligence and questionable war motives that some argued were deliberately intended to mislead the American public. Critics began to ask why no WMD were found in Iraq, and to suggest that the Bush foreign policy team had "cherry-picked" intelligence to justify an unnecessary and unwise invasion. In response, Bush and his advisers began vocally defending their intelligence and insisting that any doubts had not been effectively communicated to them by the responsible intelligence agencies.

The fact that no WMD were found in Iraq, despite almost Cinderella shoe–like efforts by the U.S., continued to haunt the administration as it began searching for an exit strategy. Opponents of the war attacked any continued U.S. presence in Iraq on the grounds that the invasion was not justified in the first place. The Bush administration also faced challenges about the legality of the invasion. World leaders like Secretary-General Annan claimed the invasion had violated the UN Charter; and UN weapons inspector Hans Blix and former President Jimmy Carter both called the war illegal.

The year 2004 saw the beginnings of a gradual transfer of authority from U.S. forces to an interim Iraqi government, with plans for a more permanent one to be democratically elected. On March 1, an interim constitution was agreed upon and approved by the U.S., followed by UN recognition and the transfer of sovereignty to Prime Minister Iyad Allawi and his government. The Allawi government oversaw the drafting of the Iraqi constitution and worked to stabilize the country until impending general elections in January 2005 and the legislative election in December of that year. Thus, a framework for the transition to a democratic Iraq was established.

Despite these initial successes, some of the Bush administration's problems began to worsen in 2004. U.S. forces in Iraq had two of their deadliest months in April and November, while images of U.S. torture of Iraqi prisoners at Abu Ghraib prison were revealed in April as well. These images created horrible publicity for the U.S. military and Central Intelligence Agency, and resulted in internal investigations and the dismissal of both high- and low-ranking U.S. officers. Even with this reaction, though, many public critics considered the administration's response to prisoner abuse too timid and limited. At the same time the insurgency also continued to spread, causing U.S. troops to attack the cities of Najaf and Fallujah in an attempt to subdue Sadr, Zarqawi, and others. As these problems mounted, experts began to warn the administration of the growing chance of full-scale civil war in Iraq.

While criticism was still rampant over not finding WMD, the focus of U.S. public opinion clearly began to shift to issues of economic costs, troop commitments, and security concerns as the chaos within Iraq continued into 2005. Bush signed a supplemental spending bill in May, authorizing an additional $76 billion for operations in Iraq and Afghanistan on top of the previous $87 billion allocated in 2003. It also became increasingly apparent as the year went on that despite proclaimed successes against the insurgents U.S. military casualties were mounting. The American public's enthusiasm for the ongoing effort in Iraq began to decline significantly. The Army declared in September 2005 that it had missed its recruiting target for the previous year by the largest margin since 1979, while the Senate began to exert pressure for a phased troop reduction. Outspoken critics in the House, such as Representative Murtha, also began to openly call for an immediate and complete withdrawal within a specified time.

At the same time, in 2005 there was significant progress in democratization. On January 30, Iraq held its first free election in decades, voting on a transitional National Assembly that would assist Allawi's government in drafting the constitution and clear the way for permanent legislative elections in December. The United Iraqi Alliance (UIA), a Shiite coalition, won a narrow majority in the transitional assembly, followed by a Kurdish party, with Allawi's party coming in third. As a result of these returns, the Sunni minority that had previously ruled the country became dangerously underrepresented and disillusioned with the new government, fueling the already raging insurgency in the central portions of the country.

The elections in December 2005 for a new Iraqi National Assembly were significantly more complex. Of the 275 seats available, 230 were allocated to provinces based on number of voters, while the remainder was distributed to parties that received a substantial number of votes nationwide but did not gain provincial seats. The UIA once again emerged victorious, but this time it gained only a plurality (128 seats) and eventually needed to arrange a coalition with Kurdish, Sunni, and secular Shiite parties in order to form a government with new Prime Minister Ibrahim al-Jaafari at its head. The election was largely considered a success in terms of fairness and turnout, despite some disruption by insurgents.

With the Bush administration's release in November 2005 of the *National Strategy for Victory in Iraq* and the ensuing public relations offensive to explain its approach, Washington's focus continued to shift toward a plan for the future and an eventual U.S. exit. Throughout the first half of 2006, Bush defended his "stay the course" strategy in the face of mounting criticism calling for withdrawal. While requesting an additional $70 billion for the efforts in Iraq and Afghanistan, Bush declared in March that U.S. troops would remain in Iraq until at least 2009, and that issues of withdrawal would be left to "future presidents and future governments of Iraq." This came in the face of mounting domestic political pressure, mainly from Democrats, to set a timetable for U.S. withdrawal in the near future.

Political pressure also had its effects within the new Iraq. With blame increasing for alleged mishandlings of the insurgency and other internal issues, Jaafari resigned as Prime Minister in April and was replaced by fellow Shiite UIA leader Nuri Kamal al-Maliki. After taking control, however, Maliki oversaw the formation of Iraq's first permanent constitutional government since Hussein's fall; he also declared that the country's troops would be able to handle security responsibilities on their own by the end of 2007, though to some observers this seemed far too optimistic.

As 2006 came to a close, the Bush administration found itself facing unprecedented pressure to articulate a clear and effective exit strategy for U.S. forces. There was also a flurry of diplomatic activity on the future of Iraq involving the U.S., Iraq, and Iraq's neighbors. President Bush met with Prime Minister Maliki in Jordan; Vice President Cheney met with King Abdullah of Saudi Arabia in the desert kingdom; and Iraq's President Jalal Talabani, a Kurd, met in Tehran with the supreme leader of Iran, the Grand Ayatollah Ali Khamenei, and its president, Mahmoud Ahmadinejad. A short time earlier, Iraq had reestablished diplomatic relations with Syria, which had been broken twenty-four years earlier. The need for imaginative and skillful diplomacy was great, for the sectarian violence in Iraq threatened to spill over into the whole region. Some observers also argued that if the Bush administration started playing a major role in helping Israel and the Palestinians reach a peace settlement, this might have a salutary effect on both the image of the U.S. in the Muslim world and the resolution of the Iraq War.

In the meantime, critics continued to attack the Bush administration's use of funds and the alleged lack of an effective strategy in the Iraq War. With the Democrats regaining control of both the Senate and House in the November 2006 elections, Bush stopped using his "stay the course" terminology because of its implications of negativity and rigidity. Nevertheless, the president continued to insist that U.S. troops remain in Iraq indefinitely until its own government and security forces were capable of stabilizing and defending the country. But the American public was becoming increasingly dissatisfied with what seemed to many like a failed strategy. But given the president's seemingly unshakable position on the war, what could be done?

The Pentagon came up with three possible options. The U.S. could either send in more troops that might shorten the war, reduce forces but stay longer, or leave Iraq altogether. But each of these options was fraught with difficulties, dangers, and uncertainties. Perhaps the president would look elsewhere for options. The bipartisan ISG had been commissioned by Congress to explore possible exit strategy options. It was anticipated that this commission would provide both ideas and political cover (especially for Republicans) to find the best way out of Iraq.

On December 6, 2006, the ISG finally issued its long-awaited report. Its main recommendations were to withdraw U.S. forces from Iraq beginning in early 2007, but without setting a definite timetable. At the same time, the U.S. was reducing it combat role and shifting more toward supporting, training, and advising Iraqi army and security units. In addition, Bush rejected the ISG recommendation for an aggressive diplomatic effort to involve Iran and Syria in a regional peace conference. At least publicly the president continued showing determination and expressing confidence that U.S. forces could stabilize Iraq and provide security for its people. At a meeting in Amman, Jordan, with Prime Minister Maliki on November 20, 2006, Bush reiterated that the U.S. would not leave Iraq until its job was finished.

Policy Options

By early 2007, in the face of continued escalating violence and increasing domestic political opposition, President Bush was increasingly pressured to change what many considered a failed strategy. He kept insisting that the U.S. would not leave Iraq until it accomplished its goals or the Iraqi government asked it to leave. Yet he expected there would be no "graceful exit." However, Iraq continued to break apart and down, and as it was becoming clear that U.S. military operations were not working, the president had to try something else. But what? There seemed to be a choice only between several poor alternatives.

President Bush's Decision to Boost U.S. Troops in Iraq

On January 10, 2007, in a speech to the nation on prime-time television President Bush announced his "new" course of action, which he called "The New Way Forward." For the first time, he took responsibility for previous mistakes, including admission that more U.S. troops should have been in Iraq much earlier, for example to hold areas cleared of insurgents. The main thrust of the president's plan was twofold: He would send an additional 21,500 U.S. troops mostly to Baghdad to stop both Sunni and Shiite militia units and gangs from terrorizing the capital; and he would take a much harder line toward the Maliki government, maintaining that if it did not take more responsibility for security and stability it would lose American support. Ultimately, as Secretary of State Rice explained to the media the next day, "It is the Iraqis who are responsible for what kind of country Iraq will be."

There was some support for President Bush's decision, mainly from Senators McCain and Lindsey Graham (R-SC). McCain, a 2008 presidential hopeful, had long advocated a "surge" of U.S. troops to Iraq, though with larger numbers. However, with a steadily mounting death toll of American soldiers (over 3,000 at the time) the president's plan fell under heavy assault. There already was strong skepticism, pessimism, criticism, and strong opposition from both the American public and Congress. A *USA Today*/Gallup poll at the time of President Bush's speech showed that 72 percent of Americans disapproved of his handling of the Iraq War, and an AP/Ipsos poll released January 11 showed 70 percent opposed his decision to send in more troops. There was fierce opposition to Bush's decision among Democrats in Congress, such as Senator Joseph Biden (D-DE), who days before had announced his candidacy for president. Biden warned President Bush to heed the experience of Vietnam—he could not prosecute a war without the support of the American people. President Bush faced equally severe criticism from fellow Republicans like Senator Hagel. Hagel, like McCain a decorated Vietnam War veteran, called the decision to send in more troops "the most dangerous foreign policy blunder since the Vietnam War, if it is carried out." A number of foreign policy experts also denounced President Bush's decision. For example, Professor Zbigniew Brzezinski, National Security Advisor under President Carter, decried the fact that he saw "not an inkling of a political strategy." Indeed, Bush's seeming focus on a reinvigorated military strategy rather than a stronger political/diplomatic gambit was a major theme of a growing chorus of opposition.

In February 2007 the U.K., still the U.S.'s staunchest ally in Iraq, announced plans to draw down its troops in Iraq. It had committed roughly 40,000 troops to the U.S.-led invasion of Iraq in 2003, but by 2005 it had reduced this number to about 9,000; and in early 2007 it had only about 7,100 troops left in the southern part of the country. The White House put a positive political spin on Britain's draw down decision, calling it "basically a good-news story." Yet critics like Senator Arlen Specter (R-PA) said, "I think it's Alice in Wonderland looking through the looking glass!"

Whether Bush's new plan for prosecuting the war in Iraq would bear fruit was highly problematic; nor was it even clear how long it would be tried or what the benchmarks for success were. Secretary Gates testified the day after Bush's speech that the U.S. would wait some months (but not up to two years) to decide whether Bush's plan was working. In early 2007, President Bush and his supporters pinned their hopes on General David Petraeus, the new commander of U.S. forces in Iraq. Petraeus was a highly respected leader and scholar who literally had written the "book" on counterinsurgency. If anyone could make the surge work ("Plan A"), it was

Petraeus. If this plan failed, there most likely would not be a "Plan B." However, in the mean-time, presumably the administration would continue to evaluate alternatives. The following military, diplomatic, and political options—including some variations of the president's decision—were still on the table:

Military Options

1. *"Stay the course."* The Bush administration had repeatedly stated that U.S. troops would not withdraw until they succeeded in their mission—that is, when the Iraqi government became more stable and secure. Moreover, the president indicated that the U.S. troop level of roughly 140,000 (as of April 2007 about 60,000 combat troops with the rest being support troops) would probably remain in Iraq until at least the next administration. This number, he added, was based largely on recommendations from U.S. military commanders in Iraq. While the president dropped the "stay the course" terminology just before the November 2006 elections, it appeared that he was not planning an exit strategy anytime soon.

2. *Withdraw as fast as possible, leaving the provision of security and stability and other respon-sibilities to the Iraqi government.* This position has been adopted by a number of war crit-ics, notably General Odom. However, the White House has labeled this policy "cut and run" and characterized it as "defeatist." The president argued that a precipitous withdrawal could leave behind an intensified civil war, a destabilized Iraq, a strengthened al Qaeda, and Iran as regional hegemon. Odom and his supporters responded that these things are al-ready true and that a withdrawal would not make them any worse. Instead, early with-drawal would cut U.S. losses in soldiers, economic resources, and political capital.

3. *Set a timetable for gradual troop withdrawal with definitive benchmarks, reducing U.S. mil-itary commitment until Iraq takes complete control.* This option was supported by those who oppose a continued U.S. military presence in Iraq like Senator Kerry and Congress-man Murtha. The ISG recommended a pullback of significant numbers of U.S. troops by 2008, but without a specific timetable. President Bush and other opponents of a timetable believed it would play into the hands of al Qaeda and others in Iraq who would just bide their time and wait for U.S. withdrawal to strike again. Still others believe a timetable would impose unnecessary and unrealistic deadlines for achieving difficult objectives.

4. *Redeploy U.S. troops to and from certain strategic areas.* This option involves a restructure of forces rather than an increase or decrease. For some advocates of this option, rede-ployment within Iraq should focus more on Baghdad and specific insurgent strongholds throughout the country. For others, redeployment should be considered on a grander scale, moving troops elsewhere in the region such as neighboring Kuwait or offshore. This option also allows for international assistance and regional conferences, with the possi-bility of setting a timetable. In essence, though, whether, when, and where U.S. troops would go would depend on a clearer definition of their mission.

5. *Accept the reality of defeat or failure and leave as fast as possible.* Supporters of this posi-tion, like columnist James Carroll of the *Boston Globe*, argue that the U.S. was already de-feated in Iraq and the sooner it recognizes it the better. They argue that the U.S. should not foolishly allow the Iraq War to drag on like the Vietnam War did.

6. *Stay ten months or ten years.* Thomas Friedman, foreign affairs columnist for the *New York Times*, wrote on November 29, 2006, that the U.S. was faced with "two impossible choices." Either this country would have to stay long enough "to crush the dark forces in Iraq and properly rebuild it," which might take as long as ten years, or "we need to leave"

within ten months or so. The worst choice, he argued, would be to continue an unwise middle ground of "stumbling along as we have been."

Diplomatic Options

1. *Organize a regional peace conference.* General Barry McCaffrey and others have suggested utilizing this option to enlist the support of neighboring states in stabilizing a new Iraq, especially Syria and Iran. Supporters of this option argued that the U.S. really could not go it alone in Iraq and sorely needed assistance from neighboring states that had a vested interest in Iraq's not becoming a failed state. The 1995 Dayton Accords that helped end the war in Bosnia were cited as a potential model for this approach. At first, the Bush administration opposed this idea. It was reluctant to call upon either Syria or Iran as it considered them more troublemakers than potential peacemakers. However, perhaps stung by repeated criticism for not talking to its enemies (even during the Cold War the U.S. talked with the Soviet Union), in March 2007 the Bush administration participated in multilateral talks in Baghdad where American diplomats shook hands with and talked directly to delegates from both Iran and Syria. Then at a regional conference on Iraq held in May at Sharm el-Sheikh, U.S. and Syrian diplomats talked privately for the first time in two years.

2. *Reinvigorate the Israeli-Palestinian peace process.* The idea behind this option is that arguably the main underlying cause of tension in the Middle East is the Israeli-Palestinian conflict. If the U.S. were successful in restarting peace talks between these two parties, the hope is that the U.S. would receive some credit in the Arab world that could have a positive spillover effect in Iraq. Critics of this "holistic" approach to peace in the Middle East argue that the prospects for success of this option are very low and it reflects more desperation than realism.

3. *Arrange for international peacekeeping.* This would involve relying on UN diplomacy and possibly a UN force to assist with peacekeeping, reconstruction, and restoration of stability and basic services for the Iraqi population. However, it would take a lot to enlist UN forces for this mission, especially since President Bush had downplayed the need for UN support when he went to war in 2003.

4. *Let Prime Minister Maliki use Iraqi forces to quash the insurgency and restore stability and security.* Professor Mark Moyar of the United States Marine Corps University advocated this option, arguing that it is supported by the early experience of the Vietnam War during the Eisenhower administration. President Bush supported at least a variation of this idea. When he met with Prime Minister Maliki in Jordan at the end of November 2006, he called upon the Iraqis to do more to solve their own problems of instability and insecurity. However, critics argued that, even given the similarities of the Iraq and Vietnam wars, there are too many fundamental differences. For example, there is no Iraqi national leader with great stature and widespread public support, as Prime Minister Maliki is a Shiite beholden to Shiite interests. Perhaps a more fundamental criticism of this option, voiced by pundits such as Thomas Friedman, is that "Iraqization" was too late because Iraq had fallen into an unmanageable Hobbesian abyss.

5. *Offer a large economic aid package to Iraqi leaders to entice them to sit at the negotiating table to resolve their differences.* This option, proposed by Anthony Cordesman, an analyst at the Center for Strategic and International Studies in Washington, D.C., focused on the lure of a big money package to attract Iraqi leaders to negotiate their differences peacefully. However, critics pointed out that sectarian differences were too serious for nego

tiation to work, and that events in Iraq had already gone beyond the point where this option may have been feasible. It was also very doubtful that given the deepening anti–Iraq War sentiment in the U.S. whether the U.S. Congress would authorize such a large financial aid inducement.

Political Options for Iraq

1. *The Biden-Gelb Plan for a three-region Iraq.* This soft partition plan aims to keep Iraq intact while protecting U.S. interests and withdrawing most American troops by the end of 2007. Its main goal is to "maintain a unified Iraq by decentralizing it and giving Kurds, Shiites, and Sunnis breathing room in their own regions—as provided for in the Iraqi constitution." This plan also calls for an international conference "to enlist the support of Iraq's neighbors and create a contact group to enforce regional commitments." This plan was based loosely on an earlier idea publicized by Peter Galbraith, former ambassador to Croatia and longtime advisor to Iraqi Kurds. Galbraith argues that the Biden-Gelb plan is probably too optimistic. He maintains that Iraq, a state artificially created by British imperialism, de facto has already divided itself into three separate regions and has ceased to exist. Galbraith concludes that Iraq is not salvageable as a unified country; all that is needed now was recognition of this reality.

2. *Seek a two-state solution.* This idea, suggested by David Apgar (contributing editor to *The Globalist*), argues that a three-way solution would make Iraq's neighbors mad, especially Turkey with its large restive Kurdish population. Apgar believes that a two-state solution is more realistic and felicitous: One state (with about 5 million Kurds and an equal number of Sunnis) would run from southwest to northeast and include all of Baghdad and the 2 million to 3 million urban-suburban Shiites in its vicinity; and the other "purely Shiite state" would be located in the southeast but would also have access to the main Baghdad airport.

3. *Use a federal or confederal structure of government in a new Iraq.* The Iraqi Congress has already passed measures to permit the division of Iraq into three autonomous regions. This has become a contentious proposal, prompting many Sunnis and Shiites to walk out of parliament upon its suggestion. One crucially important and related issue is who will control Iraq's oil, located mainly in the Kurdish and Shiite sections. A Sunni region or state will benefit from this oil only through some sort of shared political process.

4. *Pick a winner.* Reportedly, U.S. ambassador to Iraq, Zalmay Khalilzad, later appointed U.S. ambassador to the UN, had for some time tried a policy of "Sunni outreach." The idea was to make the Sunni minority feel more included and involved in plans for a postwar Iraq. However, this strategy may have had a negative impact on Iraqi Shiites who believe the U.S. should focus on their concerns; moreover, it had failed to lead to any reduction in the Sunni insurgency. According to David Ignatius, columnist for the *Washington Post*, some Bush administration officials near the end of 2006 began arguing that "National reconciliation is a fallacy" and insisted, "You have to pick a winner." This option, sometimes referred to as "the 80 percent solution," would rely on a Shiite-dominated government and an Iraqi army that was predominantly Shiite and Kurdish. The main risk, though, is that Iraqi Sunnis would feel abandoned and in desperation increase their reliance on violence.

5. *Accept the possibility that the Shiites in the South will establish a theocracy, possibly tied to Iran.* Some argued that this is a likely outcome because Iraq's Shiites are closely tied to their religious brethren in Iran. In fact, many Iraqi Shiites had spent significant time in Iran either because they were exiled there by Saddam Hussein or chose to go there to study

their Islamic heritage. However, Shiites in Iraq in the past (e.g., during the Iraq-Iran War of the 1980s) had demonstrated some independence from Iran. Moreover, the Iraqi Constitution promises a unified secular state. Finally, settling for this option would be a terrible setback to the U.S., which has expended much time and effort trying to contain or moderate the Iranian theocracy.

6. *Develop a comprehensive strategy to quell the violence and establish stability.* According to retired Gen. John Abizaid, "military power solves about 20 percent of your problem . . . . The rest of it needs to be diplomatic, economic, political." Abizaid adds that this strategy requires a new national security structure and lots of patience. Consequently, this option may not be politically realistic since most of the American people want the U.S. out of Iraq as soon as possible.

Conclusion

The initial military success of the U.S.-led invasion of Iraq marked not only an achievement for the Bush administration, but also the beginning of a new set of challenges. Since President Bush's "mission accomplished" speech in May 2003, the new state of Iraq has both made significant progress and faced difficult setbacks: the democratization process has produced a constitution and an Iraqi National Congress, but this has been hampered by conflicting factions and problems with leadership at the prime minister position and the continuing struggle over who will wield power in postwar Iraq; U.S. troops have contributed to increased stability in some areas, but the insurgency has blown into a frightening civil war; and the U.S. has continued devoting enormous economic and military resources to Iraq despite mounting political pressure and partisan bickering. Late 2006 marked a major turning point for U.S. forces in Iraq, as in November the Democrats took control of both the House and the Senate and Gates replaced Rumsfeld as secretary of defense. In the first week of December the ISG released its recommendations, forcing the president to further reconsider his already revised strategy. President Bush had to grapple with finding a new strategy to deal with a country that had almost completely broken down. He also was forced to adjust to the changing conditions within the region, including Iran's decision to play a much greater proactive role in deciding the future of Iraq. On January 10, 2007, the president announced his decision to send an additional "surge" of 21,500 U.S. troops to provide more security in Baghdad and Anbar Province. In March he decided to send several thousand additional combat and support troops to Iraq that would bring the surge number to roughly 30,000. At the same time, he told the Maliki government that the U.S. would draw down its troops if it did not step up to provide more security and stability on its own. However, the situation in Iraq may already have gotten too far out of control and beyond the point where the U.S. could exert meaningful influence. Only time will tell.

Discussion Questions

1. Do you agree with President Bush's decision in January 2007 to send additional U.S. troops to Iraq? Explain your position.
2. Which option or combination of exit options for the U.S. military in Iraq do you believe would be most successful? Why?

3. How does skepticism over the administration's original motives for invasion affect the search for an exit strategy? For example, do you believe a main reason for the war was the U.S. attempt to gain control over Iraq's oil and/or to establish long-term military bases in the country?

4. Does the United States have a moral obligation not to leave Iraq until it can provide stability and security to the Iraqi people?

5. Where do you think Iraq will be in ten years, both politically and economically? Will Iraq become a successful democracy? Or is Iraq more likely to become a failed state or break apart?

6. What geopolitical concerns should be addressed when preparing an exit strategy? In your answer, assess how the involvement of Iran and other states in the region in the Iraq War should be considered.

7. What role, if any, should the UN play in helping determine a U.S. exit strategy and assisting with its implementation?

8. How do you think history will judge the U.S.-led invasion of Iraq?

9. Compare and contrast the Iraq War with the Vietnam War, focusing especially on viable exit strategies.

10. President Bush has stated that he would withdraw U.S. troops from Iraq if the Iraqi government does not meet stipulated benchmarks to provide for its own security and stability. However, Ted Koppel, longtime ABC newsman who became a freelance journalist, makes the reverse argument: U.S. troops should stay if the Iraqi government cannot provide security and stability and leave if it does. Whose argument for U.S. troop withdrawal makes more sense? Why?

11. Do you agree or disagree with this statement made in late 2006 by Richard Holbrooke, former U.S. ambassador to the UN and architect of the Dayton Accord of 1995 that ended the war in Bosnia? "The United States has lost its capacity to shape the events on the ground, regardless of what's recommended by the commission [Iraq Study Group], regardless of what's done by the U.S. military and the presidency."

12. In late March 2007 John Burns, veteran Iraq war correspondent for the *New York Times*, stated that the U.S. situation in Iraq was "bleak but not hopeless." What do you think of this observation?

13. What lessons can be learned from the U.S. occupation of Iraq and its attempts to democratize the country?

Class Activities

1. Divide the class into three groups that will role-play Shiite, Sunni, or Kurdish Iraqis in determining an "endgame" strategy for the U.S. The groups will first meet separately to determine their recommended option, and then they will meet in plenary session to see if they can agree on a single option.

2. The class holds a regional peace conference with delegates from Iraq, Iran, and Syria. The task of this conference is to devise both an exit strategy for the U.S. and a plan for postwar Iraq.

Suggestions for Further Reading

Brigham, Robert K. *Is Iraq Another Vietnam?* Boulder, CO: Perseus, 2006.

Clark, Wesley. "The Smart Surge: Diplomacy." *Washington Post*, January 8, 2007, A15.

Friedman, Thomas. "Ten Months or Ten Years." *New York Times*, November 29, 2006, A27.

Galbraith, Peter. The *End of Iraq: How American Incompetence Created a War Without End.* New York: Simon & Schuster, 2006.

Hagel, Chuck. "Leaving Iraq, Honorably." *Washington Post*, November 26, 2006, B07.

Hurst, Steven R. "'Civil War' Debate Masks Deeper Divisions." *Rochester Democrat and Chronicle*, December 3, 2006, 4A.

Ignatius, David. "Groping for the Exit." *Washington Post*, December 1, 2006, A29.

Moyar, Mark. "An Iraqi Solution, Vietnam Style." *New York Times*, November 21, 2006, A29.

Ricks, Thomas. *Fiasco: The American Military Adventure in Iraq.* New York: Penguin, 2006.

Woodward, Bob. *State of Denial: Bush at War, Part III.* New York: Simon & Schuster, 2006.

Helpful Websites

www.antiwar.com. This website contains articles arguing against the Iraq War. See, for example, William E. Odom, "What's Wrong with Cutting and Running?" October 3, 2005.

www.democracyrising.us. This website contains articles arguing against the Iraq War. See, for example, "Time for an Exit Strategy," November 5, 2006.

www.mideastweb.org/iraqtimeline.htm. Website for the MidEastWeb, containing chronologies and histories about Iraq and the Middle East. See "A Timeline of the Iraq War," August 16, 2006.

Index

About the Authors

Edward Drachman received his B.A. in government from Harvard College, his M.A.T. in social studies from the Harvard Graduate School of Education, and his Ph.D. in international relations from the University of Pennsylvania. He has taught at Boston University, the University of Hartford, and since 1991 at the State University of New York at Geneseo where he is professor of political science and former director of the international relations program. Professor Drachman is the author of a number of articles on political affairs and several books: *The United States and Vietnam, 1940-1945* (1971); *Challenging the Kremlin* (1991); with Alan Shank, *Presidents and Foreign Policy* (1997); *You Decide! Controversial Cases in American Politics* (1999); and *You Decide! Controversial Global Issues* (2003). Professor Drachman has also been a volunteer reading tutor in the second and third grades at School 45 in Rochester, New York, and he has organized and supervised Geneseo's after-school tutoring program in Rochester sponsored by the Puerto Rican Youth Development and Resource Center.

Robert Langran is professor of political science at Villanova University and has taught there since 1959 with an emphasis on constitutional law. He has published three other books and numerous articles. He received his Ph.D. from Bryn Mawr College in 1965, his M.A. from Fordham University in 1959, and his B.S. (Honors) from Loyola University (Chicago) in 1956. He served as a lieutenant in the Army (Ordnance Corps) from 1956–1958. At Villanova he served as department chair for ten years and has received the Lindback Award for Distinguished Teaching and the Faculty Service Award. He was Villanova's varsity men and women's tennis coach and is a member of the Villanova Athletic Hall of Fame. Authored books include *The United States Supreme Court: An Historical and Political Analysis* (six editions); *The Supreme Court: A Concise History*; and *Government, Business, and the American Economy* (two editions).